D0385189

Advance Praise for *Strategic Relationships at Work*

"Receiving and providing mentoring are crucial for professional growth at any age, but too often we leave these learning opportunities to chance. This much-needed book offers a smart, practical plan for taking charge of our own development by building authentic relationships throughout our careers."

—John R. Ryan, President and CEO,
Center for Creative Leadership

"Navigating a career that hops organizations, shifts focus, and grabs opportunities to learn and shine isn't the exception these days, it's the rule. Murphy and Kram show us why you can't go it alone, no matter how talented or hardworking you are, and that the best route to cultivating great mentors is learning to be a great mentee."

—Sheila Heen, coauthor of *Thanks for the Feedback*
and *Difficult Conversations*

"In *Strategic Relationships at Work*, Wendy Murphy and Kathy Kram have created a perennial resource for people at all phases of their careers. With their engaging examples, practical guidance, and years of experience woven together, they take a fresh look at how we make critical developmental relationships and connections at work and how we can all become better at forging these connections."

—Randy Emelo, President and CEO, Triple Creek River

"We survive alone, but to thrive we need others—we need relationships with people who care about us and for whom we care. Murphy and Kram show us why and how to develop a network of people who can help us liberate ourselves, pursue our purpose, and become the person and performer we want to be. Life is tough enough—make it easier by reading this book and following the authors' insights."

—Richard Boyatzis, PhD, Distinguished University Professor,
Case Western Reserve University; coauthor of *Primal Leadership*

"With all the buzz about differentiating mentors from sponsors, the authors of this book remind us that it is all about cultivating *meaningful* relationships at work and in other important domains of our lives. These noted scholars bring the best of contemporary research to inform their very practical, story-rich guide to the variety of developmental relationships we form with peers, bosses, protégés, sponsors, mentors, and coaches. Individuals at all stages of their careers will be able to use the many tools they offer, and organizations will learn from the best practices they report."

> —Deborah M. Kolb, PhD, Deloitte Ellen Gabriel
> Professor Emerita for Women and Leadership,
> Simmons College Graduate School of Management

"Thousands of books provide wisdom on the boss-subordinate relationship. The authors of *Strategic Relationships at Work* have mined a vast collection of research-based insights on the mentor-protégé relationship—which is often as critical as boss-subordinate--to provide us with desperately needed practical advice this set of key career issues demands. An important guide for 21st-century career progress."

> —Leonard A. Schlesinger, PhD, Baker Foundation Professor,
> Harvard Business School; President Emeritus,
> Babson College; former Vice Chairman
> and Chief Operating Officer, Limited Brands

"Whether you are an expert or a novice about mentoring—whether you are a mentor, a mentee, or someone who aspires to be either, this book has everything you need. With a strong research footing, a compelling guide to action, and plenty of tools, this is one-stop shopping for building mutually rewarding developmental relationships."

> —Douglas T. (Tim) Hall, PhD, Morton H. and
> Charlotte Friedman Professor in Management,
> Boston University School of Management

"This astute book reminds us that not only do relationships matter, but that it is necessary and possible to leverage them through planning, developing, and nurturing—with genuine interest and reciprocity. It is remarkable how professors Murphy and Kram have managed to weave together many strands of research with a practical and personal tone. Not only do they provide great ideas about what any individual can do to aid in career growth, but also sophisticated advice to companies about how to build programs to stimulate sponsorship, mentoring, and other developmental relationships."

> —Allan R. Cohen, PhD, coauthor of *Influencing Up*;
> Distinguished Professor of Global Leadership, Babson College

"A magnificent prescription for taking charge of your own professional and personal development through the power of strategic personal relationships and self-reflection. Your success as a rising manager or executive is ultimately up to you, enabled by your inner circle of colleagues."

—Kenneth W. Freeman, MBA; Dean, Boston University School of Management; former Chairman and CEO, Quest Diagnostics

"By applying entrepreneurial principles to mentoring, Murphy and Kram have upended the classic definition of the mentor/protégé relationship. *Strategic Relationships at Work* demonstrates the new path to personal and professional growth is best achieved by 'career entrepreneurs' willing and able to identify, build and nurture key relationships and networks among multiple mentors to maximize career success. Unique, insightful, and provocative."

—Kerry Murphy Healey, PhD, President, Babson College; former Lieutenant Governor of Massachusetts

"Despite the easy access of social networks and the hundreds, if not thousands, of friends and followers on Facebook and Twitter, successfully navigating careers and companies can be lonely and fraught with uncertainty. As this book clearly and forcefully demonstrates, to become truly competent and successful, everyone needs to create his or her own boards of advisors who can help to anticipate and avoid obstacles to success. This is a must-read for all who seek to advance in their careers."

—Elaine J. Eisenman, PhD, Dean, Babson Executive Education

"Finally, a book that any manager can use to explain that time spent on developing and cultivating relationships is crucial to achieving business results in the 21st century. In our hyper-networked society, only relational managers will succeed and see their businesses survive. Dr. Kram and Dr. Murphy lay that truth bare."

—Robson Goulart, MBA, Organizational Development Consultant, Dana-Farber Cancer Institute

Strategic Relationships at Work

Creating Your Circle of Mentors, Sponsors, and
Peers for Success in Business and Life

Wendy Murphy, PhD

Kathy E. Kram, PhD

New York   Chicago   San Francisco   Athens   London   Madrid

Mexico City   Milan   New Delhi   Singapore   Sydney   Toronto

1 2 3 4 5 6 7 8 9 0 DOC/DOC 1 2 0 9 8 7 6 5 4

ISBN: 978-0-07-182347-0
MHID: 0-07-182347-6

e-ISBN: 978-0-07-182478-1
e-MHID: 0-07-182478-2

Library of Congress Cataloging-in-Publication Data

Murphy, Wendy M.
  Strategic relationships at work : creating your circle of mentors, sponsors, and peers for success in business and life / Wendy M. Murphy, PhD, Babson College and Kathy E. Kram, PhD, Boston University School of Management.
    pages cm
  ISBN 978-0-07-182347-0 (hardback : alk. paper) -- ISBN 0-07-182347-6 (alk. paper) 1. Success in business. 2. Interpersonal relations. I. Kram, Kathy E., 1950- II. Title.
  HF5386.M8574 2014
  650.1'3--dc23   2014010569

McGraw-Hill Education books are available at special quantity discounts to use as premiums and sales promotions, or for use in corporate training programs. To contact a representative, please visit the Contact Us page at www.mhprofessional.com.

Dedication

To our families
with love and gratitude

Dan, Keira, Alexa, and Jack
Peter and Jason

CONTENTS

ACKNOWLEDGMENTS

This book was inspired by the joy in learning that both of us have experienced within our own circles of developmental relationships. We are grateful to all of the mentors, sponsors, and peers who have supported us and continue to help us navigate our careers. And a special thanks to our students—your talent and energy has motivated this project, and it is our hope that these ideas will serve as a resource in your career journeys.

We appreciate the many dedicated professionals who contributed examples and ideas, and who provided consultation on this book, including: Susan Alvey, Lisa Bonner, Michael Campbell, Dennis Ceru, Ted Childs, Peter Cohan, Jodi Davidson, Susan Duffy, Randy Emelo, Mary Fernandez, Kathleen Fink, Laura Francis, Edward Freeman, Susie Goldring, Robson Goulart, Audrey Haas, Deb Hills, Bill Hodgetts, Steve Hudock, James Hunt, Whitney Johnson, Heatherjean MacNeil, Nancy Mellard, Tina Opie, Lisa Prior, Dave Templin, Tom Turcan, Nicole Valliere, Kim Vappie, Luke Visconti, Barbara Wankoff, Ilene Wasserman, Joe Weintraub, Kim Wise, and Carol Yamartino.

We are fortunate to have many wonderful colleagues and friends who encouraged us to take on this project and supported us throughout, including: Lloyd Baird, Richard Boyatzis, Susan Chern, Allan Cohen, Anne Donnellon, Elaine Eisenman, Elana Feldman, Fred Foulkes, Jennifer Fraone, Ken Freeman, Karen Golden-Biddle, Judy Gordon, Danna Greenberg, Tim Hall, Brad Harrington, Emily Heaphy, Carolyn Hotchkiss, Monica Higgins, Bala Iyer, Bill Kahn, Jennifer Kimball, Jamie Ladge, Elaine Landry, Nan Langowitz, Louise Lawson, Jack McCarthy, Polly

Parker, Srini Rangan, Keith Rollag, Len Schlesinger, Andrea Sigetich, Liz Volpe, Jeffrey Yip, and Jessica Young.

We offer special thanks to those who helped us bring this book to completion, including Giles Anderson, Bob Gilbert, Scott Kurtz, Tom Miller, and Jim Wilson.

We would also like to thank Babson College and Boston University (BU) for supporting this project. In addition, we want to acknowledge Babson's Center for Women's Entrepreneurial Leadership, BU's Executive Development Round Table, and the Center for Creative Leadership. Any omissions or errors of credit are ours entirely.

Finally, we thank our families for their unwavering support and patience through the countless hours, conversation, stress, and love that was poured into the creation of this book.

INTRODUCTION: WHAT ARE STRATEGIC RELATIONSHIPS?

With slews of websites offering advice on how to "mentor" and whom to do it with—to say nothing of the legions of corporations now offering formal mentoring programs—we'll pose the big question you have right here at the beginning:

Why do I need to read this book?

The surprising answer is that good mentoring isn't what most people think it is. In fact, the most effective form of mentoring for accelerating your career cannot be shrunk into a Q&A on the Internet or even within a company classroom. Rather, it's a dynamic very personal process; one that can be learned. Further, it works to benefit both sides of the mentoring equation, and, in the best case, is rigorously *informal*. We repeat, informal.

And, oh by the way, you're the one who makes it happen, whether consciously or not.

What may further surprise you is how few of our colleagues, students, and professional acquaintances consider mentoring crucial to their career development. Based on decades of research, we beg to differ.

In this book we make the case that in today's era of "Me, Inc."—when multiple jobs and career shifts are the norm—a new definition of mentoring is essential to success. Indeed, those who employ flexible, shifting networks of mentors achieve higher salaries and receive promotions faster. Our findings have confirmed this over and over.

So why don't most people already know this?

Frankly, it's because academic journals that publish mentoring research aren't very accessible. Meantime, those commendable corporate programs out there also seem to imply that mentoring is largely the company's responsibility to nurture talent, not yours. Thus, the label *mentor* has come to embody a formal one-way relationship, sort of like a direct report. But let's examine the data.

Informal Mentors Are More Effective

One of the most important findings from the extensive academic literature is that informal mentoring relationships are more effective than formal ones. This conclusion is irrefutable. Relaxed, informal relationships provide *more* of every kind of benefit.

After decades studying mentoring, you can take our word for this. As professors, it's our job. We've plowed through scores of academic studies, interviewed hundreds of research participants, and painstakingly analyzed survey findings from both our own and others' data.

Not satisfied with all that, we've also asked people to fill out complex questionnaires and to map their mentoring relationships. In addition, each of us has created and run mentoring and coaching programs, as well as assisted organizations with designing their programs. We've consulted with large and small organizations, spoken with executives and consultants, and discussed mentoring at conferences with people from all over the world. As a result, we think we know what we're talking about on a whole range of mentoring issues. But the bottom line is this: You are in charge of your own development.

You Are in Charge of Your Own Development

Ralph Waldo Emerson wrote about the virtues of "Self-Reliance" way back in 1841. But the admonition to "trust thyself" may be even more true in today's business climate. Leaders—and those aiming to be—face a more tumultuous and uncertain work environment than ever. Organizations may seem to be focusing more on their talent funnel (and ought to) as workplace challenges have burgeoned. But in actuality, they've largely off-loaded most of the responsibility for leadership development and career management on the individual—yes, you. They know you're mobile, too. Thus, the self-directed career that is managed by the individual, or the notion of self-leadership training, has unobtrusively replaced traditional formulas for success.

It's obvious that in this new environment, each of us must create stability and certainty for ourselves. But, perhaps paradoxically, you can't do it alone. Strategic relationships can assist you in adapting to constant career upheavals and in growing as a leader.

Relationships Benefit Both
You *and* Your Mentor (or Protégé)

Research on mentoring consistently demonstrates that protégés (also called *mentees*) and their mentors not only have higher salaries and climb the ladder faster, they end up more satisfied overall with their careers. Understanding this, many organizations created formal mentoring programs as part of their HR strategy. But recent research shows that if you proactively create a wider, deeper network of mentors each of the benefits—more money, quicker promotions, and greater satisfaction—can be even greater.

When you combine these findings—that informal mentoring relationships are more effective and that a network of mentors promotes better career outcomes—the conclusion to be drawn is inescapable: *Everyone* needs to become an entrepreneurial protégé. What do we mean by that, exactly? To place the idea in context, let's look back at where mentoring came from.

What Is a Traditional Mentoring Relationship?

The traditional mentor–protégé relationship consists of a junior person—the protégé—paired with a senior, more experienced colleague—the mentor. Most often, this relationship springs up within the same organization.

There's nothing new about this. Mentors and their contributions to leadership development have existed across history. In the written record, they began most notably within the traditions of Greek mythology and philosophy. The original Mentor, himself, appeared in Homer's *Odyssey* as a teacher and protector of Odysseus' son, Telemachus. Over time, the word *mentor* came to mean someone who imparts wisdom and knowledge to his or her protégé. There is a chain-like effect over time. Recall that among Greek philosophers, Socrates was a mentor to Plato who, in turn, was Aristotle's mentor.

Protégés have heralded mentors for dramatically changing their lives ever since. In today's world, consider Warren Buffett, CEO of Berkshire Hathaway, and one of the richest men in the world. He credits economist Ben Graham, author of *The Intelligent Investor*, as a critical influencer in his career development. In turn, Buffett has mentored Bill Gates, founder of Microsoft, and now a world-renowned philanthropist. This is all well and good if you can find such a sage who is also willing to spend years with you.

The Changing Nature of Work and Why You Need More Than Traditional Mentoring

By definition, traditional mentors offer wise counsel and support, and may serve as important resources, if you are lucky enough to get one. But several recent trends make relying on one traditional mentor a risky strategy.

1. **Job mobility.** People rarely spend their entire career in one organization anymore. Put another way, we are no longer dependent on organizations to define our careers, and most of us will work for more than one organization.
2. **Globalization.** We live in a connected world that constantly requires additional skills and the ability to learn from new people and experiences. This means that different advisers and counselors will be needed in different contexts.
3. **Technology.** Relentlessly advancing technology keeps us connected at all hours. Fewer barriers between work and home mean we need evolving strategies for how to engage (or disengage) in our work and personal lives; mentors can help us separate the meaningful and important from the urgent.
4. **Pace of change.** This brings us back to those Greek philosophers. Or as Heraclitus put it: "The only constant is change." What's happened between 500 BC and now is that the *pace* of change has gone into overdrive to become overwhelming.

Boundaryless and Protean Careers in Response to the Changing Nature of Work

Two of our colleagues, Michael Arthur and Denise Rousseau, have encapsulated these frenetic trends within their conception of the "boundaryless career."

Modern careers are not just dissolving time and space, but barriers and limits as well. Think about the ways: To begin with, most of us now view our career as independent from the organization that currently employs us. We've become the proverbial free agent. Even within the company, fewer fences exist between hierarchical levels due to "restructuring" (e.g., delayering, downsizing, or rightsizing). The increase in team-based work and more informal work cultures are also erasing old lines. Technology, meanwhile, is obliterating a sense of place. You may work from home or at the local coffee shop or the airport, or anywhere at all, at any time.

Without the old constraints, you may move in and out of the workforce. Or you might make non-traditional career moves, such as taking a lateral position or even stepping down to learn new skills. All the while, you may be challenged to work with diverse colleagues or clients, on a global assignment, or on a virtual team. Work is beginning to feel existential.

The larger point is that we, as agents of our own destiny, will have to adapt to changing opportunities and work requirements repeatedly. Does this sound like an environment where constantly forming nebulae of mentor networks need to coalesce and renew themselves?

Our colleague and mentor, Tim Hall, aptly calls new patterns of progression the protean career. Proteus was the Greek god who could change shape at a moment's notice to meet any conditions he faced. While not at every moment, we're all faced with the need to change our skill set and job definition many times—even professors are.

Modern Careers Require Multiple Mentors, Start Your Own Development Network

Scientists view the vast and formless nebulae they see in space as star-forming regions. A lot of things must come together, as well, to form a corporate star. And this process is easier to manage if you can gain help from a network of mentors with multiple backgrounds and perspectives.

In the academic community, we call this your developmental network; it includes a variety of relationships that support your personal development and career advancement.

Such diversity taps various mentors for different roles and in different eras, such as those who can sponsor and advocate your promotion, or coach you through a job change. Mentoring relationships are inherently developmental because they contribute to your growth and career advancement. But beyond traditional "rabbi" or "guru" relationships, support from other senior leaders and peers can be developmental, as well.

Keep in mind that your developmental network is a subset of your overall network. Its unwavering focus is on your personal and professional career growth, and requires self-awareness, a range of critical social skills, and persistence. But it's not necessarily all about you alone. To be most effective, it requires an element of altruism, such that both you and your developers will value the connections you've created as mutually beneficial. And that gets us to how mentorships should work.

You Are a Protégé and a Mentor

Whichever mentoring role you take—whether protégé or mentor—they are equally developmental. Indeed, research reveals that mentors receive as many career benefits as protégés. They also gain meaning in their work by passing on their knowledge and wisdom. This *mutual learning and growth* is perhaps the most important part of the mentoring process. This is worth repeating: Each role gains in this virtuous circle of sharing and gaining.

It's a myth that only the protégé benefits from a developmental relationship. Both protégé and mentor have the potential to develop self-awareness, new knowledge, and skills (old dogs need to learn new tricks, too). Moreover, each contributes meaningfully to the learning of the other when the relationship is based on trust, effective communication, and a commitment to the partnership.

Very successful people have learned to apply their talents in changing ways as their careers take shape. Part of that experience often includes being a protégé—sitting at the feet of the wise— and then becoming a mentor with age and experience. Media mogul Oprah Winfrey is a highly visible example of a mentor who has fostered a plethora of protégés. Her efforts at exposing them to her audience also increased their visibility helping to propel their careers. She has mentored "Dr. Phil" McGraw, helped develop the media savvy and authorship of Dr. Mehmet Oz, created opportunities for designer Nate Berkus, launched financial guru Suze Orman's television career, and made chef Rachael Ray a household name. When talking about her own success, Oprah credits one of her own mentors, Maya Angelou.

Oprah calls Angelou a "mentor-mother-sister-friend," highlighting the different roles a mentor may take depending on the needs of his or her protégé.

An Entrepreneurial Approach to Relationships

When you ask a room full of executives (and we do this, regularly), "What makes a good protégé?" you get a list of admirable traits: a protégé should be open-minded, motivated, thoughtful, passionate, willing to learn, and most importantly, respectful of their mentor's time and efforts. Leaders want their protégés to be trustworthy, loyal, diligent, and grateful. And the list goes on, as you can imagine.

This refutes the narrow conception of protégés as receivers of wisdom and exposes their active role in the relationship. To build mentoring connections, protégés need what our colleague Dawn Chandler calls "relational savvy," those attitudes and skills that enable you to build relationships that foster your personal and career growth.

We see over and over again that people can make significant career progress—left turns and employment hops, even—through skillfully employing such a wider awareness.

Take Nina for example. She'd been quickly promoted up the ranks of the menswear division of a national retailer. Her real passion, however, was cosmetics. No existing relationship would help make that switch. Encouraged by her fiancé, who worked there, and a colleague, she set out to meet potential mentors in the cosmetics area. At the company's holiday event, Nina took the initiative and introduced herself to Bob, a vice president of the cosmetics division.

She chatted with him about some new lines that she liked as well as trends she'd noticed in boutique stores. She knew what she was talking about and Bob was impressed. Clearly, Nina had a sense for the product. More than that, he'd learned something, himself, about the market. They continued to talk at company events and informally (remember that word?) over an occasional coffee. He taught her more about cosmetics and the marketplace; she gave him intelligent and thoughtful replies.

Not surprisingly, when Bob had an appropriate opening, Nina was promoted into the cosmetics division.

You can break down Nina's pathway into four distinctive routes: reflect, experiment, learn, and teach.

1. **Reflect**

   When you take an entrepreneurial approach to mentoring, you determine your personal goals and seek mentors who will propel you toward what's personally and professionally meaningful.

   Unlike Nina, you might need some help figuring out your goals. In fact it's mandatory. Even she did at some point earlier in the story. Further, when you identify appropriate career-learning building blocks, you also identify the people you need to learn from.

   In other words, you're beginning to construct your informal network of mentors. Obviously, you'll need to tinker, engaging in vicarious learning and seeing how different roles might fit. In doing so, an entrepreneurial protégé (you) becomes authentic and eager to learn from his or her mentor's experiences—which is both engaging and genuine.

2. **Experiment**

   Alex is another good example. While he held a job as a successful marketing executive for a large corporation, he felt stifled in his career. He admired his friend Sanjay, who had started his own company and seemed to have a lot of fun doing it. They had lunch on occasion. This was mutually beneficial because Alex would offer Sanjay advice on marketing strategy. After a year of talking with his wife and close friends, including Sanjay, Alex determined exactly why he wanted to leave and, more importantly, his goals.

   Alex yearned for the energy and excitement of working for a startup and building something new. Emboldened by his self-knowledge and supportive network, Alex left his secure job and comfortable salary to become the sixth employee of a software company. Now, a few years later, he's the chief marketing officer of a highly respected and successful company that's growing at a rapid pace. And, thanks to entrepreneurial mentoring, he loves it.

3. **Learn**

An entrepreneurial protégé will use feedback and ideas from multiple sources to aid in career decision-making. Good protégés also realize that their mentoring relationships, like all relationships, require give-and-take. Meaning: they must ensure that they assist their mentors whenever possible. When protégés do this well, mentors (also called *developers*) learn in the process of helping their protégés.

What's the response when you ask executives, "How do you feel when your protégé succeeds?" They tell us they're delighted for him, proud of her, I knew she/he was capable. It feels good.

This is all true, but deep down they're expressing a very human need to matter in another person's life. People like to help others who are genuinely interested in them, and who are thankful for the assistance. They are particularly enthusiastic when they feel like they also learned a lot while helping their protégé. In fact, some of the best mentors tell us they actually feel guilty about taking any credit. Indeed, they insist that they get more out of the experience than their protégé.

4. **Educate**

Charlotte demonstrates another mentoring pathway. Her relationship with one of her past college professors is a good example of the mutual learning and satisfaction that comes from a high-quality mentoring relationship, and how this can lead to a stronger developmental network overall.

After five years in the financial services industry, Charlotte began to feel restless. She found herself more interested in managing the process of change. She'd observed how the two firms she'd worked with had tackled macro environmental changes and the leadership challenges that came with them. She was fascinated.

She decided she wanted to do some systematic career exploration. She reconnected with a trusted teacher, Professor Kaye, who listened and counseled. The professor also provided names of persons working in positions that might be of interest to her. Good student that she was, Charlotte made contact.

Because of her already highly developed relational savvy, Charlotte learned about a new field and enlisted several people working in change management into her developmental network. Two years after talking with her professor, Charlotte is now enrolled in a master's degree program to prepare her for this new career. Who took the most satisfaction in this outcome?

Charlotte expresses sincere gratitude to Professor Kaye, who delights in having enabled her to make this significant change in her career. The two continue to be in touch. Charlotte often recommends her professor as a resource in the field of change management, and Professor Kaye sends Charlotte people struggling to manage effective career exploration.

Mentor and protégé thrive and endure as a result of their relationship. But this isn't always the case.

Cautionary Tales and Lessons

Unfortunately, dysfunctional relationships do occur in mentoring. Basically, people fail to achieve personal aspirations when they don't enlist others in their developmental networks, whether through selfishness or ignorance. Poor experiences are far too common. We will discuss the main reasons in Chapter 10. For now, the lesson to be drawn is that by understanding the causes of dysfunction—and the failure to engage in effective relationship building—these negative experiences can be avoided or at least minimized.

Get Going on Your Own
Developmental Network

Decades of research shows unequivocally that good mentoring relationships are critical for career success. And here's the beauty of it: both mentors and protégé benefit.

We will begin this book by explaining why having one mentor is not enough in today's tough and turbulent work environment.

To improve the likelihood of success, all of us—from new hire to CEO—must create and maintain a network of mentors. We call this your *developmental network*. But you can call them your gang of gurus, your work wonks, your support society, your advisory board, or whatever you like. Just be sure to form one.

We share stories and invite you to reflect, experiment, and learn from your own experiences—and to assess your needs and cultivate a developmental network that will enable you to thrive.

How This Book Will Help You Create
and Sustain Strategic Relationships

We start this book with an overview of mentoring and developmental networks. Then we discuss why mentoring works and how you need to take an entrepreneurial approach to creating and sustaining relationships.

In the second part, we review the strengths and limitations of formal mentoring programs, explore alternatives to mentoring programs, consider the role of leaders in fostering a mentoring culture, and underscore the critical importance of peer mentors.

The third part focuses on special challenges presented by workforce diversity, technology, and change. It also addresses the dark side of mentoring.

Finally, we highlight new trends and discuss how organizations can encourage networks of strategic relationships.

Throughout the book we include examples and stories of people whose careers and lives have been enriched because of their developmental networks. In addition, we provide opportunities for self-assessment and pose questions for reflection.

We hope this book helps you discover your inner entrepreneurial protégé and formulate a plan to create your own developmental network.

At the end of the book, you will find a brief list of recommended reading to explore further the ideas in each chapter. In addition, notes provide sources for more in-depth reading as well as original academic sources.

This is all about you, but you'll go further by sharing the journey with others.

PART 1

CREATING CONNECTIONS WITH MEANING AND PURPOSE

1

WHY RELATIONSHIPS MATTER

"No man is an island," wrote English poet John Donne in 1624. But in our workplace lives, we sometimes act like one.

Lauren is two years into her first job as a financial analyst after graduating from college. She really likes the work and wants to build her career in this organization. At the same time, she doesn't have a real sense that her work is valued. She wonders if she is doing what's expected of her. So far, her performance appraisals have been generally good but perfunctory. She likes her peers and they seem to like her, but she wonders if she really fits in and whether anyone is taking notice of her contributions. In a word, she is unconnected.

Michael has been at SunSystems for eight years. He has been promoted several times and has had several bosses. Because the industry is growing, there's no dearth of opportunity for challenge and growth. Yet he is not quite sure what he wants to accomplish in the next three to five years. He works extremely hard, and that diligence has paid off. But he's beginning to wonder if he's ignoring vital parts of his life in order to ensure his next promotion. Can he continue to be successful and have a modicum of balance in his life? In a phrase, he's questioning the meaning of work within a wider context.

Brian has been at Health Services, Inc., for 22 years. In that time, he has become a senior leader. He enjoys overseeing the operations of the main clinic, helping to set strategic direction for the future, as well as mentoring and coaching less experienced professionals. He has achieved the major goals he established for himself when he joined the company after earning his MBA in healthcare management. Others admire his success and think he "has it made." But Brian wonders, like the old Peggy Lee song, "Is that all there is?" In a sentence, he's pondering what comes next in his career and, more importantly, his life.

These are all essential questions:

1. Do I fit in? (Lauren)
2. What meaning do I, or should I, derive from work? (Michael)
3. What's ahead after achieving my goals? (Brian)

As you may have noticed, all seem to be wrestling with these issues in a vacuum. None has a set of relationships to help them sort their way through these difficult life queries and transitions, much less a developmental network. Let's go back and see how each can become "a part of the main," as Donne put it.

Lauren and Michael are young professionals trying to make their way in a complicated world. Both have aspirations (though not a clear personal definition of success). They sit, isolated, grappling with questions about what their next steps should be. They can continue to wrestle with these alone or, as we would suggest, they can enlist others in helping with their development.

Let's put this as an axiom: By tapping the experience of coworkers, senior colleagues, and people outside your workplace, you can address predictable challenges and build important relationships (with meaning and purpose) that will help you meet your goals.

In effect, you are no longer alone. Let's now explore how this might play out.

In Brian's case, a seasoned professional at midlife is wondering if he wants to stay the course or consider a change in direction. While others imagine he's all set, it's clear that he can benefit from reflecting on where he has been—and where he's headed—with trusted others. In that way, Brian can fulfill Donne's vision of humanity that "every man is a piece of the continent." That vital linkage in the workplace is through developmental relationships.

What Are Developmental Relationships?

Relationships play a key role in career success and well-being. Decades of research on workplace relationships has consistently shown the benefits of high-quality connections. These can comprise professional relationships with mentors, coaches, leaders, bosses, and colleagues—or personal relationships with family, friends, spouses, and partners.

These connections provide the social support, the sort of land bridge, to uphold your performance at work as well as generate life satisfaction. Put succinctly, good relationships enable us to cope with stress and thrive during times of change.

Specifically, developmental relationships are those whose primary purpose is learning—both task-related and personal learning—that enables career growth and advancement. We call those who impart knowledge from experience in these relationships "developers."

More often than not, each individual in these relationships is learning and developing new attitudes and skills, along with gaining a sense of identity related to the challenges they currently face. Such relationships become high-quality connections when parties feel engaged, energized, and appreciated as a result of their interactions.

True mentors, in our lexicon, offer the broadest range of career and psychosocial support. But because of the nature of careers today, such mentors rarely come in one package. All of us must create our own network of developers. The people in your network should be both able and willing to provide pieces of the career and psychosocial support you need at different career stages.

The Roots of Mentoring

At this point you probably buy the argument that you need a mentor in order to succeed. But where do you find these godlike figures?

Well, they are not omnipotent, nor is that the right question to ask. Yet it's understandable why most people think of mentors as having life-changing powers. They do, but not in exactly the way we imagine.

The idea of novice approaching master started with Greek mythology. In Homer's *Odyssey*, the first mentor was actually the goddess Athena in disguise. Odysseus, king of Ithaca, had to travel to fight the Trojan War. In his absence, he entrusted Mentor to teach and oversee his son, Telemachus. Over a decade passed, and the kingdom was overrun. Mentor advised Telemachus to begin a quest abroad to find news of his father and seek the counsel of kings and soldiers. As a result, Telemachus returns with Odysseus to put things right.

Over time, the word *mentor* acquired a specific meaning of someone who imparts wisdom and knowledge to his or her protégé. But can anyone live up to the standards of a Greek god? Some organizations have tried that model.

Business and academic interest in mentoring as a developmental tool soared during the 1980s and 1990s. Today we know that mentoring can facilitate leadership development, career advancement, work satisfaction, individual performance, and organizational performance. But we're no longer in the 1990s, much less in ancient Greece.

We now know that mentoring occurs in multiple relationships, not just in a traditional hierarchical relationship—one that may be formally assigned or spring up organically in an organization. And that's a good thing to know amid today's revolving-door work environment. A commonly cited statistic is that we'll all have seven separate careers in a lifetime, which may be a dubious claim. But the U.S. Bureau of Labor Statistics reports that the typical worker's job tenure has been about four years since 1996. The real point is that we increasingly need all the help we can get.

How Do Developers Provide Support?

Basically, there are four ways in which people can help support your developmental journey:

1. First, they can help you *get your work done.* They do this by coaching and directing you as you learn new tasks. They can also introduce you to those who can help you complete a baffling task, or they can offer just-in-time technical advice that might even save your job.
2. Second, people can help *advance your career.* They accomplish this by giving you challenging assignments, by sponsoring you for stretch assignments and promotions, and by protecting and advising you when you are in high-risk situations. (Mentors who can sponsor you are really good ones to have.)
3. Third, people can provide much needed *personal support.* They do this by listening well to your concerns, offering empathy, and counseling you when difficulties arise. They care about you as a person, not just as a contributor (a.k.a. cog in the wheel) to the work.
4. Finally, people can serve as *role models.* They do this by representing (and providing a vision of) what you would like to become as you grow in your career.

This quartet of support can be grouped into a trio of overarching themes:

- *Career support* entails those instrumental aspects of a developmental relationship that support career advancement.
- *Psychosocial support* relates to aspects that develop competence, clarity of professional identity, and self-worth.

- *Role-modeling* encompasses those aspects of the other person that are admired, that offer a source of inspiration, and that provide a vision of what you want to strive to become.

This is further outlined in Table 1-1.

Table 1-1 Types of Support

Career Support	Psychosocial Support	Role Modeling*
Sponsorship	Encouragement and emotional support	Behavior to emulate
Coaching		Work ethic and values
Exposure and visibility	Acceptance and confirmation	Inspiration and motivation
Challenging assignments	Counseling	
Protection and preservation	Friendship	
	Personal feedback	

*Anti-role modeling includes: (1) devaluing relationships and (2) work-life interface failure. We will discuss this further in Chapter 10.

Photographic darkrooms don't exist much anymore, but the concept of immersing yourself in experiences with people—developers—who can bring forth a true picture of you is what we're talking about. And the more you know about yourself—and the possibilities for developmental relationships—the more you'll be able to build connections that provide clear meaning and purpose for your life.

Developing Self-Images

Let's go back to Lauren. She's a relative newcomer to her profession and her job. She seems quite uncertain and disconnected from others at work. She's really in the dark.

Lauren would benefit from getting exposure to, and feedback from, her immediate supervisor. Spending time with selected peers and probing them on their work experiences would help, too. From them, she might discover that her uneasiness is widely shared. Together, they might not only support and coach one another but also develop strategies on how to get more feedback and coaching from their bosses.

And why not widen the circle? Friends, family, and others outside work have wisdom and support they're willing to offer. Such options are certainly better than stewing about not being "in the know."

By contrast, Michael knows all the ropes. He's well established at his company and has experienced considerable career success. Yet, like most of us, he has a vague sense that getting the next promotion may not be what life's all about. How can others help him sort out his current needs, priorities, and goals? How can he learn more about the alternatives within his company and outside? Who might be helpful, and whom can he trust to be a sounding board?

Good questions, though the answers aren't straightforward. Michael can begin his existential quest by approaching his current manager, past bosses, or other senior colleagues. This takes tact and sensitivity. But the chances are good that if mutual respect already exists, his more experienced peers will be willing to share their firsthand knowledge about wrestling with ambivalence and coming out the other side with a life-affirming plan. Theirs' may not be Michael's eventual plan. But he—and you by inference—can relate to the processes of finding it.

Strategic Relationships
Help You Face Challenges

Regardless of the challenges you face, you are not being held in concrete. You can create and sustain relationships that will enable you to move forward. This is true for anyone. Whether you're just starting out or are 15 years into your career, developmental relationships are a dynamic resource that can lead to learning and satisfaction instead of stagnation and frustration.

What's more, you have everything to gain by getting cracking on creating strategic relationships. The evidence: 30 years of systematic, empirical research shows that people who have had effective mentoring experiences tally up benefits that just don't quit. They gain greater career and life satisfaction, achieve better performance, acquire more learning and skill development, and experience less stress than people who don't have these all-important developmental relationships.

Relationships Smooth Career and Life Transitions

Let's add our personal testimony to all that empirical evidence. Both of us forged through significant transitions within the past three years.

Wendy moved to a different city and a new position at a different institution. Kathy made a decision to redefine her work after 32 years as a full-time professor. We're the experts, but neither of these decisions was easy to make.

What made it possible to survive and thrive during our respective transitions/ordeals was the support and critical thinking that our developers provided. Also—like the preacher who reads his sermon into a mirror on Saturday—we practiced what we preach. We started by apprising our developers of what we needed, indeed what we aspired to. We also enlisted new developers in order to navigate these major, scary moves.

For example, Kathy needed to reach out to individuals who'd already made a shift from full-time to half-time faculty. She needed to know how they managed writing and consulting careers outside the cocoon of a university. More than a sanity check, Kathy learned proven strategies and tactics (through coaching). And she was able to feel less alone on her new path (through role-modeling, counseling, and friendship).

Kathy also discovered that as her new training wheels went on, some old ones were carefully put in a box labeled "old friends" to be contacted intermittently thereafter. In other words, some trusted developers who'd been central to her network for years were no longer as helpful once she started down her new path. But they would never be forgotten or abandoned. Throughout, her husband Peter was a mainstay (of encouragement, coaching, and friendship). As other long-standing relationships necessarily became more distant and new relationships were begun, he was there to provide continuity and support.

Wendy, on the other hand, sought out colleagues who'd changed jobs successfully. She knew she had to ask about their strategies (role-modeling and peer coaching). She then reached out to former developers who'd helped her secure her first academic position (through coaching and sponsorship). Wendy also made contact with those who could connect her to people at the institution of interest (through exposure and visibility).

Friends who'd moved across the country—as she intended to—provided another emotional anchor and encouragement. And Wendy's husband, Dan, metaphorically held her hand and helped her strategize (through encouragement, counseling, and coaching). Once she landed the job, Wendy moved quickly to form wholly new developmental relationships. (It beat feeling overwhelmed.) This last step enabled her to learn and grow while taking on new responsibilities (through sponsorship and providing challenging assignments).

How Developmental Relationships Change Over Time

Once you understand the range of support that a developmental relationship can provide, how do you go about enlisting others? That's the real trick to mentoring.

We go into detail on the necessary underlying skills and behaviors needed for acquiring developers in Chapter 4, but at this point let's start with a few key concepts.

The most salient is that all developmental relationships go through four phases: *initiation, cultivation, separation,* and *redefinition.* These constitute a life cycle that's more like the enduring spring of nature than the casual comings and goings of acquaintances.

Depending on your history with someone, you may find it quite easy to move quickly through the initiation phase—the seeds of a mentoring relationship—to the cultivation phase. Beyond that, the depth of your connection, as well as the frequency with which you communicate, will shape how long the

Table 1-2 Phases of Developmental Relationships

Relationship Phase	What Happens in This Phase
Initiation	Aspirations become fixed expectations. Opportunities for interaction exist. Both parties see potential for learning. Meaningful, helpful conversations begin to take shape.
Cultivation	Both individuals continue to benefit from interacting. Career and psychosocial support grow. Opportunities for more meaningful interaction occur. Emotional bond deepens.
Separation	One or the other partner's needs change. Circumstances on or off the job change and impact the relationship. Negative emotions may surface because of the change in the relationship.
Redefinition	Stresses of separation diminish. New relationship is formed to adapt to partners' needs. Gratitude and appreciation increase.

relationship endures. So too will circumstances that influence your interactions,

At some point and for a variety of reasons you or your mentor-mentee, may decide that the relationship is no longer necessary or helpful. That's when the last two phases—separation and redefinition—kick in. These final pruning and transplanting steps, if you will, have their own protocols. Some of the issues encountered along the way are shown in Table 1-2.

Be Proactive

A faint heart never won a fair lady; nor does hoping and waiting for a mentor to find you. Several studies abundantly demonstrate that being proactive about initiating relationships vastly increases your ability to acquire effective developmental relationships. Start with those people who can help immediately.

For example, here's one way to enlist a senior individual to coach you, sponsor you, and help you learn the ropes: Ask him for feedback on a project he oversees that you're working on. If no such project exists, propose one and volunteer to do it.

An alternative would be to invite Ms. Big to coffee or lunch for an informational interview. Once there, ask her thought-provoking questions about how she got to this point in her career. Many experienced people will not only be flattered, if you're sincere, but will welcome the opportunity to reflect on their own career paths with someone who genuinely wants to learn from their story.

These same tactics, which are in no way ploys, will work with people outside your organization who have experience and wisdom that can enhance your knowledge and skills.

Cultivate Each Relationship, and See Where It Goes

After a few mutually satisfying interactions, the relationship will begin to grow naturally. A little like any friendship, you'll sense whether there's potential or not. A few questions to ask are: Can you sense enthusiasm and welcome? Does he or she seem to enjoy the conversations as much as you do?

The answers to these questions are good indications of whether the relationship will work or not. As time passes, you'll find yourselves in the cultivation phase of the relationship. There, you'll start to receive the kind of career and psychosocial support you've been seeking. Your mentor will be getting different but equally satisfying benefits. But, as needed, you will have to expand your developmental network, and the process begins again.

Spend Your Time Wisely

In nature, budding plants sometimes need water, sometimes sunlight, sometimes nutrients—and in different amounts as they grow. Sometimes, unfruitful shoots need to be nipped off. The same is true with relationships.

Put another way, the very nature of these relationships constantly evolves and grows as we change and move in new directions. The separation phase can be difficult, characterized by conflicting feelings and loss, but separation is healthy to maintaining a viable developmental network.

Brian, the senior executive we introduced earlier, is feeling the need to reassess his position at Health Services. More than likely, his current developers are not the best mentors on this journey. He's looking for assistance in exploring opportunities outside the organization and for objectivity in evaluating his shifting needs in his current position. Where to turn? He might gain the impartial insight he needs by enlisting an external coach, family members, or peers. In other words, he should look for someone who has no vested interest in his staying put.

Time and energy are limited, meaning regular reassessment of your developers is essential. If you're uncertain about a relationship, whether to maintain, broaden, or end it, consider discussing your options with a trusted peer or experienced coach. Again, an objective sounding board serves you best.

This doesn't always necessarily mean adding relationships. Brian had a longtime developer whom he'd confided in for years. They'd redefined their relationship many times, especially after this wise counselor moved to another role in the healthcare industry. Brian could always count on hearing the disinterested truth from him.

Ranking the Quality of Relationships

If you put Brian's relationship with his trusted advisor at the summit of a ranking of relationships, that leaves a spectrum down through great, useful, somewhat useful, useless, and way, way down at the bottom is a category that's actually harmful.

In her research on mentoring, Belle Rose Ragins devised a formal continuum of quality in mentor-mentee relationships with dysfunctional anchoring at the low end and high-quality floating at the top. Not surprisingly, she put "average quality" as the midpoint. Each type has a set of specific characteristics. But you can employ this continuum to consider the quality of all your developmental relationships.

Figure 1-1 Quality of Developmental Relationships

When you actively assign a grade for the quality of each of your relationships, you can move forward along another line between nurture and nip. Moving from negative to positive, you get Figure 1-1.

Starting in the middle, a developmental relationship of average quality serves the needs of the less-experienced party. Traditional mentoring relationships have this quality—coaching, sponsoring, counseling, and other career and psychosocial support characterize the relationship. The relationship primarily helps the "junior partner" develop new skills, attitudes, and/or a sense of identity. Mentors assist protégés in preparing for career advancement.

Both parties may be quite satisfied with the process and the outcomes of the relationship, but, by definition, the relationship of teacher-student is hierarchical. However, personal goals are met, and there is a sense of fair exchange.

High-Quality Relationships Foster Mutual Learning

High-quality relationships have a transformational effect on both parties. The learning is not one-directional. Instead, it's complementary and quite significant. In their article, "The Power of High Quality Connections," our colleagues, Jane Dutton and Emily Heaphy, have drawn attention to the unique characteristics of high-quality connections. They suggest that high-quality relationships inherently entail mutual influence, growth, and learning.

Both sides enter the relationship expecting to grow, learn, and be changed. The benefits don't stop there. Both also experience feelings of increased self-worth, heightened zest, enhanced capacities to build high-quality relationships themselves, and a desire for even more connection. To bend the old cliché, it's win-win to the nth power.

High-Quality Relationships Inspire Growth

High-quality relationships provide support way beyond average connections. Both parties become teachers and learners, acquiring new attitudes and skills, while facilitating similar growth in the other. In this altruistic exchange, the relationship inspires both to establish new personal or professional goals and, sometimes, create an ideal version of themselves never before contemplated.

Each has an expanded sense of the possible, experiences elevated moments of creativity, and reaches beyond current aspirations.

People in High-Quality Relationships Care About the Whole Person

Individuals in high-quality connections care about the well-being of the whole person (both at work and beyond). You respond to your partner's needs without expecting repayment.

This is in sharp contrast to typical work relationships, and the heightened commitment goes beyond keeping track of notions of fairness (as when only one partner gets a raise).

Forming More High-Quality Connections

In our life and research experience, we've found that truly transformative, high-quality relationships are rare. Many factors explain why this is so. Perhaps the most obvious and easiest to address are the mental models (or schemas) that individuals bring to relationships.

False expectations are disappointments waiting to happen. But when two people hold similar assumptions—about how the relationship should unfold and the roles that each should play—a high-quality connection is more likely to occur.

You and your partner cannot intuit these vital expectations. Both of you must articulate them very early in the relationship. What follows is a process of adjustment, alignment, or disengagement.

Looking back at Lauren, Michael, and Brian, each needs to enlist developers. They also must put a voice to that need, to articulate the particulars. This takes not only thought and skill, but courage. We've found that those who carefully consider what they want to say, even rehearse with a confidante, do best.

Prepare to Reach Out

High-quality connections are by their nature selfless. So preparation for reaching out must include asking yourself, "How might I contribute to the other's learning and growth?" If you are a relative newcomer like Lauren, you may decide you have nothing to teach to a more senior colleague. Not so.

Again and again, we see young professionals teaching invaluable new technical skills—and social media opportunities—to their developers. Consider also that you may have a unique perspective of your organization. It might be bottom up. But it very well may help graybeards to understand the workings of the department or division they run from your role, your age, or your tenure. Indeed, your viewpoint may seriously enlighten someone out of touch with those in junior positions.

Consider Who Is Approachable

Some people see making themselves available for developmental relationships as part of the territory for management. Others prefer to "make it on their own."

As owner of your own career development, it's your job to determine who the former are, and to focus on them. They're not too hard to distinguish from those not interested. Here are some tests: Does he or she already show interest and curiosity in you and your goals? Does she listen well or want to meet again? Has he shared some of his personal story with you? Some candidates already have a reputation for being good coaches or mentors.

If you're not sure whether someone is appropriate or not, you may have to approach someone else. However, don't mistake someone who's simply reserved for someone who's not interested. The degree of responsiveness is key. Does he or she engage in conversation even when pressed for time? Does he or she remember you or encourage you to follow up?

Hone Your Relationship-Building Skills

Determination, though, will take you only so far in building alliances. You'll need a minimum of relational skills to get started, and you'll need more over time to make them effective. We discuss these skills in Chapter 4.

At this point we provide the initial essentials. They are *self-awareness* and *social skills*, including listening, giving and receiving feedback, empathy, conflict management, and the ability and willingness to share aspects of your story. Doubt you have them all? Later on, we provide tips on skill building—inside and outside of a training classroom.

Give Relationships Time to Develop

Shared values and perspectives are the glue for a strong connection. You may sense you have such a bond from seeing the other person in action, but it will take time and conversations to confirm those hopeful suspicions.

Our research on high-quality relationships strongly indicates that shared values and perspectives bode well for the growth of a solid relationship over time. Trust your gut. If you already consider someone a role model, there is an excellent chance that a high-quality relationship is in the offing.

Avoid Dysfunctional Relationships

You may be stuck with your boss, but you don't have to be trapped in a dysfunctional mentoring relationship. Try to avoid them entirely. The best way to sidestep dysfunction is to be clear about your needs and interests. You must also practice the social and emotional skills that build relationships with meaning and purpose. And you must regularly reassess the health of relationships.

When things go awry, you need to hone in on a midcourse correction plan. For example, as Lauren began to reach out to her boss and two other superiors, she realized that her direct supervisor really didn't have his heart in it. The other two showed themselves to be genuinely interested and available. Lauren terminated her overtures to her boss and cultivated the other two. Frustration and disappointment were avoided, and no harm was done.

Sometimes, relationships become dysfunctional as they develop. Things then get a little more dicey. For example, as Brian grew discontented with his current position, he became less available to mentor and coach several junior colleagues. Unaware of his withdrawal as he explored his own career possibilities, those who had relationships with Brian tactfully and increasingly left him alone. Such adaptability goes to the selfless heart of high-quality relationships and can enable them to evolve—or be put on hold—without resentment, dissatisfaction, or dysfunction. Remember, again, that the best relationships are all about matched expectations that are mutually agreed upon.

Who Are Potential Developers?

To state the obvious, developers can come in many forms over a career, not just in the mythical form of Greek godlike Mentor, the all-knowing.

Among recent studies of developmental networks, a wide range of roles show up for developers. Some examples are provided in Table 1-3 and should get you thinking about potential developers within your reach.

Any one of the developers listed in the table can provide more than one type of support. And, as you weigh the possibilities, you may decide not just to reach out but to enhance a current relationship in quality and depth.

If you were to fill in names in the table, who would you choose?

Table 1-3 Social Roles of Developers

Organization	Family	Community	Other
Superior	Spouse/partner	Personal friend	Former work colleague
Manager/ supervisor	Parent/guardian	Romantic partner	Teacher/ instructor
CEO/president	Sibling	Counselor/ therapist	Business associate
Coworkers	Aunt/uncle	Neighbor	Recruiter
Formal mentor	Grandparent	Spiritual guide	Unmet hero
Subordinate	Child	Acquaintance	
HR representative	Relative/other		

Consider what you've learned about developmental relationships in this chapter—and the important sources of support that they offer—and make a list of who your current developers are—and/or what traits they should have.

Reflection Exercise: Identify Your Developers

Think about the people who've taken an active interest in your career—those people who've enabled your *personal* and *professional* development in the past year. Think broadly. These may be people from your work or outside of work (i.e., family, community).

List all of your developers in Table 1-4. Then rate each developer on a scale from 1 to 5 based on the assistance they provide to you. This will help you clarify why each person belongs on the list.

Table 1-4 Identifying Your Developers

1 —————— 2 —————— 3 —————— 4 —————— 5

| Never | Rarely | Sometimes | Often | Always |

Developer Name	Type of Assistance Provided			
	Helps me get work done	Helps advance my career	Provides personal support	Is a role model for me

MAP YOUR DEVELOPMENTAL NETWORK

This is a short chapter designed to lay out the essence of our approach. It starts with a story about someone who achieved extraordinary career success:

> His name was Steve. Early in his career, Steve knew that he could use some help. He was confident that his fledgling company had something to offer the world, but he needed capital to start manufacturing. One venture capitalist told Steve that he also needed to learn how to market and sell. Steve listened and sought suggestions. He met with entrepreneurial backers and start-up experts and hit it off with Mike, who taught him how to write a business plan. Mike eventually became an angel investor and an absolutely vital contributor to the company.

From Entry Level to CEO, Everybody Needs Mentors

Every CEO has a formal board of directors, but when you ask CEOs who helped them succeed, they'll refer to a mixed crew: former bosses, colleagues, spouses, friends, people who work for them, and trusted advisors. Some academics call this a "personal board of directors." Note that even leaders at the top of their industry enlist mentors at critical moments. The point is that you never stop needing your own *developmental network.*

The Steve mentioned above is the late Steve Jobs, cofounder and former CEO of Apple. His relationship with Mike Markkula, a successful marketing strategist and engineer, made history. Markkula guided the company in its early years, but Jobs had serial developers: people like John Sculley, Apple's first "big company" executive, who may have been a dysfunctional mentor, since he pushed Jobs out. A high-quality mentor was Jony Ives, Apple's brilliant designer.

To risk a bad pun, good mentoring is at the core of every Apple-like success, whether you're a CEO or a career seedling.

One Mentor Is Not Enough; You Need a Developmental Network

Thanks to people like Steve Jobs, connectivity is the essence of today's society. Each of us needs more than a Markkula, however life-changing such a mentor can be. We need a developmental network.

Your developmental network is a subset of your entire social network; it does not include all your relationships, connections in social media, or even everyone you've ever talked to about your career. In your developmental network you establish relationships with people crucial to your learning and growth. A few hallmarks of developmental networks include:

1. **Both formal and informal mentors are important.** A traditional assigned mentor may provide a lot of career leverage and expertise, but sometimes informal developers help you to think more broadly and outside the box. Having both is ideal.

2. **Relationships within and outside your workplace are critical.** Developmental relationships know no boundaries. They're found inside and outside your organization. Those inside

know the people and the culture of your workplace. They can help you strategize roles, help sponsor you for promotion, or find interesting assignments. Those outside your organization tend not to have biases that might stem from the workplace. They are also not invested in you staying in your current position and can think more objectively about your career.

3. **You learn from relationships at all levels.** Developers come in all flavors. They may be senior executives, direct supervisors, peers, subordinates, family members, brothers-in-law; in fact, they may be anyone who has a relationship with you (see Table 1-3).

4. **Relationships provide various types and amounts of support.** Developers are not created equal in the way they assist you personally and professionally (see Table 1-1).

It's helpful to know the numbers on the jerseys of the players in the mentorship game because modern work-life boundaries have become increasingly blurred. Yet, as our research abundantly shows, this increasingly wide array of folks—with you at the center—can profoundly affect your professional development.

A diagram of this phenomenon, looking a little like an atomic model with its nucleus surrounded by static neutrons and protons, is shown in Figure 2-1.

Cultivate a Variety of Relationships

In real life, these folks are swirling around you like subatomic particles. As they flash by, you probably wonder: Whom do I talk to about my job? Have I discussed my career with people at work besides my boss? Should I? How much does my spouse, partner, or good friend know about my career? What should they know? Answers are critical to cultivating and improving your developmental network. The simple point is that a wide range of people have the ability to contribute to your development. Where do you look for them?

Figure 2-1 Relationships in a Typical Developmental Network

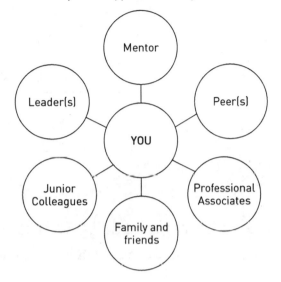

Find Mentors in Your Career Communities

Career communities are defined as any social arena in which you may find support for your development. Over the years, we've found that the most effective developers generally come from within five categories: your workplace, school, industry (professional associations, clients, customers, and collaborators), family and friends, and organizations within your community (volunteer and religious groups and so on).

Career communities do not include your spa or bird-watching club. They are places where you'd expect to find forms of career support and learning already going on, both in and outside your workplace (see Figure 2-2).

Knowing where to find helpful people is only a small part of the equation, though. Next, you have to take personal charge of meeting and working with them for outcomes that satisfy both parties. How?

Figure 2-2 Typical Career Communities

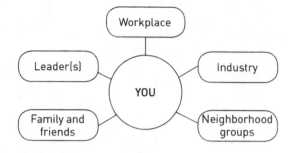

Take an Entrepreneurial Approach

The dictionary gives a one-sentence definition of an entrepreneur: "a person who organizes, operates and assumes the risk for a business venture." Similarly, taking *initiative* and *risk*s can define successful mentees.

If you ask mentors and coaches about their best protégés, active verbs appear in their descriptions: for example, mentees *ask* good questions, boldly *seek* learning opportunities, clearly *state* what they need, and frequently *thank* their developers. Succinctly put: Good work is not enough to build a career. You've got to treat your career progression as the difficult start-up business it really is.

The Entrepreneurial Building Blocks

Many studies show that three key internal elements underlie career success and satisfaction: *knowing why, knowing how,* and *knowing who.* To these, we add a fourth—*knowing where.*

These constitute what we call the *entrepreneurial approach* to relationship building. It's an approach that brings results. Let's briefly review the elements:

- **Knowing why** enables you to clarify what you seek and what you bring to relationships. Self-awareness is the most critical component.

- **Knowing how** ensures that you have the social skills, awareness of others, and self-management savvy to launch and sustain relationships with meaning and purpose.
- **Knowing who** allows you to identify those with the expertise and experience you need and who are likely to be receptive to an approach.
- **Knowing where** maps the terrain for the support you'll need to enhance your development. You will consider what career communities to tap as you create and sustain relationships. In this sense, it prepares you to focus your relationship-building efforts, and develop good questions.

There are many ways to develop these career-enhancing competencies, including what we call "structured reflection" and learning conversations. In Chapter 4, we launch your own entrepreneurial approach.

But first, we show how to analyze your current developmental network in Chapter 3. We walk you through the story of Emma, who's had a few twists and turns in her career.

Along the way, we give you some tools to assess the structure of your own developmental network. At the end of Part 1 of this book, you'll be ready to unleash your inner entrepreneurial protégé. Let's start by mapping your current developmental network.

Reflection Exercise: Your Developmental Network Map

Refer to the list of developers you created at the end of Chapter 1 to fill in the map (see Figure 2-3).

1. **Think about your career communities.** What are the appropriate career communities that describe your developers? Often these are the areas of life where we meet or interact with them. The most common communities include work, family, school, local community, professional organization, or industry. Depending on your life stage, some people

Figure 2-3 Development Network Map

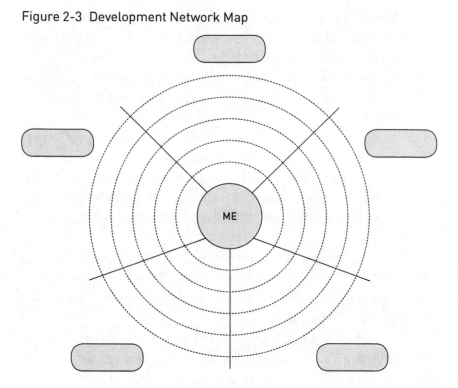

break down categories further, such as college, high school, graduate school, former workplace(s), neighbors, specific clubs or religious organizations, and so on. Fill in the open rectangles with your categories.

2. **Consider the strength of each relationship.** Look at how you rated each developer and consider how "close" you feel to that person overall. Plot their initials in small circles on the map with a line from "me" to each developer to create a visual developmental network map. Consider using different colors to represent the different types of support each developer provides.

ANALYZE YOUR DEVELOPMENTAL NETWORK

To illustrate how a developmental network can help you through the twists and turns of a career, we'll introduce you to Emma. You'll get to know her well in this chapter—and more importantly you'll come to understand the whys and wherefores of a vibrant career-building resource.

For over a decade, Emma had built a global career in financial services in three increasingly prestigious firms. She'd been promoted with each move. In fact, she'd recently been elevated to vice-president. It was clear that she enjoyed the work and the people. In addition Emma had created a small side business out of her eco-conscious fashion hobby, first in designing accessories and more recently in designing clothes. This work inspired her, and she wondered if she could risk doing it full time.

Stuck between worrying and dreaming, she asked herself: "Can I really leave the security of my big-time job and walk away from years of hard work?" A better question might have been: "Do I really have to make such a momentous decision alone?"

Whom *could* Emma talk to about her ambitions and fears? Was there someone at work she trusted, or should she look outside of the workplace? Did she need to gather many opinions?

A Formal Mentor Is Just a Starting Point

Did Emma need to gather many opinions? The answer is yes: One mentor cannot fulfill all of Emma's, or your, career support needs. But the one you might turn to first may already have been assigned to you.

Back when Emma landed her first job, the company assigned Dee to be her formal mentor. Dee answered lots of questions and helped Emma understand the company's culture and her role. Over their year together in the mentoring program, they developed a good rapport.

But two years after their formal relationship ended, Emma was trying to decide whether to stay or leave. She felt she could discuss this issue with Dee. While Dee really wanted her to stay, she advised Emma to choose the place that would give her the best opportunities to learn. Emma did leave. They still keep in touch, although less and less frequently.

As this illustrates, formal mentoring can contribute a lot to your career development—and we explore mentoring programs in depth in Chapter 5. But it can only take you so far.

Our research shows that *informal mentors*—those relationships that develop naturally over time—are often more effective. Indeed, much of the academic research on mentoring deliberately avoids the term *mentor*. Reason: it carries a heavy connotation—as in a top-down grooming process—and because mentoring is not limited to formal programs.

Informal Mentors in the Workplace

Informal developers at every internal workplace level—senior executives, supervisors, and peers—can work wonders. Their deep understanding of the territory allows them to give tailored advice, coaching, and feedback. They're capable of identifying the people you need to meet and the skills you must have in order to prepare yourself for new opportunities in your organization and sometimes beyond, thanks to their networks. For example, here's how an informal mentor helped Emma:

> When Emma arrived to head the emerging markets group at her next job, she had some trepidation: She'd never managed such a large team. She went through the firm's "onboarding" seminars with Clair, another director and newbie. They quickly become each other's resource and friend.

> The two commiserated over being "new" and learning the bewildering systems and corporate acronyms. Most importantly, they started to share strategies for negotiating some difficult budget cuts and for motivating their teams as the recession lengthened and lay-off fears mounted.

> In addition, Clair owned one of Emma's early handbag creations. She admired Emma's creativity and encouraged her to keep experimenting.

Your Career Will Transition, So Prepare by Diversifying Your Relationships

Between the ages of 25 and 45, the average person in the United States will work for nine to ten different organizations, according to the U.S. Bureau of Labor Statistics. That's right, about one organization every two years.

All this bouncing around excludes promotions within an organization—which are challenging enough. Most changes will entail some kind of lateral jump, upward move, or total career change. The pace is more sedate in the European Union; people there tend to stay about 10 years, on average, although transitions within organizations may be just as frequent.

Another form of career musical chairs emerged with the onset of the Global Recession in 2007. This is the so-called "gig economy"—which refers to those people who are employed on a contingency basis, project to project. It also includes those people who are precariously hanging on in vulnerable employment situations, informally employed through family businesses, or in transition economies.

Regardless of your perch, the fact remains that your boss and coworkers will no doubt change often. This means that your relationships with people outside work are likely to be the most stable. Indeed, you might call them your constant rock in a storm-swept economy.

Relationships Outside of Work Can Be Sturdy During Change

Non-work relationships are especially important for encouragement and emotional support through career transitions.

Decades of work-family research bear out the commonsensical conclusion that supportive family members, spouses, and partners can buffer stress. Newer studies show something less intuitive: this kind of support positively impacts work results and satisfaction in tumultuous times.

Although most of us don't consciously think of family members this way, they—and particularly parents and spouses—are part of the developmental networks of most successful people.

In fact, when people cannot talk shop to a parent, spouse, or partner, research shows that they typically express deep distress. The reason is easy to understand: work often undergirds one's identity, and people need others to share their goals and concerns. This was certainly true of Emma.

Emma's father, Tom, an engineer by training, was a longtime manufacturing executive. He took pleasure in hearing about Emma's industry and in sharing his related investment know-how. Beyond lending an ear and his experience, Tom helped Emma negotiate her first salary. He did this by doing meticulous research and by suggesting thoughtful strategies.

Tom developed a lot of confidence in Emma's judgment, and their relationship deepened as she took on increasing leadership responsibilities. He'd walked the same difficult path and therefore got a lot of satisfaction from the respect she showed for his hard-won wisdom. Everyone likes to be listened to. Over time, Tom become Emma's principal sounding board for big career decisions, the go-to guy for discussing the pros and cons of any major decision.

All Careers Are Boundaryless

We're all likely to engage in careers without traditional boundaries, whether that means changing jobs, being on a global team, or working virtually. Today's permeable work environment allows many of us to be effective in the office, at home, on the road, or in their local coffee shop. Even the most traditional organizations require continual learning and adaptation. New approaches must be adopted, new opportunities seized. It's because of this porousness that cultivating relationships inside and outside your company is so important.

Relationships help you remain steady when everything is rocking about you. Meaningful relationships provide the connectedness, perspective, and stability to help you to thrive.

What Should Your Developmental Network Look Like?

How your developmental network takes shape will depend on what you need. You must scrutinize multiple factors when assessing your developmental network and how to improve it. These include—but are not limited to—your career goals (or whether you need help in formulating them), work challenges, personality preferences, career and life stage, and those who are accessible as potential developers.

Let's analyze the characteristics of a developmental network to explore patterns of relationships. In Table 3-1, we summarize each according to size, diversity, density, tie strength, and multiplexity (the degree to which your developers are broad-gauged and cover a variety of support areas).

Table 3-1 Developmental Network Characteristics

Characteristic	Explanation/Questions
Size	How many developers do you have? This relates to having the right number of developers in your network.
Diversity	How much diversity is in your network? The focus here is on important differences among developers, including experience, expertise, social context, and background.
Density	How interconnected is your network? Who knows whom? This is about how and what people know about you and each other across different contexts.
Tie strength	How intimate are your connections? This concerns the quality of your relationships, often indicated by the frequency of interaction and emotional closeness.
Multiplexity	How many types of support do your developers provide? This addresses the versatility of each relationship and the range of support provided by your developers.

Size: The More the Merrier?

Size does matter. Research by our colleague Monica Higgins has shown that the bigger your developmental network, the greater your satisfaction at work. In fact, having an expansive (within reason) developmental network has been linked to better performance and more promotions. You are also more likely to stay put where you have more developmental connections. So, in fact, the more the merrier is true—to some degree.

However, diminishing returns set in at some point: Less time and energy is available within a large group. It takes hours and effort to identify and deepen those relationships with the most potential for mutual learning and growth. The trick is in finding a balance between breadth and depth in order to meet your needs.

Most people report that they have three to five close relationships in their developmental network at any time. One study found that extraordinarily successful people have an average of 16 developers over their entire careers. When we consult with midcareer professionals, most indicate 12 to 15 developers overall. Again, quality trumps quantity. And timing is everything—in this case, plugging into support at the right moments across an evolving career.

Diversity: What Differences Matter for You?

"Variety is the spice of life" in both the old saying and in mentoring relationships. Diversity encompasses different professional experiences, different educational backgrounds, and different personal demographics, such as age, gender, race, and so on. The business case for diversity is about tapping broader markets and talent pools.

Different Perspectives Provide New Insights

It only makes sense that diverse relationships provide wider information and resources. Different social circles and contexts have their own wisdom. Nurturing such relationships opens your perspective and challenges your thinking. They also offer fresh insights and approaches to your career and life.

For example, when a senior male executive has a high-quality developmental relationship with a junior female executive, the potential for mutual learning is off the charts, not simply because of gender and experience. They come from different worlds. Mutual enlightenment is the result. Indeed, amazing things happen in organizations we've worked with that try to retain high-performing women by matching them with senior male mentors. Both groups report not just very positive outcomes, but dawning understanding.

The women said they suddenly "got" the politics at the senior executive level; mysteries were revealed around the activities and protocols needed to gain visibility and promotions. Equally enlightened were their senior male mentors, who spoke of a revelation in their understanding of the unique obstacles women face on the way up.

Diverse Relationships May Offer Future Prospects

Emma's performance out of the gate deeply impressed Bryn, a recently promoted executive vice-president and rising star.

Bryn thought Emma had lots of potential. In a meeting with one of their biggest clients, she had prepared a quartet of scenarios in anticipation of the discussion around their client's acquisition plan (it was standard to anticipate a couple). During a coffee break after this attention-grabbing performance, Emma approached Bryn and started to ask questions, but they had to return to the client meeting.

She followed up, and they've met quarterly since to discuss emerging-market strategy, trends in the industry, and her career. Bryn has become even more impressed with Emma.

You Will Find New Opportunities to Learn

Relationship diversity works. Meaningful dialogue across gender, racial, and generational boundaries can boost individuals' developmental opportunities as well as the organization's bottom line. Research supports this conclusion empirically.

Different groups come to know and appreciate the others' points of view. Each person feels empowered and heard. With the right training, recognition, and support, these interactions can be about mutually expanding knowledge and understanding, that this process goes both ways.

If your organization's culture values diversity, it'll be easier to enlist dissimilar people into your network. Outside the workplace, connections can be made through shared interests, professional organizations, or volunteer groups. Be on the lookout. We discuss achieving diversity in depth in Chapter 9.

Broaden Your Range Across Career Communities

It's good to tap a number of social arenas and career communities for developers. The number of social arenas tapped we call the range of your developmental network. Research reveals several benefits for range breadth: more job offers, better performance in your job, and more satisfaction with career and life.

Emma's story shows why:

Pilar, an independent banking consultant, had encouraged Emma to apply for the director of emerging markets position and helped her land it. They'd met at a conference three years earlier. Back then, Emma had approached Pilar to ask questions after Pilar had made a presentation. They ended up having lunch the next day and kept in touch.

Pilar grew to see the subtlety of Emma's mind and told her she'd be good at deciphering and weaving the complex strategy required to succeed in the firm's emerging markets business. Pilar knew whereof she spoke. Before starting her consulting company, she had worked there herself. That's why she was able to answer Emma's questions with relative ease.

Pilar also introduced Emma to colleagues who shared insider knowledge of the business and culture. Emma saw that this experience, even if a way station, would open up new doors for her career.

Density: Who Knows Whom?

Density is about the interconnectedness of your developers, the degree to which people know one another.

Your developers may be interconnected if they come from the same career community. The extent to which your developers interact with one another may affect you positively or negatively, depending on your goals and needs at the time.

Density Is Good and Bad

Communication is easier and faster when people are more interconnected. They develop higher levels of trust and psychosocial support since they're often aware when you need it most. That's the good news of proximity.

But if you're looking to change careers, in-group knowledge is not particularly helpful. Everyone may think alike and have typecast you in your current role. Therefore, they have little to tell you, much less the ability to offer tips on opportunities far afield; nor can they expose you to new ideas. In other words, what may be warm and fuzzy emotionally may be stultifying for a career. That's the less than good news.

Emma shows why it's good to mix it up:

> Emma had worked with Yen as a resident assistant in college. She thought he seemed to know everyone. They'd helped each other dealing with difficult students back then and had creatively generated funds to run campus programs.
>
> Although Yen was in the technology field, she'd often speak to him about her career progression and challenges. He always seemed to have a new way of connecting her to interesting people, and he made her laugh. Yen liked talking to Emma, in turn, because she gave him good advice on negotiating with difficult people and strategizing his next move.
>
> In other words, they had nothing in common except their problem-solving natures and maybe senses of humor. But Emma learned to piggyback on Yen's zest for meeting new people.

Brokers Connect You to People

In a sense, Yen was a relationship broker. Extensive research by Ron Burt, author of *Structural Holes: The Social Structure of Competition*, underscores the importance of having such people in your network.

Like Yen, brokers are developers who seem to naturally have wide access to information and resources. This comes through their relationships with people you otherwise would never meet; without them as brokers there would be a gap or hole in the network structure between you and those contacts.

In the proper mix between range and density, you need to cultivate such people. Maybe they're gregarious, outgoing, or have some kind of heightened extroversion gene, but they can make life-changing introductions and connections for you.

Assess the Density of Your Own Connections

Talking in person isn't the only way to broaden your network. Indeed, Internet companies create value through the so-called "network effect." The classic idea is that the value of a product or service is dependent on the number of others using it. Likewise, your own developmental network can become more valuable to you (and others) if you get yourself out there through social media.

Several apps can analyze your Facebook or LinkedIn connections, for example, indicating where electronic relationships originate—and who knows whom.

We often recommend such assessments to reveal patterns and opportunities. It might also help you identify career communities and find new developers.

Tie Strength: Invest in Strong and Weak Relationships

Strong and weak ties don't refer to flashiness in neckwear. Rather, we're talking about the need to balance relationships that both nurture and nudge, support and challenge.

Strong relationships form over time with a developer you feel close to—you become emotionally connected. Close relationships provide psychosocial support, enhancing your sense of competence and professional effectiveness. The people in these relationships with you know you well, influence your thinking, and have earned your trust. They have the power to persuade you. Strong relationships make up the stable *core* of your developmental network, but you need weak ties (not weak people) in your developmental network as well.

Weak Ties Connect You to New Opportunities

In a classic paper, sociologist Mark Granovetter reveals that weak ties are anything but weak in their potential effects. He argues that weak relationships are particularly effective when you're looking for a job or trying to accomplish something at work. This is because weak ties are more likely to be brokers like Yen. By definition, brokers have access to information—on new jobs or on how to complete a task—that you might otherwise never hear about. They know things, ranging from a specific skill set to opportunities.

Maybe we shouldn't call these relationships weak at all. People who have many weak ties at work also tend to be more connected to people at higher levels in their organization. These are the kinds of powerful folks who can sponsor you for your next promotion or recommend you for high-profile assignments.

Weak and strong ties overlap when memberships in diverse career communities turn up people who can act as brokers. This sounds a little knotty, but the following tale of Emma illustrates how strong a weak tie can be:

> Emma met her friend Zoë in college. Their friendship was based on a rare overlap: both were majoring in a business field—Emma in finance and Zoë in marketing. But they were also both double majors in fine arts, and what was the likelihood of that?
>
> Although their careers placed them in different functions, they both worked in large, public firms and found themselves facing similar stressors at each new promotion. Over the years, they were able to vent and counsel one another through some difficult decisions.
>
> Lo and behold, when Emma relocated overseas, Zoë, whose company had a division there, was able to connect her to Jay and Lisa, who helped Emma adjust. These weak ties helped Emma adjust and build a new network.

Blessed Are the Weak

From years of working with people on their careers, we've found that weak ties—relationships that are not close and where communication is infrequent—can be crucial. Interestingly, these are often people we see as role models—both personally and professionally. Frequently, they're in positions of power and influence, or whom you sense are interesting and could be helpful. But because of modesty or reluctance, you just haven't connected with them yet.

Sometimes they're people recommended by other developers or those you meet at conferences or networking events. We're not talking about a relationship contemplated for manipulative reasons, a notion that makes many people uncomfortable with the somewhat loaded term "networking." To reiterate: developmental relationships are, by definition, mutually beneficial. So what's holding you back?

Invest in Relationships Strategically

Our time and energy are not limitless. But you must find enough of each to maintain a constant balance of weak and strong relationships. They're sort of the yin and yang of an interconnected developmental network that's helpful to both sides.

Multiplexity: One Versus Many Aspects of Support

Multiplexity combines the idea of *who* is in your developmental network with the concept of *what* type(s) of support they provide.

Developers who provide multiple types of support (i.e., multiplex ties) tend to represent stronger relationships. They have the ability to think broadly and holistically about your career and life. Reason: they know something about you from across a variety of domains. Sometimes, they can be downright selfless. Take Emma's former supervisor, for example:

Emma had a strong ongoing relationship with Anton, one of her former bosses she had when she was on the way up. While working for him, he'd pushed her to sharpen her presentation skills and also gave her exposure to upper-level executives. He'd been delighted by her progress. More than that, Anton knew about Emma's fashion "hobby."

One day over coffee, Anton surprised her with an insightful question: "Why couldn't you become an entrepreneur? You have the business experience."

Emma nearly dropped her cup, but she knew he'd carefully considered the matter from her point of view. His next words confirmed that he had her best interests at heart:

"It would be a tremendous loss—for the firm and for me—but do you really want to be here for the next decade?"

If you've been counting, you'll know that Emma's developmental network has three developers at her current workplace—as well as developers from industry, college, family, and her previous workplace. It's outlined in Figure 3-1.

This is the end of Emma's story, but we're hoping it is the beginning of yours.

Abundantly evident in Emma's adventures is that the different layers of relationship support can originate from different career communities. Each mentor can contribute to development,

Figure 3-1 Emma's Sample Developmental Network Map

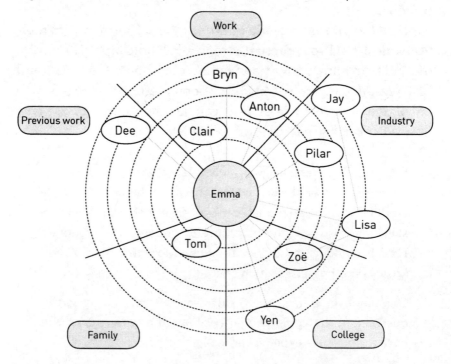

both personally and professionally. Over time, many relationships take on characteristics of multiplexity.

In the next chapter, we discuss how you can be entrepreneurial in your approach to your own developmental network. But as we say goodbye to Emma, we ask you to ponder what you've learned in this chapter.

Reflection Questions

The following questions will help you analyze patterns in your own developmental network. Review your map as you read and answer the questions.

1. **Size.** Do you have the right number of developers to help you reach your goals? Should you enlist more people? Or do you have too many and need to manage those relationships more effectively?

2. **Diversity.** Consider the people you have in each category. How similar or different are they in terms of experience, expertise or function, background, gender, race, age, and so on?

3. **Density.** Which developers in your network know each other? Is your network very closed (does everyone know one another?), or is it open?

4. **Strength of connections.** As you look at your map, are all your developers very close or are some more distant?

5. **Connections to power and influence.** How many would you characterize as influential and/or well connected?

TAKING AN ENTREPRENEURIAL APPROACH TO RELATIONSHIPS

People who've built strong and responsive developmental networks are more confident about relationship-building and navigating their career than their less-connected peers, who may feel isolated and unsure about their career prospects. Over a decade of research on developmental networks demonstrates this conclusively.

Similarly, investigation reveals that mentors and coaches like helping to develop positive people. It turns out that developers enjoy fielding their protégés' sincere questions and are flattered by their keen interest.

To illustrate why, consider two young professionals who are representative of people we've worked with. Both are recent graduates of excellent undergraduate business programs with concentrations in marketing:

Cary and Kelly each landed similar good starting positions as marketing analysts at Procter & Gamble. Over two annual review cycles, both received outstanding performance appraisals and were optimistic about their prospects for advancement. But from this point on, their stories diverge.

Later that year, Cary was excited to get an offer to become an assistant brand manager. It represented a big salary jump as well as more challenging responsibilities.

Kelly's career, though, had remained static. He's not sure why, but he harbors a vague sense that if only somebody would notice his contributions, there would be a promotion for him.

The variable lies in how these two equally ambitious professionals approached building relationships from the time they joined the company. The differences are striking.

Cary, from day one, personified proactivity; he struck out on his own to get to know the right people throughout the company—his peers, his boss, and many other senior colleagues.

Kelly, on the other hand, put his nose to the grindstone. His exclusive focus was on doing the best work he possibly could. His assumption was that excellent performance—in and of itself—will be appropriately rewarded. It's an idealistic perspective many of us start out with in the workplace.

Cary recognized the importance of good work just as much as Kelly did. But he also knew that building relationships in which he could learn from others, while demonstrating what he could bring to the job, pays dividends in wider, speedier support and recognition.

It's not that Kelly is self-reliant while Cary is self-aggrandizing. It's more that Kelly is hiding his light under a bushel basket. Something underlies these two very different approaches to relationships. Let's go deeper.

The Entrepreneurial Approach

Four foundational elements govern an entrepreneurial approach to relationships and developmental networks:

1. The first is *self-awareness*. It comprises knowledge of your personal values, your professional and personal goals,

your attitudes and preferences in work and relationships, and your talents, strengths and weaknesses.
2. The second is *awareness of the career landscape*. This includes knowledge of the immediate opportunities for growth and advancement within your organization, as well as keeping tabs on career trends beyond your organization or industry and how these may affect you.
3. The third is *relational mindset and skills*. These are the combination of attitudes and relational acumen that enable you to reach out to potential developers and to deepen current relationships.
4. The final one is *selecting potential developers*. This is the ability to identify developmental partners who can provide mutual learning opportunities.

These four fundamentals align with the career pointers we discuss in Chapter 2, which are knowing why, knowing how, and knowing who. Many studies have shown that these core competencies contribute to career success and satisfaction. As noted, we've added a fourth, knowing where. This last directional pointer helps ensure that you systematically consider opportunities at your company and every other appropriate venue.

Taken together, these principles focus your relationship-building efforts. They also help you hone insightful questions for those whom you decide to enlist in your developmental network. (See Table 4-1.)

Knowing Why: How Can I Build Self-Awareness?

Career experts agree that self-awareness is the first building block for satisfying career and life decisions. It gives you impetus. When you know what's important (by examining your personal values), self-awareness also reveals a personally meaningful goal. But in order to course-correct, you need two other things: an accurate sense of your strengths and weaknesses and an understanding of your "personal genius" (by determining

Table 4-1 Developmental Network Characteristics

Knowing Why: Self Awareness	Knowing Where: Awareness of Career Landscape	Knowing How: Relational Mindset	Knowing Who: Potential Developers
Values	Research	Proactivity	Senior leaders
Goals and interests	Opportunities	Effective interactions	Peers
	Obstacles		Junior colleagues
Talents and skills		Social skills	Professional associates
Areas for improvement			Family/friends
			Inside/outside work

what you love to do and excel at). The resulting self-awareness also generates the confidence that enables you to reach out to others.

> Cary and Kelly took widely dissimilar approaches to self-awareness. Cary was self-reflective early. In college, he took courses with regular reflective practices. They required him to keep weekly journals. In them, he'd write about how concepts that he was learning about in class might be applied broadly.
>
> Kelly, by contrast, took a number of specialized marketing research courses. True, they equipped him to land his first job, and it was a good one. But he was unaware that knowing himself deeply would be an important element in his career advancement.

Make Time for Reflection

You don't need a college course to develop self-awareness. But Kelly should have learned that regular reflection on your experiences, in and out of work, provides clarity; it offers unclouded insight into your preferences, your personal values, your interests and talents, and, ultimately, your personal goals. All must be crystal clear in order for you to make the right next step in your journey.

This doesn't just happen. You have to make time for it. And to use those minutes and hours efficiently, we suggest employing several well-tested tools. Among these are journaling, pausing to reflect during and after meaningful conversations, reviewing performance feedback carefully, and soliciting feedback from supervisors and others. A variety of assessment tools are also available through your organization and online.

Try Journaling or Blogging

The technique of journaling is frequently used in schools, executive programs, and by individuals. Some discover its value in a classroom setting, working with a career counselor, through professional associations, a self-help book, or an online resource.

In some industries, it's also quite common for individuals to use blogging or social media to gather feedback on their ideas and reflections. Less personal than journaling, these electronic tools do provide input from others who share interests and values. Common to all methods is a set of guiding questions:

- What happened? Write a brief (three to four sentences) description of events that occurred.
- How did you feel? What did you think?
- What did you learn from the experience?
- How can you use what you've learned in the future?
- What *actions* will this lead you to take in the future?

Capture Your Experience for Future Reflection

The purpose of structured reflection is to sharpen your self-analytical skills. Opportunities can arise in many ways—a conversation with your boss, a disagreement with a coworker, a mistake at work, a difficult conversation with your partner, or a recognized accomplishment. The trick is to capture the experience on paper (or virtually) and to reflect on it. That is, use work-based experiences as data for improving your relationships and performance.

Then as you reread your reflections, you'll discover patterns. These offer insight into what's important to you and help reveal future directions.

Our colleagues Tim Hall and Lynn Daudelin offer useful rules for structured reflection:

Guidelines for Structured Reflection
1. Write in a journal or blog regularly.
2. Choose a specific time of the day or week to devote to writing.
3. Capture insights as they occur (keep your journal handy).
4. Don't worry about spelling, punctuation, or complete sentences (just write).
5. Date each entry (to provide chronology and perspective over time).
6. Explore creative ways to record your thoughts (a poem, a picture, colors, etc.).
7. Adopt a spirit of inquiry (go with the flow, be curious).
8. At regular intervals, read what you've written.
9. Allow contradictions to occur and explore them for more learning.
10. Observe yourself as you think and learn with your writing.
11. Share ideas with others (it leads to new insights and new material).
12. Trust that you will discover relevant information (if you believe this has value, it will).

Beyond increasing your self-awareness, structured reflection will provide you with the data you need and uncover questions you want to explore with potential developers. For example,

> From his start at P&G, Cary found that reflecting on his experiences gave him plenty to talk about with his boss, peers, and selected senior colleagues.
>
> With his boss he discussed his evolving interests in the job and the company. This elicited conversations about next steps

and the skills he should develop. During his third year, he got to know a more senior colleague. Sharing his well-informed reflections on experiences and goals led to an introduction to the person who offered Cary his next position.

Reflect on a Regular Basis

Habitual reflection clarifies your thinking and makes you a better conversationalist. Remember, intelligent conversations, as opposed to work-related chatter, are the starting point for strategic relationships.

No one likes being unprepared, especially when an opportunity arises to talk with a senior executive. What happens in such an interchange if you haven't already examined your preferences, your interests, your skills, and your goals? Nothing meaningful.

But if you've done at least some reflecting, you'll be able to do more than stammer. You'll have informed questions that may set a new relationship in motion.

Reflect on Conversations with Others and through Assessments

Conversations with people interested in you can enhance your self-awareness.

Most organizations have structured appraisal systems that regularly provide feedback on your performance. Feedback is also available in widely used assessments of your personality style (such as the DiSC or MBTI assessments), your leadership style (such as the LPI), your personal values, your career interests, and current knowledge and skills.

If these are not available through your organization, such self-awareness tools can be found in books and online. All provide a starting point for meaningful conversations. We define these as talks with a boss or other experienced colleague, with friends and family members, or with any developer who's also a good listener and really cares about your personal success and happiness.

Discover Your Passion

The overarching goal of reflection and self-exploration is to discover your "personal genius."

Herb Shepard defines "personal genius" as that which you are passionate about and really enjoy doing. The only way to figure out what your personal genius is is to observe yourself in action, at work, and in life. Take note of the activities that give you positive energy and satisfaction. Then consider what it is about these activities that you enjoy. Where else, especially in the workplace, might you find work that engages you similarly?

Self-awareness evolves throughout our career journey. Our priorities, goals, and interests are likely to change over time. Therefore, the practices we suggest are relevant not just early in your career. They apply whenever you sense a need to move on, to grow, or to respond to external changes.

That also means that if you're like Kelly, all is not lost. It's never too late to reflect, journalize, and avail yourself of assessment tools. In fact, we've seen managers and executives discover the value of these practices after 15 or 20 years in the workplace. Sometimes this awareness comes from what's called "the gift of a crisis." External conditions related to family, economy, or industry can all be catalysts that inspire you to reassess your situation at work. In doing so, you'll be better prepared to move on by engaging others in meaningful, purposeful dialogue.

Knowing Where: How Can I Broaden and Deepen My Understanding of Career Opportunities?

Journalists talk about the "five Ws and Hs" of a news story: who, what, where, when, why, and how. Self-awareness is the "why"; the first step in figuring out whom to enlist in your developmental network. But just as important in writing your personal news story is knowing "where" opportunities in the workplace might align with your goals, preferences, interests, and skills.

When there's a good fit between what you want and what a job offers, positive attitudes and good performance are likely outcomes. And there's another benefit from an overlap of your goals, preferences, and skills with the expectations, demands, and rewards of a position: You become more positive and adaptable.

Research Career Opportunities Inside and Outside Your Workplace

Why guess about your job fit? Instead, do some research on what's out there, not only in your organization, but in any industry, related or not. The better informed you are, the more realistic choices you have.

If you're sensing a lack of fit, this is an indication that it is time to revisit both "Knowing Why" and "Knowing Where." Career information is abundant online and through social media. And those should be the first places you investigate for digging up realistic alternatives. Old-fashioned face-to-face interactions work, too. Like a good reporter, you'll need to do legwork to query individuals in professional roles you'd like to learn more about.

Combine Your Research with Insights from Others

It's a good idea to alternate online research with informational interviews. Mix the latter up among people you want to meet, both at your workplace and outside it.

Your self-awareness and familiarity with possibilities will help you develop solid questions—insightful queries that will tease out the experience and insight of those whom you talk with.

What's in it for them? Reporters already know that most people enjoy being asked about their career history and what they know about a job or industry. They like being the center of attention and the big authority. You'll also discover that a 30-minute informational interview is no imposition. People often give not just their time but introductions to good sources of career information.

Let's return to Cary and Kelly for a how-to and a how-not-to:

From the get-go, Cary was sharpening questions about next steps in his career. He'd already learned the importance of self-reflection and of self-awareness in career development. And he intuitively understood that questioning colleagues, friends, and family could help him to clarify his path and goals.

During his second year on the job, he began talking with marketing colleagues in positions he considered interesting. He armed himself with questions about how they'd gotten to where they were; he also quizzed them on the advantages and disadvantages of certain roles. In doing so, he isolated the most attractive possibilities and how best to move toward them.

By year three, Kelly hadn't made much progress in identifying career possibilities. Nor had he developed penetrating questions based on his goals, preferences, and skills. Reason: He hadn't clarified them. But he could have used them. They're the essential catalysts for launching discussions with those who might help him.

Kelly needs to explore "knowing where." Hopefully, someone who cares about Kelly's potential will light a match under him to do so.

Continue Learning and Exploring to Develop Your Career

It's not possible to know all there is to know about alternative career possibilities in today's tumultuous economic environment. Indeed, maybe it's a good thing that most of us won't have the same job or employer over the life of our career. That's a sign of opportunity as well as peril. But like the Boy Scout motto, you've got to be prepared. How?

If you're looking for inspiration, read the biographies and autobiographies of individuals you admire, like Steve Jobs. He certainly triumphed over adversity, and his story may strike a chord with you. Looking for industry knowledge and trends? There's no shortage of career fairs, career centers, professional associations, industry trade groups, and industry publications. All can stir your career juices.

Knowing How: How Can I Create and Sustain Strategic Relationships?

The old joke is, "How do I get to Carnegie Hall?" Punch line: "Practice, practice, practice." In *Blink*, author Malcolm Gladwell popularized research by Anders Ericsson that it takes 10,000 hours of deliberate practice to become an expert.

Fortunately, you don't need 1,250 eight-hour working days to create relationships with meaning and purpose. This may be a relief to introverts. Indeed, psychologists have been arguing for years that people should build on their strengths. If you are not a social butterfly, we do not expect you to become one.

You do, however, need to be open to relational learning, to be proactive, to manage your interactions, and to have enough social awareness and social skills to connect with potential developers. And then you must practice at whatever pace you're comfortable with. Let's explore some attitudes that will make this easier.

Do You Have a Relational Mindset? Are You Open to Learning in Relationships?

Do you believe that others are willing and able to help you? It is a basic assumption that good protégés and good mentors share alike, with the caveat being that people are willing to help as long it doesn't consume too much of their time.

Having a relational mindset signals two things: You believe others are receptive to helping, so you are, therefore more likely to ask for help—seeking advice, perspective, information, or feedback. It also implies reciprocity for helpers and a willingness to assist people who contact you for the first time.

These assumptions will make you proactive in initiating and building relationships with individuals whom you admire for their expertise and wisdom—and maybe even earn their friendship. Let's see how Cary and Kelly handled this:

Cary had internalized a relational mindset during his college days. Since day one at P&G, he knew that building relationships with peers, supervisors, and other colleagues was as important as mastering the technical aspects of the work. This allowed him to create a developmental network that secured him a desirable promotion.

Kelly's natural style is to be more of a lone ranger—self-reliant, self-contained, and self-actuated by focusing on his individual performance and productivity. Assuming he's content in his position, there's nothing wrong with this approach.

But the problem is that Kelly doesn't want to be left alone. He wants to get ahead. He'll be lucky to bump into someone on the job who'll become a developmental partner. Therefore, in order to increase the likelihood of his finding someone to help him, he needs to develop his own version of a relational mindset.

Relationships Are Good for You

Developing a relational mindset offers deeper benefits than just learning from others.

Neuroscience shows that engaging in positive social interactions increases a feeling of well-being. In fact, behaving altruistically or with empathy triggers the release of oxytocin, the hormone associated with human bonding and intimacy. Thus, the trust that's fostered benefits you *and* your developers. You both feel good.

Increase the Potential for Mentoring Moments

Practice does make perfect. It also provides the occasional *mentoring moment*. These are serendipitous interactions that change how you think or act. They can range from obtaining almost mundane support needs—such as tips on how to get work done—to an awakening about your future career.

Foster More High-Quality Connections

When you're open to relationship learning, you hone your ability to have interactions that reshape your thinking, sometimes minutely, sometimes radically. In other words, a relational mindset unlocks *high-quality connections*—whatever the intensity or duration—that can contribute to your learning and growth.

Are You Proactive? Do You Reach Out Broadly and Often?

It's both a truism and a fact that if you proactively initiate relationships, you're likely to receive more of the support you need. After all, the law of averages is working in your favor. We see this with go-getter Cary, who naturally reaches out to people to build his marketing résumé. The corollary is that people are more interested in you and responsive to you—whether you are asking for help, advice, feedback, or information—when you regularly make the effort to interact.

But what if you don't know how to break the ice? Here are some good conversation-starters. You'll need to tailor them to the person you're dealing with and your interests.

Good Questions for New Developers
1. Could you tell me about your career path? How did you get to the position you are in today?
2. What are the most important things you've learned from each promotion or change?
3. What are the best (worst) things about your current job? About your current organization?
4. How would you advise someone who wanted to follow a similar career path?

Introverts Can Be Proactive Too

If the thought of never eating lunch alone terrifies you, then you are probably an introvert and need regular quiet time to recharge. Another distinction is that introverts think hard before talking while extroverts talk to think. Either way, creating a developmental network is essential for both introverts and extroverts.

Interestingly, introverts may be more comfortable seeking relationships with a purpose and with preparation than are extroverts. It's more natural for introverts to dive deep in. This means that our goal is to give extroverts extra focus during such key conversations; to make sure that they address areas of concern that they've pondered. Or more broadly speaking, we aim to empower extroverts to harness the power of relational learning.

The following short quiz assesses your current skill at initiating developmental relationships:

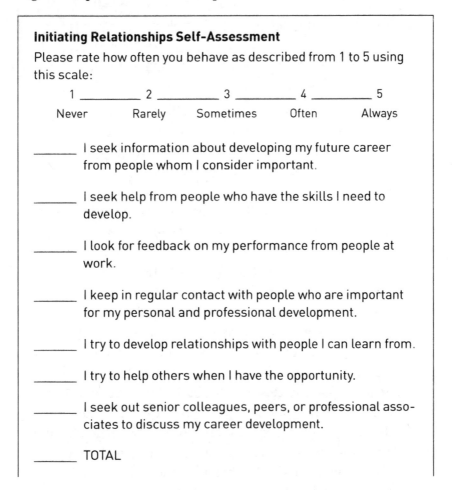

Initiating Relationships Self-Assessment

Please rate how often you behave as described from 1 to 5 using this scale:

1 _____ 2 _____ 3 _____ 4 _____ 5

Never   Rarely   Sometimes   Often   Always

_____ I seek information about developing my future career from people whom I consider important.

_____ I seek help from people who have the skills I need to develop.

_____ I look for feedback on my performance from people at work.

_____ I keep in regular contact with people who are important for my personal and professional development.

_____ I try to develop relationships with people I can learn from.

_____ I try to help others when I have the opportunity.

_____ I seek out senior colleagues, peers, or professional associates to discuss my career development.

_____ TOTAL

Tally your score:

7–14 It would benefit your career and the careers of those around you to initiate and foster more developmental relationships.

15–27 You make efforts to seek and provide developmental assistance, although you may not always follow up or consistently touch base with people who are important to you.

28–35 You are highly aware of the importance of developmental relationship initiation, both seeking and contributing developmental assistance.

Do You Manage Your Interactions? Do You Build Trust and Leave a Good Impression?

When you create a good connection with a developer, you reap the rewards of support and growth through the relationship. That's the whole idea. But how can you manage these interactions most effectively? Here are some ways:

1. **Prepare for meetings.** Reflect on your purpose for the interaction and jot down notes concerning what you hope to learn. Bring them to the meeting. Being prepared demonstrates that you care about your developer's time and emotional investment in you.
2. **Listen carefully.** Don't get so wrapped up in your questions that you fail to listen carefully to your developer. This means being fully present in the conversation. Attentiveness enables you to ask good follow-up questions.
3. **Strategic self-disclosure.** Personal comfort is important to bonding. One way to increase it is through relevant self-disclosure. Revealing vulnerability fosters trust. Such disclosures tend to be reciprocal—if you reveal a weakness, your developer will likely share one, too. It also provides valuable insight into how you and your developer can help each other.

4. **Convey appreciation.** Simply thanking people for their time and effort can go a long way—both at the end of a meeting and as a way of following up.

5. **Keep in touch regularly.** The best way is to give a progress report on your experience with your mentor's advice or what you've been working on since you last spoke. Follow-up questions also keep your developers engaged. Relationship maintenance over long gaps between meetings requires frequent updates. These are essential to maximizing your limited time together.

6. **Create opportunities for mutual learning.** Don't forget to think of what's helpful to your developer. Ask yourself: what interesting articles or books have I read? What new trends or ideas might be useful to him or her? Are there speakers or events that would be useful? The point is to find ways to build common interests and have discussions in which you both are learning.

Do You Have Social Awareness and Social Skills?

Equally important to building valuable relationships is what Daniel Goleman, psychologist and author of *Social Intelligence,* refers to as social awareness and social skills.

Social awareness begins with *empathy*—your ability to sense other people's emotions accurately and to actively communicate your understanding of their perspectives and concerns. It also includes *organizational awareness*—your ability to read and navigate social networks as well as maneuver within the politics of your organization.

When you demonstrate empathy and awareness of the social context in which you're building relationships, chances are good that you'll be able to establish positive bonds with developers. And honing these abilities takes practice, practice, practice.

Apply Thoughtful Communication Skills

And there's yet another skill: You'll also need finely tuned communication skills, such as active listening, giving and receiving feedback, managing conflict, and appropriate self-disclosure.

What's the point? What's the payoff? Jean Baker-Miller, in her work on growth-enhancing relationships, noted that "five good things" come from high-quality relationships: zest, empowered action, increased self-worth, new knowledge, and a desire for more connection.

Relationships Energize You and Your Network

According to research by Ryan Quinn, high-quality developmental relationships do more than foster learning and professional development. They actually release positive energy. And it's reciprocal.

Moreover, that energy sets in motion a virtuous cycle of learning, engagement, and growth. Indeed, if you want to make a change in your behavior or learn a new skill, you are more likely to embrace such a challenge and succeed if you're fueled by the energy that comes from positive connections. It gets you twitching in anticipation just to think about it.

Of course, part of social awareness is being attentive to energy dynamics as a form of feedback. You need to constantly gauge how people are reacting to you and your ideas, and whether they can and want to support your learning. It's sort of your own internal dynamometer test of the power you're receiving.

Be Realistic and Respectful

Realistically, you won't get lots of time with developers until they get to know you. This is especially true of industry leaders, keynote speakers, and busy executives. Sheryl Sandberg, COO of Facebook and author of *Lean In*, talks about how awkward it is for young people to approach her and ask, "Will you be my mentor?"

This gets back to how loaded the word *mentor* is; it reflects how people have their own interpretation of what a mentor needs to do. For people to take on this role, they need to see that you have interests in common. People will choose to invest time in you if they see that you are talented. Most often, they make such a determination based on your performance, or if they think that you have potential and you could benefit from their help.

Your goal is to make them aware of your talents and get them that information in a way that captures their attention, while also showing that you respect their time. Again, preparation is key!

Knowing Who: Who Are on My List of Potential Developers?

Rolodexes are gone, but their function remains in whatever electronic or paper address book you keep. The point is that you must constantly review and update your list of current and potential developers. This will enable you to accurately target your efforts.

Revision is inevitable, especially if you think about the shifting variables of goals, knowledge and skills, preferences, or simply the constant reactions needed to cope with changes and upheavals in your job specs or industry.

Change may not only be in the air but in your head. Perhaps your self-awareness has increased in the last year. You now realize that you are ready to consider graduate school as the means for enhancing your professional skills and opportunities. Or, maybe thanks to research, you've stumbled onto an organization with a mission that's more aligned with your personal values.

Relationships Change; Invest When They Are Mutually Beneficial

Parting is such sweet sorrow. But sometimes it's necessary. Needs change, relationship partners move on, and a connection can go stale. Sometimes the relationship is just no longer mutually satisfying. The question becomes whether to revitalize the relationship or invest energy and efforts elsewhere. We have personal experience to share on these difficult choices.

About five years ago, Kathy (one of the authors of this book) began to sense that her role at the university was less aligned with her changing needs and preferences. This simply reflected growth and an evolution in her goals, not dissatisfaction.

During her first 20 years as a professor, Kathy was passionate about her teaching and research. She embraced several important service responsibilities at her school. But after she'd done these things more than a few times, she began to experience burnout—a vague sense that she was no longer thriving. This was coupled with a related decline in energy.

Kathy realized that she needed help in figuring out what was going on at this point in her career. She also understood that she might have to initiate some new relationships in order for her to get a handle on her confusion.

Two individuals came immediately to mind in Kathy's ongoing developmental network. They were good friends and peer coaches. Sure enough, both were able to listen, empathize, and make valuable suggestions. Those suggestions were: to reach out to individuals who may have experienced what she was feeling; to contact people doing work that piqued her interest; and to get in touch with people she might enjoy spending time with at this point in her life.

What Kathy realized, only in retrospect, was that she was entering a major transition. This sea change required substantial changes in her priorities, her expectations of herself, and her work. Comparing her developmental network today with what it was five years, we can see what happened. In almost rank order of importance for getting through the crisis, we can see new relationships, transformed relationships, and relationships that have taken a backseat for the time being.

Reassess Your Developmental Network as Needed

Regardless of your age or career stage, it's essential to review your developmental network and work situation. You want to see whether enough change had rippled through your life to warrant updating your developmental network with fresh blood.

It's not a bad idea to do this periodically. But the time of maximum need is when you are feeling that something is out of alignment. Here are some examples of that little voice of warning that goes off in your head:

> Perhaps your organization has vastly altered its strategic direction, which does not bode well for your future growth in your division.

Or you realize that you have to move on in order to learn new skills.

Maybe a critical developer has left or no longer has the interest or time to coach and guide you.

Changes in your family situation require you to redefine your work boundaries.

Possibly, your own reflection might have made you aware of latent skills and interests you didn't even know you had.

This aspect of the entrepreneurial approach is truly self-administered. You can begin by reviewing the list of individuals that you identified at the end of Chapter 1. Look again as well at the developmental network you created at the end of Chapter 2 and your reflections at the end of Chapter 3. Do you have relationships in your network currently that could help you navigate? Are there distant developers who might be more helpful now?

Are there people who are not on your list or in your developmental network who you think could be helpful to you, given your current challenges? If you are at midcareer or beyond, are their individuals whom you'd like to mentor, coach, or influence in some way? Is there anyone with whom you would like to initiate a conversation that may lead to a new connection with mutual learning?

These efforts, in turn, will undoubtedly strengthen your relational mindset, your proactivity, and your social skills.

Be Intentional; Invest in Relationships Strategically

When you make choices about investing in new relationships or deepening existing relationships, other relationships may inevitably weaken. This is a natural part of managing your developmental network; strong ties may loosen as you interact less often and your needs change.

Likewise, new developers will require more of your time in the initiation stage and increased interaction in the cultivation stage than current developers do. Nevertheless, some emotional bonds will remain strong regardless of how often you interact. Try to be realistic about how close your developers will be in relation to your current goals and challenges.

At the end of the day, you are responsible for navigating your career. Relationships that matter are the ones that support you in this process. Remember, you (in whatever label you've given your role—mentee, protégé, mentor, coach, sponsor, learning partner, developer, rah-rah supporter—need to take an entrepreneurial approach to relationships to both give and receive the help each of you needs to be happy and successful.

Reflection Exercise: Creating Your Ideal Developmental Network Map

Now that you've created your current developmental network in Chapter 2 and evaluated it in Chapter 3, follow the two-step process below to create your ideal developmental network map.

Step 1: Summarize Your Personal Goals and Challenges

Essential to self-assessment is creating clear goals and identifying challenges. In order for others to help you, you must be able to articulate your needs and hopes.

Extensive research by Edwin Locke and Gary Latham on goal-setting has resulted in many organizations using SMART goals—specific, measurable, attainable, relevant, and time-bound goals. Another important aspect of goal-setting is getting feedback on your progress and achievements.

Considering both immediate challenges and longer-term goals will help you to approach others with purpose and ask good questions.

Goal-setting may cover such situations as getting promoted, gaining insight on how the organization works (who the key people are and what they do), exploring a different role or function, learning about an individual and his or her career strategies, understanding a different organization or field, and so on.

Identifying challenges may include the ability to handle a difficult boss or coworker, being assigned an onerous task (e.g., budget and personnel cuts), a new assignment or collaboration, a new idea and how to communicate it, and the like.

Take a few minutes to list your current goals and challenges:

Goals and Challenges

Goal or challenge 1:
Goal or challenge 2:
Goal or challenge 3:

Step 2: Identify Whom to Enlist and How

Look back at your developmental network map from Figure 2-3. Then, based on your goals and challenges, consider the following:

Whom Should You Enlist?
- Assess your current developmental network. Whom should you get to know better or deepen your relationship with?
- What type of help is missing?
- Is there anyone in your broader social network who could be helpful as a developer?
- How can you leverage your current network to enable you to meet new developers?
  - Is there someone who is well connected who may be able to introduce you to developers in your area(s) of interest?

- o Is there someone whom you've never talked to about your career or asked questions about his or her career?
- o How will you meet developers outside your current network? (Consider professional associations, conferences, interest groups, volunteer organizations, online communities, and so on.)

Good job so far. Now you're prepared to create your ideal developmental network map—the document that will help you reach your goals and meet your challenges (see Figure 4-1).

Some potential developers might be unknown at this point. Use a placeholder if it's clear you need a new developer. This should also prompt you to create an action plan to meet that person.

Figure 4-1 My Ideal Developmental Network Map

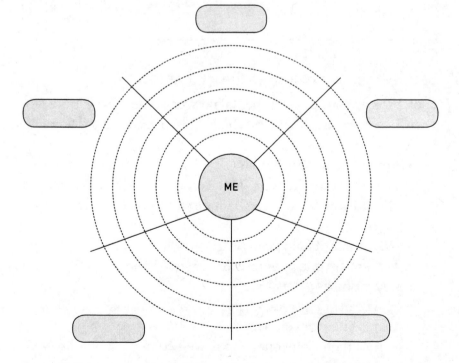

PART 2

LEARNING FROM MENTORS AT WORK

5

FORMAL PROGRAMS FOR PROFESSIONAL DEVELOPMENT

"Perfect," you might think. "My company has a formal mentoring program. Now someone else will find me a mentor."

Sure, formal relationships are one way for you to find developers, in either role—as mentee (protégé) or mentor. Over 70 percent of Fortune 500 companies have implemented formal mentoring programs for targeted employees. Yet desired outcomes from these formal programs often remain out of reach.

Should you participate in a formal mentoring program? Well, yes. But you should know a few things first. At a glance, formal mentoring programs appear to be a panacea for individual development and organizational retention. The reality is that mentoring relationships require patience, commitment, and time. And the biggest challenge is setting realistic expectations for participants and organizations.

Given that informal relationships are generally more effective, the more that formal programs create conditions similar to informal relationship development, the more likely they are to be successful. Formal programs offer you an opportunity to learn about mentoring, to experience a matched mentoring relationship, and to develop the self-awareness and social skills you need to build other relationships that comprise a robust developmental network.

If you are an individual worker, you might want to examine this chapter to see if your company has the right components in place for the program you are considering. We offer you a few key tips on how to succeed as a participant starting on page 103.

If you are an employer thinking about sponsoring a formal program, we outline strategies for linking this initiative with other leadership development, career planning, and succession planning systems and programs. Mentoring programs are most effective when they are aligned with business culture, talent development practices, and the business strategy.

For example, many formal mentoring programs address retention problems that relate to high-potential midcareer women. However, establishing such a program—which matches senior executives with midcareer women—may cause disillusionment if the senior executives don't embrace the program's goals and requirements, they don't have the emotional intelligence to mentor high-performing women, or the culture is so competitive that it is difficult to develop trust and, in turn, high-quality relationships. Our point is that a diagnosis of the context and the forces that will support or undermine a formal program needs to be the starting point.

In this chapter, we provide an overview of the myriad types of formal mentoring (developmental) relationships. The popularity of these programs reflects the array of potential benefits for both individuals and organizations. To capture these benefits, we highlight practices and tactics that lead to realistic expectations and reduce disillusionment or the number of dysfunctional relationships. Formal mentoring programs work when leaders create conditions that promote success and participants take responsibility for fostering their relationships.

Formats: What Are Typical Roles and Responsibilities in Formal Programs?

Mentoring programs may play an important role in your development if they are well designed. Traditional mentoring relationships are composed of a more experienced, senior leader in the role of *mentor*—or sponsor, coach, learning partner, developer—and a less experienced, junior employee in the role of *mentee*—or protégé, coachee, learning partner, associate. We use the terms mentor and mentee for clarity and because these terms are most commonly used in practice, but any of these labels is appropriate.

In Chapter 1, we introduce the issue that the term *mentor* has become synonymous with someone who formally passes on wisdom to an inexperienced or junior colleague. As we've discussed, the idea of mentoring is a much broader concept. In fact, mentees receive a wide variety of support (see "Types of Support," Table 1-1) and benefits as do their mentors (see below). With this in mind, companies use a variety of formats to create access to mentoring for their employees. The language that is used to describe these programs, often from the perspective of the person expected to provide support, signals its purpose and helps form expectations.

We do want to remind you that it is the mentee's needs and goals that should be driving the relationships and that he or she should take an active role in managing the focus of the relationship within the organization's framework. In Table 5-1 we review the most common labels for these program roles and define general responsibilities.

Before implementing a formal program, leaders should conduct a thorough needs assessment and determine what issues the program will address. Each of these relationships supports all participants if the programs are successful. More importantly, participating in a formal program should help participants practice skills that will enhance the effectiveness of their developmental network.

Table 5-1 Typical Roles and Responsibilities in Formal Programs

Role	Responsibilities
Mentor: More experienced, senior manager/executive within the same organization	Focus on a broad range of issues and offers many types of support to help the mentee succeed. May offer mentee assistance in managing career, learning new skills, personal support, and role modeling (see Table 1-1 for a complete list).
Sponsor: Senior leader within the same organization	Advocate for protégé's promotion, connect to senior leaders, and prepare him or her for more senior roles in the organization.
Coach: More experienced person in the organization or external.	Instruct on (or help coachee discover) a specific task or skill needed in order to be more effective. Guide coachee in a process of improvement. Ask questions to prompt reflection and generate actionable learning.
Step-ahead mentor: Colleague one level higher than the mentee in the organization	Focus on developing mentee's knowledge and skills needed for promotion to the next level. Serve as a resource on how to get things done in the organization and provide encouragement.
Peer mentor: Colleague with more experience in a similar position/role within the same organization	Teach new knowledge and skills. Provide encouragement.
Peer coach: Colleague at a similar level who may have complementary skills/experience	Share learning opportunities and grow through reflection and practice.
Reverse mentor: Less experienced or junior person in the same organization	Focus on knowledge sharing, particularly current topic/technical expertise and generational perspective. Emphasize leadership development and mutual support.

Role	Responsibilities
Co-mentor: Pairing of more experienced, senior colleague with less experienced, junior colleague in the same organization	Combines traditional mentor relationship and reverse mentor relationship; may be analogous to learning partner or developer (below). Focus on new skills, leadership and career development, and mutual support.
Learning partner: Someone at any level in the organization (any role mentioned above)	Help your partner focus on developing/improving a specific task or skill. Provide feedback and advice as relevant. Often within the context of an educational or training program.
Developer: Someone at any level in the organization or beyond (any of the above roles)	Focus on the needs of the individual seeking help, may provide one specific type of support or a range of different kinds of support to assist in career and personal development (see Table 1-1).
Mentoring circle facilitator: One facilitator or two to three facilitators with complementary skill sets/experiences matched with a group of three to six mentees	Helps the group focus on relevant issues and offers many types of support to members. Mentors and mentees have opportunities to connect with one another as peer mentors within the circle as well. Alternatively, could be composed of peers only, started with the guidance of an outside facilitator—called peer mentoring or peer coaching circles.

Benefits: Why Implement a Formal Program?

Over the last 30 years, research has exploded concerning the benefits of mentoring, and the business press has touted its importance, so much so that many of us no longer question that we need a mentor. We want to know how to get a mentor. In formal programs you are given a mentor (or mentee), so why not take advantage of the opportunity?

Once you see all of the potential benefits of mentoring relationships (see Table 5-2), you begin to understand why so much effort goes into implementing formal mentoring programs and why organizations are willing to invest in new ideas concerning sponsorship (Chapter 6), reverse mentoring (Chapter 6), and peer mentoring (Chapter 8).

Table 5-2 Benefits of Mentoring Relationships

Benefits for Mentees (Protégés, Coachees, Learning Partners, Developers)	Benefits for Mentors (Sponsors, Coaches, Learning Partners, Developers)	Benefits for Organizations
Career/job satisfaction	Career/job satisfaction	Talent management (succession planning)
Life satisfaction	Giving back	Retention
Salary increase	Salary increase	Recruiting
Promotion	Promotion	Performance
Improved job performance	Improved job performance	Productivity
Self-confidence	Reputation	Social equity and diversity
Optimism	Employee loyalty	
Motivation	Organizational commitment	
Learning		
Skill development	Skill/competence development	
Organizational commitment	Leadership development	
Lower stress		
Less work-family conflict		
Clear professional identity		
Changing jobs/careers		
Cultural learning/ adjustment		
Leadership development		

Benefits for Mentees

Why should you seek a mentor? When you have a high-quality relationship, you may receive all three types of support—career, psychosocial, and role-modeling. The exchange of support is how all these benefits accrue to you and your organization.

Here are some specifics. Instrumental or career-focused support has significant impact on mentees' objective outcomes, including compensation, promotion, and/or improved performance. In contrast, psychological (psychosocial and role-modeling) support has significant impact on subjective outcomes, such as increased satisfaction and confidence. Role-modeling has its strongest impact on mentees' satisfaction and skill development.

It is notable that mentees rate a program's effectiveness based on the amount of psychological support they receive. Unfortunately, this reflects our outsized cultural expectations of what mentoring must entail and stereotypical ideals of a mentor. Mentees often come to a formal program expecting their assigned mentor to provide psychological support and to actively sponsor them for challenging assignments, and ultimately for promotion to the next level. Many individuals who sign up for the mentor role are able and willing to provide one or the other, but not necessarily both. Aligning expectations for the relationship, thoughtful selection and matching, and careful consideration of the talent-development needs of the organization are important steps toward minimizing the disillusionment that occurs when participants' expectations are not met.

This mindset about the ideal mentor also helps explain why when Sheryl Sandberg (COO of Facebook and author of *Lean In*) clearly provided career support to a junior woman, her mentee did not think of Sandberg as a mentor. It is successful people like Sandberg, who have the most demands on their time, who are sought after as mentors, and yet often mentees' expectations of unlimited amounts of time and support are completely unrealistic.

If you take an entrepreneurial approach to relationships, you will be better equipped to recognize when you are receiving support and to foster that valuable connection rather than expect any one person to fulfill all your needs. Each relationship has the potential to provide the opportunity for mutual learning. With this in mind you can seize the opportunity provided in a formal program to create and sustain a relationship that matters.

Benefits for Mentors

Why should you engage with mentees? When you have a high-quality relationship, you also benefit from mutual support and learning in the relationship. Mentors who provide instrumental support—in the forms of teaching mentees new skills, advocating for a mentee's promotion, or helping them secure challenging, high-profile assignments, for example—also find that their reputations are enhanced at work and that they are viewed as people who develop talent. Serving as a role model and/or providing psychological support—in the forms of encouragement, counseling, on professionalism thus motivates a mentee to achieve—result in feelings of satisfaction and giving back to the next generation. It should come as no surprise that mentors also reap benefits such as increased compensation, promotions, and the loyalty of their employees.

Mentees often teach mentors in unexpected ways.

Take for example, Adam, a senior marketing director, who is matched with Karen, a new product manager, to help her learn more about the strategic positioning of the firm and become a stronger candidate for the next level of responsibility. Karen shared a number of analytic tools (learned in her MBA program) that were very helpful in scanning the market potential of new product ideas. She also knew of a number of websites that provided up-to-date forecasts relevant to the industry that were unfamiliar to her mentor Adam. Her facility with web-based tools became a major resource to him.

We recommend a shift in mindset. If you are in the role of mentor, consider your mentee as one of the many contributors to your own developmental network.

Benefits for Organizations

Why implement a formal mentoring program? Organizations looking for opportunities to develop targeted groups of employees—often emerging leaders, women, people of various minority backgrounds, or newly promoted managers—find that mentoring relationships help develop both the focal population and their leadership pipelines.

Participants in these programs often increase their contributions to the firm through improved productivity and performance. In addition, fostering relationships among employees is a retention tool because it increases job embeddedness, the web of connections that explains why people stay. Finally, many organizations attract employees by highlighting the opportunities they offer for mentoring during recruitment.

What Are the Key Components of Successful Programs?

Mentoring programs are usually run by talent management divisions or areas of the firm tasked with overseeing career advancement, training, and/or resources for employee development, often in human resources or diversity and inclusion offices. They may also be administered internally or cross-functionally as stand-alone programs. While mentoring programs exist in a variety of formats, there are eight key components to any successful program (see Table 5-3):

Goals Aligned with Organization's Strategy

How does this program fit with your organization's overall strategy? What issue or problem does it address, and how does it fit in with your current goals?

These questions are critical for leaders to answer before launching any mentoring program. When the program has clear

Table 5-3 Successful Mentoring Program Components

Program Component	Description
Goals aligned with the organization's strategy	How does this program fit with your organization's overall strategy? What issue or problem does it address, and how does it fit in with your current goals?
Active support of senior leaders	Leaders at the top of the organization serve a key role in publicizing the strategic importance of your program, encouraging participation, and providing recognition.
Program coordinator	An individual or team responsible for creating materials, managing communications, and managing resources. Also serves as a third-party consultant for participants and facilitates program implementation.
Selection and matching	Participation is voluntary. Participants should have input regarding their interests and needs. The mentor should not have direct reward power over the mentee.
Education and training	Connect the purpose of the program to organizational goals. Set expectations for roles and time commitment. Communicate resources and support for the program. Facilitate initiation stage of the relationship. Offer opportunities to hone relational skills.
Ongoing support	Provide additional programming like guest speakers or sponsored lunches, and formal check-ins with participants early in program. Resources should be easily accessible.
Periodic feedback and evaluation	Provide first feedback early, then at three to six months. Give assessment at one year and incrementally, as appropriate. Generate feedback to improve program and evaluation accuracy. Metrics are based on program goals (e.g., skill building, leadership development, etc.).
Aligned with HR systems and organizational culture	Does a mentoring program complement your existing HR programs, or will this be a new approach? Do you have a collaborative or competitive culture? Will senior leaders champion the program? Thinking through these issues will help in planning and program design.

goals, it is easier to define selection and matching criteria, to set expectations for participants' roles, and to determine the amount of training needed.

Common goals include supporting transitions to a managerial role, diversity or part of an affirmative action initiative, grooming of employees with high potential, facilitating transitions to global assignments or repatriation, part of leadership training, and options for career development and learning.

Evaluate the Program Based on Its Purpose

The purpose of the program informs administrators of how they should evaluate its success. A large consumer products organization that Kathy (one of the authors of this book) worked with wanted to accelerate high-potential junior executives' learning and preparation to assume more strategic senior executive roles.

The company had been through a major reorganization, a number of new strategic leadership roles were added, and several senior executives were about to retire. Senior management wanted to create a 12-month leadership development program for a group of 30 high-potential junior executives. This program involved a classroom component composed of four one-week sessions throughout the year, as well as a mentoring component. Rather than assigning one-to-one relationships, however, the decision was made to create mentoring circles of one senior executive and seven junior executives (who were part of the program).

This design fostered hierarchical mentoring as the senior leader facilitated the mentoring circle, served as a role model, and brokered relationships with other senior executives who could offer assistance to the mentoring circle members. Peer mentoring was also fostered among the junior executives as they learned new strategies and tactics from their colleagues who faced similar challenges. Finally, the senior executives met periodically as a group to reflect on their roles as facilitators of the mentoring circles, thus deepening their understanding of how to guide others' development and developing greater self-awareness of themselves as mentors, coaches, and facilitators.

Plan for the Long Term

Considerable planning and up-front work is necessary to create conditions for mentoring circles to thrive. In the example above, Kathy provided external consulting to a team of internal human resources design specialists. They prepared guidelines for the two participant groups and held educational modules that provided opportunities for individuals to develop the relational skills needed to participate effectively in the mentoring program. Beyond the immediate benefits of participating in a well-functioning mentoring circle, participants were asked to consider how they could apply these learning experiences back on the job. The longer-term objective was to create a developmental culture in which members were motivated and equipped to form high-quality connections with seniors, juniors, and peers on the job.

Active Support of Senior Leaders

For any program to be launched successfully, there must be a clear message about its strategic importance from the top of the organization. It is essential that C-suite executives and the top management team openly embrace the initiative and serve as ambassadors for the program in order for there to be broad-based participation. Senior leaders should be engaged at the first step in ensuring that this new initiative aligns with the organization's strategy and develops both people and the company.

Get Visibly Involved—Even Participate

Formal programs with the active support and sponsorship of senior leaders in the company get better results and have greater longevity than those implemented without such support and sponsorship. Sometimes this involvement is limited to providing the funding for the necessary program infrastructure as well as speaking at the kick-off meeting. However, it is better when senior leaders are actively involved in selecting the participants (both mentors and mentees) and perhaps even serving as mentors.

When the mentees are midlevel managers slated for executive roles, it may make sense for senior managers to participate as mentors. When the program involves middle managers serving as mentors to senior associates or first-level managers, senior managers may instead be part of a panel that speaks to the participants as a group about their experiences with mentoring, and what they hope will occur for the program participants. In either scenario, the senior managers are serving as role models for mentoring and as sponsors for the program. Both give legitimacy and strength to the initiative.

Programs Without Support Are More Likely to Fail

We have also observed the unfortunate demise of programs that are started as grassroots efforts (sometimes by employee resource groups) without the active support or understanding of senior leaders. While at the outset there is sufficient enthusiasm and volunteerism to get the program launched, without the "blessing" of management, these initiatives often lose their focus and active involvement when difficulties in the business call participants' attention away from such a developmental activity. Only the active support of senior management can keep such programs thriving during stressful times.

Program Coordinator

There must be a designated leader or coordinator(s) of the program who takes responsibility for creating materials, managing communications (in partnership with the executive team), and managing resources. The program coordinator serves as a critical third-party consultant for participants—answering questions, clarifying expectations, and consulting with either party who may need additional support or strategies for making the relationship a success. In addition, there needs to be someone (or a team) who facilitates program implementation and assessment for the organization. We also recommend a steering committee, comprised of representatives of the various constituencies, that will be involved and/or affected by the mentoring program. The team ensures that program design meets participants' needs and provides assistance to the coordinator(s) in evaluating and interpreting feedback.

As a program coordinator herself, Wendy (one of the authors of this book) designs and facilitates orientation, is visible and available at events, and meets with individual mentors or mentees as needed—often over coffee or on the phone. Beyond discussing their experiences and progress in the formal mentoring program, entrepreneurial mentees and mentors will reach out to her as an additional potential developer to discuss their goals and careers.

Selection and Matching

Do you like to have input on how you spend your time at work? Most of us do, which is why employees who participate in goal-setting and are given some autonomy at work are more motivated and satisfied than those who are not. Voluntary participation works better because when you opt in, you are more likely to be committed to the program and make time for it. Not surprisingly, the more time that mentees and mentors spend together, the better the quality of the relationship, although increasing the amount of interaction after you get a chance to know each other is most beneficial.

Select Committed Mentors

In their study on formal programs, Frankie Weinberg and Melanie Lankau found that mentors who are more committed to their organization are more likely to serve as role models to their mentees. It follows that you should select people with high organizational commitment to serve as mentors. Such participants are likely to commit to making the time to foster their relationship. In addition, leaders need to support their employees by allocating time for the program and recognizing participation as an important contribution to the organization.

Get Participants' Input on Matching

Part of the process of mentor and mentee selection should include participants' input, particularly their interests and/or development needs. Participants who are similar to one another (demographically and/or common interests) tend to develop strong relationships. This is a challenge for programs with an explicit focus on diversity, which we discuss further in Chapter 9.

When diversity and inclusion are overarching goals of a mentoring program, education and training on building relationships across differences is equally important. Reviews of research on mentoring by Tammy Allen, Lillian Eby, and colleagues have shown that when participants feel they had input into the matching process, they receive more support, particularly role-modeling, and are more satisfied with the experience. Participant input matters for the program's effectiveness and reputation.

Program Type and Size Dictate Feasibility of Matching Methods

Organizations can use a variety of tools for matching, such as questionnaires, interviews, statements of interest, work history, personal knowledge, and so on. In order of increasing cost, matching can be administrator-assigned, choice-based, or assessment-based.

Pairs are often administrator-assigned when the administrator has personal knowledge of participants, there are particular organizational goals (e.g., diversity, cultural integration), or the program pairs mentees with external mentors. Programs that are choice-based invite participants to submit requests through priority lists or selection activities. This method is positive from the perspective of participant input; however, it takes more time and also runs the risk of disappointing participants as multiple mentees may prefer the same mentor and vice versa. The size of the company affects how this works, as larger organizations will simply take mentors off of the list (e.g., electronic profiles disappear or become unavailable) as they are selected by mentees, whereas in smaller companies this may create competition among mentees selecting from among a smaller pool of mentors.

Finally, assessment-based matching is the most structured, using personality inventories or technology to match participants. Using this method, participants can increase their self-awareness through the assessment tools and readily share their strengths and weaknesses to focus their work together.

Find What Works for Your Program

Successful programs often use a combination of complementary skills and a similarity of interests to make their pairings. The size of the program may also help determine the feasibility of the matching method. Formal mentors should not have direct power over the mentee (i.e., do not match a mentee with his or her boss's boss). While bosses can be great informal mentors, and in fact supervisors who provide career-related mentoring to their employees are better performers, the inherent conflict of interest is an unnecessary complication in formal mentoring relationships.

In the programs Wendy has administered, which use a combination of methods, she finds that the matching criteria need to be flexible. It is unlikely that you (or any technology) will be able to perfectly fulfill the needs of every participant or meet every request. The goal is to make pairings that give participants the best chance of making a healthy and helpful connection, and then to train them appropriately.

Education and Training

Orientation to a formal program is a critical time for leaders to explicitly connect the purpose of the program to broader organizational goals and initiatives. Training should set clear expectations for participants in terms of their role requirements and time commitment, and it should provide access to organizational resources and support. The objective is to introduce participants to one another in the framework of the program and facilitate the initiation stage of their relationships. Finally, it should also provide opportunities for mentors and mentees to connect with others in the same role.

The amount of training and the quality of training seem to affect participants differently. The number of hours spent in training impacts the amount of psychological support that mentees feel they receive, yet mentors feel that more training helps them provide a higher-quality experience, more career-related support, and role-modeling. In contrast, the quality of the training affects the career-related and role-modeling support that mentees experience and increases the psychological support that mentors feel they provide. Regardless, it is clear that training improves the quality and support provided through the relationship.

Training Should Complement Existing Employee Development

Training should fit within the portfolio of educational tools that the organization has for employee development and complement existing activities. Based on the organization's culture and the objectives of the program, training may occur separately— mentees only and mentors only—and/or together for the launch of the program.

It may be more comfortable for participants to start separately when you need to have frank conversations about role expectations for a new program or if you are doing self-assessments to give them time to process this feedback. We believe that any training is helpful, but the more that training provides a forum for increasing self-awareness and interpersonal skills the better participants will be prepared to contribute to the relationship.

Everyone Needs Training

We have found that senior executives often resist the idea that they need training and education in order to provide mentoring to their assigned mentee. Yet when these same individuals do not get the training, they often begin the matched relationship at a disadvantage: they have not internalized the goals of this particular initiative, they have given little thought to the unique perspective and resources that they can bring to their assigned mentee, and they don't get to deepen their understanding of high-quality relationships and their role in building and sustaining such connections through a shared educational experience.

Ongoing Support

Organizations can offer ongoing support for participants through additional programs beyond orientation. Examples include continuing self-assessment and/or interpersonal skills training—such as how to manage conflict or provide feedback, relevant guest speakers or panels, and sponsored coffee breaks or lunches. Formal check-ins with participants by program administrators early in the program—six weeks to three months in—can help facilitate open communication and reduce the likelihood of a negative experience for either party.

Make Resources Easily Accessible

It is also critical to make any resources available and easily accessible, including program materials, suggested activities or topics for participants, current articles, social media links, and answers to frequently asked questions. Materials can be posted on an internal website, which can also include announcements and discussion boards for questions/answers and information that might be accessible to everyone or just mentees or mentors, as appropriate.

Formal Relationships Are Part of Employees' Developmental Networks

We advocate framing participation in a mentoring program as one way for participants to enhance their developmental network. This sets the stage for participants to connect with others beyond their assigned mentor or mentee for support. In particular, we encourage participants to discuss with each other (i.e., mentors with another mentor, mentees with another mentee) how their relationships are progressing.

Connections may occur informally, or the program might be structured in mentor groups and mentee groups so that each participant has a set of peers assigned and meetings are organized or sponsored by program administrators. A natural outcome of these connections is knowledge sharing—tips for how to start conversations, ask good questions, and develop rapport—and mutual reflection which generate action plans for future interactions. This is peer mentoring at work.

Periodic Feedback and Evaluation

Periodic feedback and program evaluation are critical to ensure that the program meets organizational goals and supports participants' development. You should solicit confidential feedback on the relationship as well as the program itself. One-on-one meetings and phone calls are useful, but electronic surveys are a more cost-effective mechanism as long as the data are kept confidential. In group settings, we have found that participants are more likely to give feedback when it has been validated by their peers—others are having similar experiences (positive or negative!).

Ask for Feedback Regularly
In meta-analyses of mentoring studies, Tammy Allen and her colleagues note that participants require a minimum of six months to establish a strong enough relationship for it to have an impact. We believe that the three- to four-month mark is a reasonable time to solicit a first round of feedback. Thereafter, we suggest gathering data at the halfway and one-year mark, and then periodically, depending on the goals of the program. We have seen formal programs ranging in duration from six months to three years. Successful relationships often continue beyond the established program.

Use Feedback to Provide Resources and Improve the Program
Program feedback should be used to improve subsequent training and support activities at the organizational level as well as to provide resources to individuals that have encountered challenges. Assessment data should determine if the program is meeting the organization's goals and provide data for leaders to evaluate its on-going effectiveness.

The goals for a particular program, as well as the context in which the program exists, will determine which assessment

Table 5-4 Recommended Program Assessments

Focus of Assessment	Timing of Assessment
Feedback on training	Beginning of the program, after each module
Program progress—what's working, what's not working, what needs to be added or changed (process feedback)?	2–3 months out, midpoint of the program, end of program
Satisfaction with program	End of program
Retention	End of program, 2 years out
Promotions	End of program, 2 years out
Improved performance	End of program, 2 years out
Job satisfaction	End of program, 2 years out
Developmental relationship initiation	Beginning and end of the program
Developmental network size and quality; change over time	Beginning and end of the program
Satisfaction with developmental network	Beginning and end of the program

measures are appropriate. We have found the assessments shown in Table 5-4 to be most commonly used in time-bounded formal programs. Furthermore, we recommend adding a developmental network assessment.

Aligned with HR Systems and Organizational Culture

How does a mentoring (or coaching, or sponsorship, or learning partners) program fit with your organization's current leadership development process? Is a mentoring program a natural fit with the culture, or will this be a new approach for your organization?

These are important questions as you consider implementing a formal mentoring program, with implications for participant recruitment and selection as well as the amount of training you will need to provide. Relationship-focused initiatives are generally easier to establish in a culture that values collaboration. However, a program like this could also be a way for an organization with a competitive culture to connect with its employees and foster interpersonal skills, particularly if it is framed as a leadership opportunity and there is visible, high-level support for the program.

Mentoring Is Part of Employee Development

We suggest positioning a mentoring program as one of a portfolio of employee development opportunities facilitated by human resources. Do not underestimate the importance of commitment, participation, and support from your executive team in order to ensure that the program is seen as a legitimate activity and has the ongoing resources it needs to be successful.

Such resources may include program administrator(s), materials, website maintenance, and allowing time for employees to participate. Formal mechanisms for recognition are also useful, such as crediting participation as part of personnel development on annual reviews. We discuss leaders as creators of a mentoring culture in depth in Chapter 7.

How to Succeed as a Participant (mentor or mentee)

Following are tips that can help you to do well as a mentor or mentee in a formal mentoring program:

1. **Bring self-awareness and personal goals to the relationship.** Spend time reflecting on your needs and formulate goals for your own learning in the program. These goals may change or get refined in conversation with your mentor/mentee. Use Part 1 of this book as a foundation for thinking about your career and for how you can learn in high-quality relationships. Take some self-assessments and/or 360-degree assessments if they are offered by your organization or seek out resources online. Think about your results and have conversations with trusted colleagues to help you interpret your strengths and weaknesses, and to develop comfort in this kind of dialogue. Come prepared

to meetings with information to share and questions to discuss in order to make progress on your goals.

2. **Be entrepreneurial in your approach.** Remember, entrepreneurs take *risks* and *initiative*, both key aspects to establishing relationships that matter with the new people you will meet in a formal program. As we highlight in Chapter 2, the "best" mentees ask good questions, actively seek learning opportunities, clearly state what they are seeking in terms of guidance and support, and regularly express appreciation for their developers' time and interest. And good mentors have similar skills as well as accumulated knowledge and wisdom to share. Relationships grow over time, but an entrepreneurial approach will enhance your communication and facilitate the development of mutual support.

3. **Reach out for support from peers and program leader(s).** Look around the room during your orientation to a formal program and consider each person a potential developer. In particular, those who are in the same role as you—whether you are mentee or mentor—will be helpful resources in navigating the program and making the most of your formal relationship. Quite naturally, your colleagues can serve as sounding boards, provide sources of information and support, and share thoughtful insights from experiences in the same role. (We discuss peer mentoring in depth in Chapter 8.) Program leaders and facilitators can also clarify expectations and provide resources to create a productive learning experience.

4. **Consider this relationship as part of your developmental network.** Your formal mentor or mentee should be one of many developers in your network. Learning how to be a good mentee or mentor in a formal program is an extraordinarily useful skill. Given that informal relationships are most often based on mutual attraction and similarities, the skills you foster in developing rapport and strategic self-disclosure in an assigned relationship will enable you to engage in the intentional diversification of your developmental network.

As we discuss in Chapter 3, diversity in your network is an important resource, and to approach diverse others, you will need these capabilities (for more ideas, see Chapter 9). In addition, these skills will strengthen your ability to develop your colleagues and employees.

A Strategic Approach to Mentoring and Talent Development

Ultimately, the decision to implement a formal mentoring program should result from a talent development goal that is established collaboratively by senior leaders and HR staff members responsible for talent development. We call this a strategic approach because the talent development goal should be aligned with the business strategy as well as the current HR practices and culture that will support implementation. Ongoing monitoring and evaluation of the program is essential so that participants are afforded the support and learning that they need in order to build high-quality relationships within the formal program. As this process unfolds, participants will deepen their understanding of developmental relationships and the skills to proactively build other relationships that matter. (See Figure 5-1.)

Figure 5-1 A Strategic Approach to Mentoring

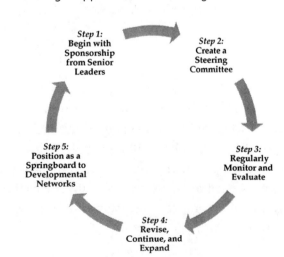

Step 1: Begin with Sponsorship from Senior Leaders

The sponsorship of senior leaders is necessary to ensure that formal programs support the organization's strategy. While the initial impetus for a formal mentoring program may come from employee groups that feel they are lacking guidance and sponsorship to be successful, it is unlikely that a response to this request will have longevity without the active support of senior leaders. If for no other reason, training and education are essential to the success of matched relationships. Plus ongoing monitoring of the relationships combined with peer group support and continuing education input can help relationships deepen over time. These require time and financial resources, both of which must be allocated by those with the authority and budget to do so.

If the culture of the organization is such that individuals are not recognized for taking time to develop others, it will be difficult for invited mentors to fully embrace their role in the program. Senior leaders are in the best position to model positive engagement and to acknowledge others for their participation. Over time, this will bring about a reward system that values developmental relationships. We realize that in some organizations senior leaders will have to be convinced that a formal mentoring program is worthwhile. Here, a small pilot that can be bootstrapped with local funds and demonstrates results may be what wins over their support.

Step 2: Create a Steering Committee with Representation from Relevant Groups

While a single staff person is often assigned to develop the program and oversee its implementation (i.e., program coordinator), it is very useful to establish a steering committee representing the various constituencies that will be involved and/or affected by the mentoring program. This ensures that the program design is responsive to participants' needs, and minimizes the degree of resistance that is often encountered with the implementation of yet another HR program.

So, for example, if the program is targeted to support the development of high-potential engineers who are aspiring to advance into management, you want to include a few engineers who are potential mentees, as well as several managers who are likely to serve as mentors. If there is considerable demographic diversity among constituents and you aim to develop a diverse talent pool at senior levels, make sure your steering committee reflects this as well. When a steering committee represents all stakeholders, it is likely to produce a program that is widely accepted and aligned with the employees' needs and the organizational culture.

Step 3: Regularly Monitor and Evaluate

Monitoring the matched pairs during the entire length of the mentoring program is important. Particular gaps in learning can be identified and addressed, participants have the opportunity to provide feedback to the program coordinator and sponsor(s), and, at the same time, participants have the opportunity to learn from each other. Thus evaluation and feedback can be solicited at the same time, electronically from individuals or face-to-face in groups of mentors and groups of mentees. These groups can be structured and facilitated to foster shared reflection and peer coaching on how to be most effective in developmental relationships.

Step 4: Revise, Continue, and Expand

Regularly assessing developmental initiatives provides opportunity to revise and expand programs in order to be more effective. Many organizations have discovered the limitations of one-to-one formal matching programs. They are quite labor-intensive and serve only a small number of participants at a time. While some organizations have expanded their reach through online matching programs supplemented by mentoring guidelines, in most cases these are not likely to have the depth and impact of face-to-face learning.

Consider alternatives, such as convening mentoring groups composed of motivated participants willing to learn skills and develop new perspectives (necessary for career advancement) through their dialogue with one another. We have observed these "mentoring alternatives" to sometimes have one senior executive facilitate and be a role model for the group and others that remain self-managing after a trained facilitator gets them started with essential guidelines that ensure confidentiality, psychological safety (a sense that it's safe to be vulnerable in the group) and a shared commitment to participants' learning.

Step 5: Position as a Springboard to Developmental Networks

As noted in Part 1 of this book, all of us benefit more from a network of developmental relationships than just one mentoring relationship. In fact, many formal mentoring programs still convey the view that one assigned mentoring relationship is sufficient for employee learning and development. We strongly recommend that one-to-one matching programs be introduced as a first step in learning about mentoring and developmental networks.

Ideally, participants will have the opportunity (as part of the education and training component) to assess their own developmental networks, how the currently matched relationship might fill a developmental gap, and an action plan for moving forward. Ultimately, participants should be prepared and encouraged to enlist other potential developers as a result of the formal program.

Reflection Questions

Consider what formal development programs exist in your workplace or professional organization(s).

1. If you are an individual employee seeking to enhance your developmental network:

   a. Do the purpose and goals of a particular program align with your needs?

   b. If so, how might you become a participant in the program?

   c. If no such program exists, who might you talk with about the need for an initiative that will help you and others with similar development needs?

   d. If you are currently a participant in the program but the program is not meeting your needs, whom can you talk with about this (e.g., program coordinator, your supervisor, an informal mentor)?

2. If you are a leader in your organization or a talent development specialist:

   a. To what extent are formal professional development programs aligned with the business strategy?

   b. Are the necessary components in place to ensure positive results from the program?

   c. Are results evaluated on a regular basis to ensure that the program and its practices are still relevant and optimal?

   d. Is there a need for a new program targeted at a particular group of employees? What kind of developer role makes sense given the development needs of this group?

MENTORING ALTERNATIVES: SPONSORS, COACHES, REVERSE MENTORS, AND MENTORING CIRCLES

Do you need a sponsor or a coach? Or could a reverse mentor teach you something new? The popularity of formal programs has created opportunities for connections of all kinds. In this chapter we highlight the most novel and widespread approaches to developmental relationships. Sponsor, coach, reverse mentor, or mentoring circle—each of these offers an effective alternative to naturally occurring mentoring and can enhance your learning and development at any career stage. An important question for you to ask is: how can these alternatives contribute to my developmental network? (See Figure 6-1.)

These mentoring alternatives share the key characteristics of all developmental relationships: trust, mutuality, and the

Figure 6-1 Mentoring Alternatives

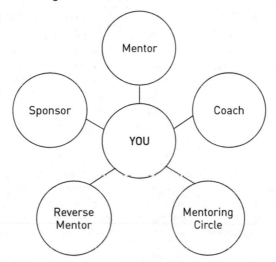

provision of some type of support—whether instrumental or psychosocial. Here, we contrast the roles of sponsors, coaches, reverse mentors, and mentoring circles with traditional mentoring relationships and share examples of effective initiatives. Recall that "true mentors" may also serve as sponsors or coaches over time. (See Table 6-1.)

Sponsorship

Sponsors advocate for your promotion, connect you to senior leaders, and prepare you for more senior roles in the organization. In order to be a sponsor, one must hold a senior-level leadership role and have power and influence in the organization. While sponsorship has always been one of the possible instrumental or career support functions of mentors (see Table 1-1), this specific role has been highlighted recently as critical to women and minorities' success in the workplace.

Sylvia Hewlett's recent book, *Find a Sponsor*, advises everyone to seek out sponsors at work in order to propel you through your next promotion and through your career. A critical piece of Hewlett's advice though is to "distribute your risk"—you need a few sponsors in your developmental network if your goal is to

Table 6-1 Comparison of Developmental Roles

	Mentor	Sponsor	Coach	Reverse Mentor
Purpose	Personal and professional development	Advocate for protégé's promotion, connect to senior leaders, prepare protégé for more senior roles	Develop the capabilities of executives or high-potential performers; often task-oriented	Support mentee's learning goals, foster cross-generational relationships, develop mentor's leadership skills
Focus	Focusing on both immediate and long-term development issues	Increasing protégé's visibility and opportunities	Increasing coachee's professional competencies	Focusing on immediate development needs; knowledge sharing
Role	Leader at any level above the mentee within the organization	Senior executive within the organization	Coach internal or external to the organization	Junior/less experienced associate within the organization
Methods	Holistic discussions that support career development and growth	Expansion of protégé's perceptions of capabilities, mobilization of network on protégé's behalf, advise on executive presence	Professional development, facilitation of transitions, sounding board, remediation of derailing behavior	Share knowledge, exchange of ideas, expansion of senior person's technology skills, facilitation of each other's learning
Outcomes	Objective and subjective career success	Promotion	Performance improvement and promotion	Content/technical knowledge and skills, cross-generational relationships, leadership pipeline
Duration	Longer term or program specified	6 months to 1 year	Flexible—may be one time or as needed	6 months or as needed

move up the hierarchy. As with any developmental relationship, the results are mutually beneficial for you and your sponsor.

Sponsorship Is Instrumental Support

It's important to remember that sponsorship is *instrumental support* by nature. You will attract sponsors based on your performance. Sponsors expect protégés to be self-directed, demonstrate trust, and show loyalty. This means assuming responsibility for delivering 110 percent on objectives and making your sponsor look smart for supporting you. Although a high degree of trust must be built between sponsor and protégé, do not expect your sponsor to offer personal counseling or a shoulder to cry on—that is why you need other developers in your network.

A couple of years into her buying career at Filene's (now Macy's), Wendy was sponsored by one of her senior managers, Rick Seeger. She worked hard as an assistant buyer in the ready-to-wear division, and as she began to have an impact on the business, she interacted more frequently with Rick. Though Wendy and Rick had little in common, she watched as a strong relationship developed between him and one of her male peers based on their shared interests in golf. As far as Wendy was concerned, it was more important that Rick trusted her analysis and insights on the market.

When Wendy was promoted into her rotation as an area manager in stores, Rick was also promoted from divisional manager in ready-to-wear to general manager/vice president of children's, juniors', and shoes. Within months, Wendy was again promoted into the shoes area as a buyer-in-training, and she then advanced to a buyer in children's. It was clear to her (and her colleagues) that Rick had advocated for her promotion into these roles and supported her career. And she delivered results—in her first year as a buyer, she was the only one in her division to meet aggressive gross margin goals. It was a mutually beneficial relationship.

Rick was an informal sponsor to Wendy, illustrating that the support of a sponsor can be critical for getting promoted. As Monica Higgins explains based on her research, a *sponsor* provides high instrumental or career-based support and low psychosocial support—sponsors do not need to be your friend. The key role of a sponsor is to push you and advocate for you to get to the next level. In order for your sponsor to back you in conversations with other executives, he or she has to know your strengths, trust that you will perform, and understand your goals.

Mentors Can Be Sponsors

We want to remind you that mentors can provide sponsorship if they are in a position of influence. Deb Hills recalls how her mentor listened and supported her through a decision to leave her job as a consultant in client services when it became clear that she wanted a more operational role. "He had approached me and offered to help guide my career, and that's what prompted me to open up to him. I was thinking—I care about my clients and solving their problems, but I am more interested in our internal problems." She left the firm later that year. A few weeks later over dinner, her mentor mentioned an upcoming reorganization and an opportunity in human resources. When Deb expressed interest, he connected her to the partner who oversaw that function. Today, Hills is the chief people officer at The Parthenon Group.

Informal Sponsorship Is More Effective Than Formal Sponsorship

Because of the high level of trust required for sponsorship, CEO Luke Visconti of DiversityInc. feels that it is difficult to formally assign protégés to sponsors. Visconti explains, "You need to genuinely like your protégés to advocate for them. You have to be passionate about them in a meeting with other leaders and believe in their capabilities in order to promote them effectively. There has to be chemistry, where they've earned your respect based on performance over time."

Visconti suggests an alternative way to formalize sponsorship—make leaders responsible to find their own protégés and make these leaders accountable to the goals of the firm. Have leaders—including the CEO and other top managers (two to three levels down)—find three people to sponsor and then track the relationships. If diversity is a goal, support leaders by connecting them to minorities through resource groups and other initiatives where they can meet potential protégés and track their progress.

Similarly, Ted Childs, former vice president of global workforce diversity at IBM, has continued to help a variety of organizations to develop their women and minority talent. Whether it is a branch of the armed forces or a large pharmaceutical, technical, or financial company, he maintains that senior leaders must direct their subordinates to actively sponsor talented candidates from all constituency groups in their divisions. When diversity is a clear goal, and there are consequences for *not* achieving this goal, people will get serious about building relationships with people who are different. This becomes easier to execute, and more critical to their business results, when they see it as important to have talent at all levels that looks like both their talent pool and evolving marketplace. And, as we discuss at length in Chapter 9, this usually requires a level of self-awareness and relational skills that many managers don't have. It is up to the CEO and other leaders of an organization to make sure that there are sufficient sponsors with the requisite skills.

Sponsors Need to Have Power and Influence

If you are looking for a sponsor, do not make the mistake of simply seeking out a role model. A sponsor really has to be someone in a position of power and influence. Who brings in the revenue? Who are respected for their work and performance? Women in particular tend to look for someone whose leadership style they admire rather than simply an outstanding executive with power. Again, your goal is to have more than one sponsor as well as other mentors and peers supporting your career.

Your goal is have two to three people in your developmental network who are in positions of power and influence to sponsor you. You will attract more sponsors if you:

- Perform at a high level in each role.
- Take on challenging tasks/assignments and succeed.
- Share insights and take credit for your accomplishments.
- Seek out and prepare for interactions with senior executives.
- Ask good questions and promote your ideas.
- Follow up after your conversations by providing relevant updates or links to resources.

Companies recognize the important role of sponsors and are starting to formalize sponsorship programs. In the next chapter, we highlight the new sponsorship program at KPMG as an extension of its developmental culture.

Coaching

Coaches can enhance your knowledge and understanding of how to navigate your organization and industry. Traditionally, executive coaches were hired to help fix the toxic behavior of leaders on the top management team. Today, the coaching industry has grown tremendously and expanded its focus to include developing the capabilities of high-potential performers at all levels in companies. Coaches can be internal or external to your organization; many managers are trained as coaches, or your company might bring in external coaches for specific skills and expertise.

Coaching Versus Mentoring

Like sponsorship, coaching has always been one of the possible types of instrumental or career support provided by mentors (see Table 1-1). How is coaching different from mentoring then? The scope of mentoring tends to be broader than it is for coaching. Mentoring is a more holistic approach, focused on the whole person and his or her career. In contrast, coaching tends to focus on developing a particular skill set, changing or expanding behavior, or teaching during a specified time frame (e.g., transition to manager).

Sometimes personal development is required for professional development, and so while many professional coaches and consultants are relied upon for career guidance, their counsel often expands to include the nonwork domain. The boundaries of the coaching relationship, as with any relationship, depend on the objectives and goals established at the outset.

External Coaching for Senior Leaders

Susan Alvey, owner of Pemberton Coaching, shared Frank's story with us as an example of a coachee's journey with an external coach:

> Frank was tired. He was constantly buried in work, and his wife was upset because he was never home for dinner. As the executive vice president of sales and marketing, Frank had hundreds of employees, and with the recent reorganization his group had gotten even bigger. Members of the senior executive team (of which he was a part) were reorienting, trying to improve their leadership overall and had the resources to hire some external coaches.

> Frank was not good at delegating. His strengths—his relentless commitment to getting the work done and driving results—were working against him as he tried to do it all. Susan Alvey, an experienced coach, had uncovered this issue in their first meeting. It was hard for Frank to let go because it felt like letting go of his commitment. They decided that his goal should be to get home for dinner at least twice a week. In order to do this, he would have to offload work—and he wanted to hit that target.

> They systematically assessed Frank's direct reports. Who on his team did he see as capable of taking on more? What would it mean for him to work in a more collaborative way? What did

his employees need from him? As Frank began to ask talented people to do more, he was surprised at how they rose to the occasion and began to excel. Some needed skill development; others just needed his support. Frank would try delegating to one person and report back to Alvey. He then repeated this process with several employees.

Habits were hard to change. When someone would come into Frank's office with an urgent problem and say, "*We* have to do something," he would hear, "*I* have to do something." After sharing many examples of these situations with Alvey, he recognized the pattern. His job became more about helping others learn to solve their own problems. And as he began to delegate more, Frank was making it home for dinner more often.

In their work together, Alvey began to shift Frank's attention. She asked him, "Where should you be spending your time?" Frank listed more strategic things that needed his attention. Their goal became to make this strategic time a priority.

Although their coaching sessions were focused on work, as Frank was home more, he got more involved in his family life. He became a den father for his son's Cub Scout troop. He came in saying, "Susan, none of these other fathers listen to me!" How could he facilitate a collaborative relationship when there was no formal hierarchy? He was used to people listening to him because of his position at work. This became another forum for Frank to stretch his leadership skills.

Internal Coaches

Many organizations have a hybrid approach to coaching for their employees. They hire external coaches for the very senior executives of the firm, and they maintain a full-time staff of professional coaches to work with individuals at all levels of the organization. This ensures that all employees are eligible for coaching when they have identified development goals that would benefit from this kind of helping relationship.

Some organizations are exploring how their coaching resources might be expanded by incorporating peer coaching into their leadership development programs as well. Not only are aspiring and current leaders expected to develop their coaching skills, but they also have the opportunity to coach their peers in the context of an educational program and beyond.

For example, a prestigious New York financial services firm hired a team of leadership development experts to design and deliver a leadership program to its high-potential women. As part of the team, Kathy was asked to design a peer coaching component of the program. The women executives completed a 360-degree feedback program and had three hours of coaching with an external executive coach (hired by the consulting team). During the educational component, which included three sessions over six months, participants worked with peer coaches in the classroom. At the last session, they were asked to commit to development goals and an action plan, which they shared with their peer coach. Then, after the last session, participants would follow up with one another, holding each other accountable and providing helpful coaching as well.

Internal Versus External Coaches

When considering whether to enlist an internal or external coach in to your developmental network, it is useful to consider why you need a coach. External coaches have the advantage of bringing an outsider's perspective as well as varied experiences with other organizations. Internal coaches, on the other hand, know your organization well and are more likely to understand the political and social nuances than is an external coach.

If you are contemplating a career or job change, you may feel safer working with an external coach. If, on the other hand, you are looking for guidance on how to better navigate the current realities of your workplace, then an internal coach may be preferable. There are no hard and fast rules for this decision. In part it will depend on what resources are available and provided by your organization.

Fidelity Investments makes both internal and external coaches available to employees at all levels of the company. Dr. Bill Hodgetts, vice president of enterprise coaching and assessment, describes Fidelity's coaching capabilities as consisting of different cadres of coaches. First is a cadre of external coaches that can be engaged on an as-needed basis and is mostly utilized by senior executives. Midlevel executives have the opportunity to work with an external coach should it be their preference. The second cadre of coaches is internally trained and certified by Bill Hodgetts to serve as "debrief facilitator coaches." There are now 150 trained coaches of this kind (usually from the HR organization) who are on call to help employees at all levels of the organization to process and develop action plans after a 360-degree feedback process. Finally, to reduce the attrition rate among expatriate employees, they introduced 10 "global navigation coaches" for those traveling on assignments abroad. These coaches are trained to support expats before, during, and upon their return, in order to facilitate adjustments at both ends of the assignment.

Hodgetts emphasizes they have been successful with their coaching capability because they remain flexible and competent. In essence, annual training of new coaches makes it possible to meet the developmental needs of employees, and having external coaches identified allows the organization to expand its capability when the individual prefers to work with a coach outside of the company. While there is only one full-time coach on staff at Fidelity, there are close to 200 internal coaches who have been certified and trained to serve when needed.

At the Center for Creative Leadership (CCL), a top-rated global provider of leadership education, it is common practice to combine external coaching with leadership development programs so that participants benefit from both internal and external coaching. The CCL coach (external) helps with the interpretation of assessment data and with the development of an action plan that aligns with current development goals. Fellow participants in the leadership development program serve as internal peer coaches who provide support and accountability as participants move forward with their action plans. As a result, participants are not required to choose an internal or external coach, but have the opportunity to benefit from both. If an organization wants to build an internal coaching capability of its own, CCL will train and certify selected employees to serve as coaches in their organizations as needed.

Establish a Coaching Dialogue

At its core, coaching is about asking good questions. James Hunt and Joseph Weintraub, authors of *The Coaching Manager*, emphasize that establishing a *coaching dialogue* helps the coachee to self-assess, reflect, and actively participate in his or her own learning through action planning. This requires a high-quality, trusting relationship between coach and coachee, but not necessarily affection or emotional intimacy.

A coaching dialogue is different from a typical discussion because the coach is focused on inquiry rather than advocacy. This means asking questions to explore issues and allowing the coachee time to reflect and process his or her experiences. Feedback is provided based on observations. Often, top management teams will look for coaching when they are not functioning well together.

Joe Weintraub, codirector of the Coaching Inside the Organization executive certificate program, was called upon by one of Babson College's former presidents to provide coaching for the college's top management team. Weintraub agreed on the condition that they invite an external coach to support the process with him and that everyone involved would take a behavioral style self-assessment and have a 360-degree review as a foundation for discussion. He was also clear that as an internal coach and technically in a subordinate role, this would be a single one-on-one feedback and coaching session with him and that any long-term coaching would be with the external coach.

The president and cabinet's goal was to improve effectiveness, and everyone agreed to participate. Weintraub sat down for his session with the president himself and was immediately asked, "How long is this going to take?" At the end of a very productive session, in which the president demonstrated significant investment in the improvement process, Weintraub provided some feedback: "You know, your session took two hours. This is the longest I've spent with anyone. Yet at the beginning, you came off as disinterested and seemed to want this to be over as quickly as possible. Do you know that you sometimes have a rough edge?" It was important feedback because Weintraub explained it was a style that would not be effective given the culture of the college. Several of the cabinet members continued their sessions with the external coach for a few months. The president and his cabinet then began several good years of collaborative service to the institution.

When Should You Seek Out a Coach?

Are you having difficulty working with colleagues or collaborating effectively? Are there specific tasks that give you trouble or times of the year when being productive is more challenging? Have there been significant changes in your company or to your role in the company? Are there internal politics or relationships at risk that would make it better to get an external view of the situation? Or would deeper knowledge of the culture and business practices help you navigate?

A coach can be an excellent sounding board during times of transition and/or when you need to focus on learning to improve your workplace performance. Consider the resources available to you including employee resource groups, leadership development programs, internal coaches on staff, or external professional coaches.

Reverse Mentoring

Your professional network will be more robust if you include a range of talent, including those who are younger or less experienced than you since they come into your organization or industry with a fresh perspective. The practice of reverse mentoring has been around for decades. It gained widespread notoriety in 1999 when Jack Welch, former CEO of General Electric, ordered his top executives to learn about the Internet from junior employees. This format flips traditional mentoring—the more junior and/or less experienced partner in the relationship is the mentor, and the focus is on supporting the more senior and/or more experienced mentee's learning goals.

Mutuality and Reciprocity Make Good Relationships

Mutuality and reciprocity are particularly important for reverse mentoring relationships because both individuals learn and teach (on different matters). The role reversal—particularly the senior leaders as mentees—can be a big hurdle for effective relationships. Executives who are used to being in charge often have a difficult time adapting to the role of learner, particularly when there is a wide age and experience gap.

Ask your executives: What makes a good protégé? They will tell you: people who are curious, open-minded, hardworking, thoughtful, and respectful. Now ask them: Why wouldn't you want to role-model that for your junior colleagues?

Knowledge Sharing and Skill Development

The primary purpose of reverse mentoring is *knowledge sharing* and *skill development;* therefore, it is essential to match participants based on their developmental needs and competencies as well as commonalities that facilitate rapport. So, for example, while a new employee may bring knowledge of technology that a manager needs to learn, the more senior, experienced employee knows how to get things done in the organization and has industry experience to share. They will have a stronger bond if they can connect based on these complementary development needs as well as shared values, hobbies, or interests. There is potential for both parties to learn new knowledge and skills as well as develop greater empathy across generations.

Leadership Development

The secondary purpose of reverse mentoring is *leadership development* for both mentor and mentee. Growing leaders is primarily about personal development and providing support for your people to develop. People from the millennial generation (those born in the United States in approximately 1978 to 1999) tend to be uncomfortable with ambiguity and want immediate feedback. As reverse mentors, they are tasked with creating some of the structure in their interactions with mentees and responding to their mentees' needs. This pushes them to be creative and focus on someone else's learning instead of just themselves. They undoubtedly get immediate feedback in the sessions from senior-level mentees who acquire new skills or are frustrated and need further coaching.

Reverse mentees are often humbled by their lack of new knowledge and skills, and are reminded of what it's like to be new in the organization. Mentees are able to help mentors learn how to teach more effectively, get work done in the organization, and access resources. Both parties are mutually supported, gain critical skills in cross-generational communication, and build connections across the organization.

The Hartford's Reverse Mentoring Program

At The Hartford, a large insurance company, employees needed to learn how to leverage social media and other digital technologies internally as well as for their customers. Recent strategic analysis had shown that most customers were finding information from blogs, reviews, and online conversations. Potential customers and partners were already using these tools, so the company risked losing business without a strong digital presence. In addition, over the next few years their millennial employee base was projected to rapidly increase resulting from baby boomer retirements. Alarmingly, industry turnover among young employees was abysmal, hovering at around 15 percent. Each of these is a compelling reason for initiating a reverse mentoring program and a clear rationale for allocating resources to a formal program.

Program coordinator Lisa Bonner and her team were excited, but in such a traditional organization as The Harford she said, "We needed senior leaders buy-in to get commitment from participants." Bonner and a team of early career professionals and social media enthusiasts had created and implemented an internal social network for employees to connect and collaborate for social as well as business purposes. For young teams within this large, geographically dispersed organization, being able to share documents, ideas, and solutions in real time online was already improving creativity and productivity. The value was clear to them but the rest of the company wasn't yet onboard.

CEO Liam McGee enrolled in the program as a mentee himself along with other key company leaders, a clear signal to employees of the importance of the reverse mentoring initiative. The company adopted the existing social networking platform, which then hosted the application process including profiles for mentors. Millennial mentors were evaluated based on technical and communication skills as well as their reputation for keeping information confidential. "It was necessary to create a very safe environment where executives felt comfortable shutting the door and having a real conversation," explained Bonner.

Mentors were assigned from a different function and several levels below their senior-level mentees in the hierarchy to prevent conflicts of interest. Matching also included common personal interests that might serve as a basis for building a relationship. Finally, mentors were required to commit a minimum of four hours per month, which included research, preparation, and peer coaching along with their own meetings. The Hartford's reverse mentoring program team created guidelines for structured sessions to facilitate their meetings.

The results of this pilot program of 16 pairs were overwhelmingly positive, and the company rolled the program out to the next two levels. The collaborations between mentors and mentees resulted in learning by both parties. Mentees found that their mentors were talented and savvy users of technology, and they learned how to use technology to enhance their own careers. Millennial mentors felt more connected to their colleagues and gained insight into the company. For mentors, this was essentially a stretch assignment, which exposed them to senior leaders who were impressed. In turn, many mentors were quickly promoted, in part because of sponsorship from their mentees.

During the project, both mentees and mentors generated new ideas and insights into their business and customers. Overall, the company's workforce became increasingly comfortable with the new internal communication network. Most importantly, the initiative created momentum for interesting conversations and creative ideas to explore that would benefit the company and its employees. Reverse mentoring at The Hartford has been rolled out as a national program and is now a model for other companies.

When Should You or Your Organization Consider Reverse Mentoring?

Millennial and Gen X employees often have more technological knowledge than their bosses and other senior executives. Thus they can serve as reverse mentors to leverage technology that helps drive strategic goals. New employees bring fresh ideas, a global perspective, and updated content knowledge in many fields, particularly IT, engineering, and the sciences.

As an entrepreneurial protégé, you should be attuned to learning from people at all levels and seek opportunities to grow through these relationships. Organizations also benefit from reverse mentoring in creating greater understanding, information exchange, and collaboration across inherent generational divides. Reverse mentoring leads to a range of outcomes including learning, innovation, improved individual and organizational performance, reduced turnover, and increased satisfaction.

Mentoring Circles

A problem that many organizations face is a diminishing number of high-level mentors available for their broad employee base. This is predominantly the result of the hierarchical pyramid structure but may also be a function of geographic constraints, travel schedules, and business cycles. One creative way to formally make developmental relationships more accessible to every employee is through mentoring circles. In this format, one to three mentors are brought together with four to eight mentees for the purpose of accelerating the development of the mentees.

Early piloting of mentoring circles quickly demonstrated that the mentees learned as much from each other as they did from the senior mentors in the group. The group of mentees served as peer mentors to each other. Over time mentoring circles have adopted different structures and practices—in some instances peers are a self-managing group who are given some initial training and guidelines for creating a well-functioning peer mentoring or peer coaching group. In other instances an outside facilitator from HR provides periodic assistance. What is common to all these models is that each individual has the opportunity to build several developmental relationships characterized by reciprocity, mutuality, and trust.

Mentoring Circles at Work

Companies often use mentoring circles to support the career development of high-potential women and minorities, increase millennial employees' exposure to upper management, and empower project team leaders to develop their competencies and job performance. Since this is a relatively new strategy for fostering developmental relationships, we expect that there are many more applications yet to be discovered. We know of several examples which show prodigious results worth highlighting here.

At CBIZ, a professional services company, Nancy Mellard, executive vice president and general counsel of the employee services division, began working in 2006 with WFD Consulting on a development program, "CBIZ Women's Advantage," designed to support women's career development. This was a multidivisional program covering employees in tax, accounting, insurance, and HR consulting. The business challenge addressed through what came to be called "networking circles" was to increase retention among high-performing women.

Over the last several years, approximately 1,000 CBIZ women have participated in year-long mentoring circles. Circles have 10 to 12 participants and are provided eight modules/topics and guidelines. Participants report having developed self-confidence and clarity of their own development goals. Some attribute a recent promotion to having participated in this developmental opportunity. Valued consequences of these circles are the mentoring and coaching skills of members and the enduring relationships with women in other divisions that are sustained.

Since this initiative began in 2006, two additional networking circles have been added to the program. Networking Circles II is for graduates of the first program, and the primary purpose of these groups is to foster business development through strong connections with women in other divisions of the company. The third group is Women's Lead Groups, which continues the cross-divisional connections that support new business development. Each circle has a suggested curriculum (eight topics over one year), and the facilitator role is rotated among members.

In a given year, CBIZ has five to eight circles ongoing that actively support and develop up to 12 members per group. Approximately $1.2 million per year in new business development in the last three years can be attributed to the peer mentoring and exchange of business contacts that occur in these circles.

Employee Business Resource Groups Create Circles

Another way for employees to access supportive relationships is through the formation of employee business resource groups (EBRGs), an extension of affinity groups. These are based on shared characteristics or life experience. At Sodexo, a quality of life services outsourcing firm, mentoring circles have grown out of EBRGs and have goals that reflect their target population. Jodi Davidson, director of Diversity and Inclusion, explains that the mentoring circles have evolved over time and each operates differently depending on its focus.

For example, there is the Honor resource group composed of employees with military backgrounds whose mentoring circles focus on transitioning effectively to a corporate career and then on professional development. The Pride resource group connects LGBT employees with allies who focus on reverse mentoring and professional development simultaneously, and the Intergenerational group (IGEN) offers generational roundtables to explore intergenerational issues. The combination of mentoring circles and resource groups at Sodexo illustrate how formal programs may evolve from informal developmental initiatives. Fortunately, leaders at Sodexo recognized the value in these grassroots efforts and now provide access to resources to encourage these connections.

Mentoring Circles Outside the Workplace

Mentoring circles can also exist beyond organizational boundaries to bring together people in similar positions with common needs and concerns. Dr. Dennis Ceru teaches at Babson College and has served as a mentor to circles of CEO/entrepreneurs for years. His consulting firm, Strategic Management Associates LLC, brings together like-minded CEOs of small to medium-sized firms with the assumption that every business faces a core set of issues at different times and in different ways.

Ceru explains that all CEOs are lonely (it really is lonely at the top!) and value an external perspective on their business from knowledgeable peers. As trust builds and their relationships become established, peers also offer encouragement, counseling, and friendships that support each other through some of the personal challenges of running a company. Mentoring circles may run from one to five years, depending on the needs of participants and their businesses. As a result of these circles, CEOs make better decisions, improve their risk assessments, and end up with higher valuations of their companies when they sell.

Similarly, Kathy participated in a mentoring circle composed of five women professors in her field who were also serving in senior leadership roles within their respective universities. While we didn't call the group a mentoring circle (it spanned about five years prior to the use of the term), we met every other month and spent our two hours together checking in on our individual challenges and receiving coaching from other members of the group. Over time, we developed guidelines for the group which allowed those who needed more air time that particular meeting to make this known during a brief check-in at the beginning.

Then we would allocate the rest of our time accordingly. Another similar men's group has been together for about 20 years, composed of academics and practitioners in a related field. They set aside a half-day each month or every other month, with a similar purpose and process.

Why Should You Participate in a Mentoring Circle?

Do you have a deep interest in the topics the mentoring circle is addressing? Are you in a new role? Do you need to learn new skills or gain a different perspective on your work? Do you have particular skills or expertise to offer to the group?

Sometimes the mentoring circle structure takes the pressure off of individuals and allows them to focus on others' issues and learn from others' experiences until they are comfortable sharing their own challenges. Participants find it useful to get input from diverse voices in high-functioning circles, and facilitators may become coparticipants themselves.

Reflection Questions

As you look at your current developmental network (Chapter 2) and reflect on your current development needs and goals, consider the following:

1. What formal development roles exist in my organization, if any?
2. Which of these roles would be a timely addition to my developmental network?
3. What actions can I take to initiate a request to join a particular program?
4. If no developer roles are sanctioned in your organization, do you want to discuss the potential of such a formal initiative with your boss or with the talent development staff?

CREATING AND SUSTAINING A DEVELOPMENTAL CULTURE

What do companies like Google, Zappos, and JetBlue have in common? They are as well known for their work culture as they are for their products, and their leaders play a critical role in shaping that culture. However, in today's rapidly changing and networked world, a strong culture should also help develop your workforce. Developing people through mentoring should be viewed as a holistic practice embraced by leaders at every level.

This requires a shift in mindset. Mentoring should be an important part of everyday interactions, beyond formal programs and targeted initiatives. You should pay attention to culture when you choose where to work and lead. Your organizational culture will either enhance or undermine efforts to build and sustain high-quality relationships.

What Is a Developmental Culture?

Our colleague Tim Hall defines a developmental culture as one that combines challenging, meaningful work with support and caring for employees. A developmental culture exists when the work itself provides learning opportunities, the reward system values individuals' efforts to coach and develop others, and opportunities abound for individuals to form collaborative relationships with others. In this chapter, we outline essential strategies for creating and sustaining a developmental culture.

When low trust levels and strong competitive dynamics characterize an organization's culture, efforts to build or sustain high-quality relationships in which both parties are learning are more likely to fail. Ironically, mentoring and sponsorship become even more important in these environments because you need people looking out for your best interests when the rules aren't always clear. It will take effort from leaders first, followed by the commitment of individual entrepreneurial mentors and protégés to forge change.

Culture: Part of a Strategic Approach to Mentoring

In Chapter 5, we recommend a strategic approach to mentoring. From this perspective, before adding any programs, you should complete a thorough assessment of current human resource and people development practices. This step will lead to an understanding of what actions might be necessary to ensure that formal efforts to create developmental relationships succeed. In this chapter, we further discuss two major elements of a strategic approach:

1. Assessment of the current context, including culture and practices
2. Leaders as role models, creators of culture, and sponsors of programs

Many organizations are already focusing on developing people from a more holistic perspective. Thinking this way enables leaders to put formal programs into context and support their employees' efforts to learn through relationships. KPMG is one such example:

There are multiple initiatives at KPMG that foster a culture of mentoring and development at the firm. Barbara Wankoff, director of Workplace Solutions within KPMG, explains that its efforts are for the company to be "a great place to build a career through the developmental process of building skills, gaining experience, and achieving success in each role." Workplace Solutions delivers training and provides tools for managers in the role of PMLs (people management leaders). PMLs evaluate employee performance and give feedback through the annual review process. The group has also established several formal mentoring programs over the years. These programs span the firm, as 7,684 employees, more than one-third of its U.S.-based workforce, have indicated that they have a mentor, and 4,699 employees have served as formal mentors. Internal research has shown that employees with mentors feel more connected and view the firm more positively than those who do not have mentors.

Most recently, the company piloted a sponsorship program in partnership with its KNOW initiative (KPMG Network of Women), which has chapters in 62 of the 90 KPMG offices across the United States. To launch the new program, KPMG carefully defined sponsors as proactively advocating and putting their professional capital on the line to push for their protégés' promotion. Several sponsors raised the issue that they were already doing this as mentors or in their PML roles. However, Barbara explained that *not everyone* acted as a sponsor in these roles. Therefore, the goal of the sponsorship program was to raise awareness and instill this responsibility in people taking on the role of sponsor to do this deliberately for women and minorities.

The management committee and board took on roles as sponsors in the pilot, and they were matched with high-potential protégés throughout the company. To introduce the program more broadly, Workplace Solutions created training that included several videos of women leaders talking about being sponsored or being sponsors themselves and how it helped their career. Importantly, a male managing partner also contributed a video about how he sponsored a woman and her subsequent success. The firm learned a few key insights from the pilot that will help it manage its people and continue the sponsorship program.

Going forward, KPMG will encourage all employees to be more aware of their career goals so that they are alert to opportunities for connection and can reach out informally to potential mentors and sponsors. Leaders at KPMG understand the research findings that men tend to do this more naturally, whereas women tend to align themselves with those who have shared values and experiences. The sponsorship program can assist women in making these connections. However, there were barriers to the relationship if the sponsor and protégé were not in the same line of business or region. Thus future participants will be matched in the same geographic region and within the same domain of expertise.

The key is to support everyone in being more deliberate about building relationships. As Wankoff explains, "Our people have a lot on their plate. Our role is to understand how we can support them so that the best talent is recognized and moves into leadership roles."

How Do Your Current Culture and Human Resource Practices Influence Relationship Building?

In our strategic approach to mentoring, the first step is to begin with sponsorship from senior leaders. The leadership team should assess the current culture and practices of your organization in order to identify which policies encourage relationship building and which undermine developmental relationships. In the second step, the steering committee can identify unmet needs and potential gaps in development for different employee groups; in other words, where and how to focus programming efforts. Here, we briefly discuss the nature of culture, climate surveys, action learning, and appreciative inquiry. Each has its role in developing a culture and practices that lead to effective mentoring and developmental networks.

Culture Guides Behavior in Organizations

Organizational culture reflects the basic assumptions and values that guide behavior in organizations. Culture is most obvious to newcomers who are taught how to think and feel in the workplace based on the stories they are told about the organization's founding and the way it solves problems and adapts to the world. It is also communicated through the workspace and decor, symbols, and formalized values.

When the underlying values of an organization are clearly articulated and behavior is aligned with these espoused values, it is easy for newcomers to learn the ropes and quickly decide if they fit. And if learning and development are a part of the espoused values, people will feel empowered to reach out for mentors, sponsors, and peers to support their learning at every career stage. For example, both IBM and Procter & Gamble won awards for their HR development practices in 2013, specifically as the "best companies for leaders." This is directly related to how their CEOs during the period leading up to this year (Sam Parisalmo [IBM] and A. G. Lafferty [P&G]) modeled the way and actively supported programs and performance management systems that fostered high-quality developmental relationships among employees.

Both organizations were recognized for their developmental cultures. In both instances performance management systems include "developing others" as an important factor in performance reviews. Their education and training programs for every target population have leadership development, coaching, and mentoring included in the topics covered, and the infrastructure of these programs frequently includes mentoring and coaching relationships created during the formal program experience.

Climate Surveys Help Assess Culture

Companies will often use climate surveys as a first step in determining whether their culture is supportive of development, and in what ways it might be necessary to change practices in order to become more so. Organizational climate surveys assess how employees make sense of their workplace. Climate is about how people perceive the systems, practices, and policies they experience and observe. It is the behavioral evidence for the culture of a place.

Generally, an organizational climate is stronger when people interact more, when people communicate more often, when their work is more interdependent, and when leaders share a clear strategic vision for the work. One example of a climate survey that can be used in most organizations is the following, which we adapted based on the work of our colleagues Tim Hall and Phil Mirvis:

Developmental Climate Assessment

Using a scale of 1–4, please rate how much you agree or disagree with each of the following statements.

1	2	3	4
Strongly Disagree	Disagree	Agree	Strongly Agree

Current culture and HR

_____ The mission of my organization includes a concern for people.

_____ Human resources is an integral part of my organization's strategic planning.

_____ My organization values all kinds of diversity, including age, gender, ethnicity, culture, and so on.

_____ My organization provides training and education to develop people at all levels.

_____ There are opportunities for people to learn in their jobs and everyday work activities.

_____ Job assignments are based, in part, on the development needs of individuals.

_____ People are recognized for serving as coaches or mentors in my organization.

Leaders

_____ The top leaders demonstrate the organizational values; they "walk the talk."

_____ In general, managers really understand the needs and priorities of their people.

_____ There are role models at senior levels of the organization who support their people.

_____ Managers are evaluated on their efforts to develop talent.

_____ Leaders and managers at all levels participate in training and education to develop themselves and their people.

_____ TOTAL

Tally your score:

12–24   Your organization does not explicitly support a developmental culture although there may be individuals who do so informally. New initiatives or outside help may be necessary to begin efforts to change.

25–36   There are some programs in place and individual leaders who foster a developmental culture, although more could be done through HR, leadership, and the organization to promote these efforts. New initiatives may increase opportunities for talent development.

37–48   Your organization clearly embraces a developmental culture and recognizes people who are role models in developing themselves and others. There are talent development opportunities, both formal programs and informal efforts, supported by leaders and the organization as a whole. New initiatives are promoted by leaders and embraced by participants.

The results of a climate survey often lead to an agenda for change, which includes modifications to existing HR practices and the introduction of specific mentoring and coaching initiatives that are actively supported by senior leaders in the company.

Leverage Results from Climate Surveys

A good example of how a climate survey can be leveraged to create a developmental culture is found at Wilhelmsen Lines, the largest and most profitable division of Wilhelmsen Ltd., the largest global shipping company in the world, which is based in Oslo, Norway. Ingar Skaug was brought in as CEO in 1989 after a tragic airline accident in which the top executive team perished. Early on, Skaug realized that the culture of the place was not sufficiently adaptive to meet current and future challenges. The control-oriented hierarchical structure and culture of disempowered employees prevented timely learning and development of new knowledge and skills.

Skaug began his tenure as CEO by creating a clear vision and a set of values (in collaboration with his new senior leadership team) and then communicated them to all employees through a series of meetings in which he discussed the vision and values and invited questions and input from all employees. After a year of traveling across the globe and meeting with all employees, Skaug realized that a climate survey was needed to provide feedback to every department and division on how well values were being practiced.

After several years of learning how to structure the feedback and provide coaching to all managers and employees who needed to improve their styles, Wilhelmsen Ltd. arrived at a process that included an annual climate survey. The climate survey was designed to assess how well the corporate values (honesty, loyalty, cooperation, and responsibility) were being followed from employees' points of view. Over the years, practices have been modified to support the values, and values have been elaborated on in response to major changes in the competitive environment.

For over 15 years, these annual climate surveys have been conducted, and the results are studied and acted upon by managers at every level in the company. For example, after two years of climate surveys, organizational development strategies were defined and implemented to make sure that people understood expectations and were rewarded for good performance. In addition, peer coaching is fostered to help every employee benefit from effective feedback and coaching on their performance and style.

Developmental Culture Links to Financial Results

Alongside the results of the climate surveys are the financial results of Wilhelmsen Ltd. It is clear that the two are highly correlated. When a strong, developmental culture exists—emphasizing constructive feedback, learning partnerships, and development programs—financial performance and growth increase. It is interesting to note that during and following a major acquisition or merger, which has occurred several times in the last 15 years, the climate survey and financial performance dropped during the period of significant change. Then, because of management practices put in place to navigate the change, climate surveys after the period of change improved, as did financial performance.

Action Learning Develops People and Generates Solutions to Problems

During the last 20 years, organizations have become increasingly interested in action learning (AL), an approach to working with and developing people that uses work on an actual project or problem as a way to learn.

In an AL session, participants work on a business problem of strategic importance to their organization and are accountable for the recommendations they develop when they present them to senior leaders. Both large and small firms have found this a very valuable method for engaging people in strategic business problems in a format and process that leads to personal and leadership learning, as well as new collaborative relationships with their partners in the work.

The methods of AL foster a developmental culture in several ways. First, AL teams often bring together people with complementary expertise who don't know each other. This is an opportunity to build new connections and to experience collaborative problem solving on a real business problem. Second, there is often a learning coach assigned to each team who helps team members experience the value of critical reflection—not only about the problem at hand, but also about their own approaches to learning and how these can be strengthened. Finally, significant business problems are usually effectively addressed, offering the organization new solutions to critical issues.

AL is often used as a tool in formal leadership development programs. Participants have an opportunity to practice new leadership ideas in a team with their peers on a business problem of strategic importance to the company. During a 6- to 12-month program, people regularly reflect on what they are doing and learning with their peers with the help of their learning coaches. Indications of success include new solutions to business problems, new relationship-building skills, and new developmental relationships.

Appreciative Inquiry Focuses on Positive Change

Appreciative inquiry (AI) focuses on identifying the best in people as a methodology for positive change rather than problem-focused change. Founded by David Cooperrider and his colleagues at Case Western Reserve University, this approach fosters a developmental culture because it surfaces and strengthens existing capabilities and potential. The appreciative inquiry process mobilizes people to innovate around their collective strengths, thus developing one another and the organization's capacities.

AI has become a widely used approach for creating developmental cultures that foster continuous learning, innovation, and development. In the last 15 years, as companies in all industries have faced unprecedented change and competition, this approach has successfully transformed the cycle of discouragement in the face of significant challenges with no apparent answers into a cycle of positive inquiry that leads to shared hopes and aspirations as well as action plans by utilizing the organization's capabilities to move in a chosen direction.

Our colleague Ilene Wasserman explains: "An AI approach begins with structuring an organizational analysis around positive questions in order to bring out existing strengths, opportunities, aspirations, and results (SOAR). A trained facilitator can help leaders identify the critical questions and frame them to bring out these positive attributes. Then, with a shared vision and development goals in mind, an action plan that is owned by all those who participate in the AI intervention is developed."

Leaders Model Action Learning and Appreciative Inquiry

Green Mountain Coffee Roasters (GMCR) provides a good example of an AI approach. Since its founding in 1981, Bob Stiller, president and CEO, has been a strong advocate for building a corporate culture that supports individual growth and development (through collaborative relationships and effective teamwork), and for making a positive impact through sustainable growth around the world.

In 2003, Stiller sponsored the first of many leadership summits (a term often used to describe large group events that focus on creating a positive and viable vision for the future). Almost every year since, a set of positive questions are asked:

- What have we been doing well?
- Where are the opportunities for us going forward?
- What capabilities make us unique?

GMCR employees have been essential participants in developing and implementing action plans that lead to continued success.

While Bob Stiller was the driving force behind this appreciative inquiry approach to maintaining a strong, positive, and developmental culture, the tenets of AI have become part of the fabric of GMCR such that it continues as a regular process since he retired in 2007. The leader has an instrumental role in introducing AI and AL processes because these often require additional resources to sponsor training and follow-up events, as well as outside experts who can help with critical design issues that must be addressed in order to realize potential benefits.

How Can Leaders Create, Model, and Actively Support Developmental Relationships?

Leaders significantly influence the quality and availability of developmental relationships in their organizations through their decisions about what initiatives to promote and through their behavior in relationships with others. Many studies of culture focus on the leader's role in creating, modeling, and reinforcing organizational expectations and norms. This includes how they react to critical incidents or crises, how they allocate resources and rewards, and how they manage people processes in general—along with HR. Thus for individual leaders to foster a developmental culture, they must articulate it as a value and behave consistently. So what do successful leaders do to foster high-quality relationships?

1. **Serve as a role model.** At any level of an organization, a leader (whether first line supervisor or senior executive) can serve as a role model by actively mentoring junior colleagues and peers and by participating as a mentor or mentee in formal programs. Creating opportunities and making time for developmental interactions signal to employees that learning through relationships is valued. Leaders serve as role models by effectively developing their own direct reports and others.

2. **Share personal stories.** Leaders who share stories of their own learning through relationships validate the impor-

tance of developing others and of spending time on relationship development. As beneficiaries of mentoring relationships and as mentors or mentees, your examples demonstrate the critical role of relationships in career development. Some leaders may hesitate since sharing stories, especially of being mentored, may require showing vulnerability and talking about weaknesses. However research has shown that leaders who display their weakness to their employees are actually more well-liked and respected than those who don't. Above all, sharing that you are human and that you pursue learning opportunities highlights the critical role of continuous development in the organization.

3. **Support your direct reports.** Supporting your direct reports through developmental efforts includes identifying needs for skill development, facilitating learning in a given role, encouraging exploration beyond their current roles, and discussing career opportunities. This means spending time with people beyond the annual review process. Your role is to strategize with employees, allocate time for their development, and give them credit for their efforts to develop their peers and subordinates.

4. **Sponsor new initiatives and formal programs.** When leaders promote new initiatives, participate in formal programs, and actively demonstrate their support by showing up at orientations or training sessions, these actions give importance and legitimacy to such programs. Leaders who introduce and/or sponsor action learning, appreciative inquiry, and/or regular climate surveys are creating processes that will enable a developmental culture in which on-the-job learning can regularly occur through collaborative relationships among people who together come up with innovative solutions and approaches to complex issues at work. Through both words and actions, these steps enable leaders to create a learning culture in which employees are encouraged to learn through relationships with others.

A good example of an innovative developmental culture is the story of "the Spirit of Mentoring" initiatives at the quality-of-life services outsourcing firm Sodexo:

Jodi Davidson, director of diversity and inclusion initiatives at Sodexo, has helped create and grow what is known as the "Spirit of Mentoring" initiative at Sodexo since 2004. Sodexo provides quality-of-life outsourcing primarily through food and facilities services in education, government, and healthcare settings among other things. Davidson explains, "Spirit of Mentoring focuses on expanding diversity in our leadership pipeline and engaging and retaining our talent pool. Given the large and decentralized nature of the business, an on-going challenge is that our workforce may feel more affiliated with our client, or with a particular industry. An employee might say, 'I work in healthcare, I can't imagine working in education.' So an overarching goal is cross-knowledge sharing so that our employees show up as leaders across settings and help our clients solve their problems."

The initiative began with the IMPACT program, which was launched in partnership with an external consultant and included 45 traditional mentoring relationships. IMPACT ensured strong representation of minorities and women and intentional cross-cultural and cross-functional matching. Its focus has shifted over time to emphasize participation of high-potential managers with P&L (profit and loss) responsibility, and the cohorts have grown to up to 150 partnerships per year.

IMPACT mentees and mentors are provided training through an orientation, a day-long in-person launch session, and various webinars throughout the year. Pairs are expected to connect monthly. Mentees are encouraged to job shadow their mentors or engage in a business project with their mentors, who can provide them with real-time feedback. IMPACT staff members check in with each mentee and mentor at the two-month mark and survey participants at the six- and twelve-month marks. As IMPACT has grown, applications to participate have exceeded the capacity of the program. To offer expanded access to mentoring for all managers and professionals who wish to participate, Sodexo has invested in alternative programs via a web-based platform. These informal mentoring options are available for newly hired and frontline managers to help them accelerate their understanding of the company and expand professional development opportunities.

Another avenue for employees to access developmental relationships is through Sodexo's nine employee business resource groups (EBRGs) Peer2Peer mentoring. The EBRGs are organized by fellow employees around particular dimensions of diversity and provide a support system for participants. Groups offer either one-on-one informal mentoring and/or mentoring circles for employees who want to further their professional development, learn particular skills, or cultivate new relationships. The company provides resources and support for employees to engage in this type of learning.

As a part of Sodexo's diversity scorecard index, managers are granted credit for engaging in mentoring. Sodexo's impact analysis (a "soft" ROI) indicates a $2 return on every $1 spent based on enhanced productivity and employee retention, as well as client satisfaction and retention. In addition, intangible gains are assessed: Is mentoring helping people to develop new skills and better prepare for advancement? Are mentors helping people develop self-confidence and professional clarity? Are mentors and mentees learning the relational skills required to effectively build and sustain developmental relationships beyond the formal program?

Davidson shared that mentees consistently indicate that, as a result of participating, they think more strategically, have improved their skills for leading change, have improved interpersonal skills, and have higher confidence levels. Mentors report they are better at developing people, have improved their interpersonal skills and communication—particularly listening and asking good questions—and have expanded their knowledge of the industry. Most recently, Sodexo has begun to leverage its web-based application to expand mentoring networks and developmental relationships beyond the more traditional initiatives previously offered (see Chapter 9).

What Structural Changes Enhance a Developmental Culture?

Leaders in a position to influence HR strategy and practices can make sure that performance management systems include recognition and rewards for mentoring others and champion strategies that support a developmental culture.

Changes in Job Design

Good job design goes beyond the most efficient way to accomplish tasks. We know that on-the-job experience plays a key role in learning and that experience is the primary way that professionals grow. A developmental culture focuses on creating opportunities for learning within roles. Leaders foster an environment that enables employees to solidify and enhance their skills through stretch assignments and collaborations. The Center for Creative Leadership has identified three characteristics of *challenging assignments*:

1. Transitions that put people in new situations with unfamiliar responsibilities.
2. Tasks that require people to drive change or build relationships.
3. High-responsibility, high-latitude jobs, which give people decision-making power and a chance to experiment.

It is critical that leaders consider person-job fit, since roles that are developmental to one person may not be for another, and explain the developmental features of the job to the individual. Relationships then become a key source of learning at the outset.

Changes in Routines

Managers at every level can hold weekly staff meetings that incorporate peer coaching into the work itself. In one company, we observed that the director of marketing would bring his immediate staff together every two weeks on a Monday morning for two hours. While many items were on the agenda at each meeting, the first was always a "check-in" when staff members would give headlines regarding the current challenges they faced and the kind of input from others that would be helpful. Depending on the headlines, the director would facilitate a discussion of each of the challenges mentioned where staff members were expected to ask good questions and/or provide information that would be helpful to the person with the challenge. This process became a regular part of work for everyone in the group and provided an ongoing opportunity for peers to form developmental relationships with each other.

Changes in the Reward System

All the mentoring programs, enriched jobs, and climate surveys will not lead to a developmental culture in which developmental relationships and developmental networks thrive without a reward system that aligns with the values that are driving the organization.

As soon as actively developing employees and creating a climate for their learning and growth become valued features of an organization's culture, the reward system must acknowledge, recognize, and reward individuals who take the time to actively mentor, coach, and sponsor others. If a reward system continues to prize bottom line results only, employees who aspire to advance to senior levels of the company will be inclined to let go of some of their mentoring involvements so that they can continue to do what is valued.

Companies that want effective talent development practices alter the performance appraisal system to include objectives and measures related to developing others. While financial performance is still a critical indicator of success, so is regularly helping others develop new capabilities through stretch assignments and relationships that provide coaching, sponsorship, and mentoring along the way.

The Succession Planning Process

The succession planning process is another system (closely related to the reward system) that should align with the core value of creating a developmental culture that fosters learning and development for all employees. While most industries now convene groups to debate the potential candidates for executive roles in an organization, some still lag behind in the criteria they use to rank those who are identified as having potential.

When an individual is identified as having high potential based on the successful turnaround that he or she achieved with a failing division, this is critical information for a succession planning committee. It suggests that this candidate has the skills to identify the strategic challenges faced in accomplishing this kind of transformation and gets it done. However, decision makers should also consider how the people faired during the turnaround period. Did they demonstrate care and concern for the people side so that employees could leverage the difficult situation for learning opportunities? Did they actively develop direct reports and others who were essential to the challenge they were hired to address?

In many instances those responsible for these systems will have to invent new processes to support outcomes that reward excellent developers of talent. This may require not only changes in the criteria for performance assessment (to include developing others as a measurable outcome), but also new feedback channels that invite input to these processes from subordinates and peers who work with the individual on a regular basis. Sometimes these new feedback systems require skill training in giving and receiving feedback so that the data collected are provided in a constructive manner and can be useful in planning for future development. In such instances, training and education can be brought to the mix to ensure successful implementation.

Allocation of Resources

Allocating resources to formal programs, education related to mentoring and coaching, and new initiatives such as action learning or appreciative inquiry demonstrates their value to employees in a concrete way. In 2009, when Barry Salzberg, CEO of Deloitte LLP, championed the construction of Deloitte University, a learning and development center, he sent a clear message that the firm valued developing employees. There is nothing like putting resources behind a program to solidify its legitimacy and status, particularly in large organizations. Even in smaller firms, supporting the dedication of peoples' time to learning and development initiatives signals their value.

Employee-initiated mentoring programs can take off when senior management is willing to allocate extra funds for the infrastructure required to make them viable and successful. In one medical devices company, the employee resource groups (ERGs), one by one, began to create mentoring circles which met for six months on a monthly basis. Their mission was to develop leaders from among their particular ERG (e.g., women, people with disabilities, Hispanics, African Americans, LGBT). The drivers of these initiatives quickly discovered that they needed assistance to ensure that the groups would function as intended and that they would be able to assess the value of these initiatives on an annual basis. After the first year, the HR and talent development staff partnered with them to provide consulting expertise from the outside, as well as the funding for the necessary training and education.

Over the next four years, participation grew tremendously so that there were waiting lists to participate, and those serving as mentees wanted to join a new group as mentors. Each group consisted of two mentors, five mentees, and a connector (experienced mentor who made sure the circle was functioning properly). In addition, a learning agenda evolved for each cycle of mentoring circles with topics for each monthly session and a panel of senior executives who would speak to the community to deepen understanding of how the topic is relevant to the firm. Investment in this grassroots initiative clearly produced substantial learning and development, new developmental relationships, greater loyalty to the firm, and for many, promotion to the next level.

In Table 7-1 we summarize these strategies for creating a developmental culture:

Table 7-1 Strategies for Creating a Developmental Culture

Systemwide Initiatives	Leaders' Behavior	Structural Changes
Climate surveys	Establish role-modeling	Job redesign
Action learning	Sponsor new mentoring programs	Changes in reward systems and succession planning practices
Appreciative inquiry	Support direct reports	Allocation of resources

Reflection Questions

If you are considering whether to go to work at a particular organization, consider asking the following questions of current and/or past employees:

1. What is a typical day like around here? How often do you interact with others and what are your conversations about?
2. What does it take to be successful in this organization? What does it take to be promoted?
3. How do newcomers learn the ropes and get to know how to be successful?

If you are a *leader* (at any level in your organization), consider the following questions:

1. How often do you and others have the opportunity to ask for help and advice on challenging business situations?
2. Are the talent development practices providing sufficient opportunities to learn, build developmental relationships, and give back to others?
3. What can you do to model effective mentoring, coaching, and other helping behaviors to your peers and subordinates?
4. Are you in a position to sponsor a climate survey, action learning, or appreciative inquiry in order to establish a systemwide process that leads to a collaborative and developmental culture?

8

MAKING THE MOST OF RELATIONSHIPS WITH PEERS

Oprah Winfrey once said, "Lots of people want to ride with you in the limo, but what you want is someone who will take the bus with you when the limo breaks down." Who will ride the bus with you? Now that you are seeking sponsors in high places, considering a professional coach, and perhaps continuing the quest for that "true mentor," we don't want you to miss the most available and accessible mentors: your peers.

While mentoring has been a hot topic for anyone concerned with career advancement for 30 years and formal mentoring programs have become ubiquitous, an unintended consequence is that peer relationships have fallen off the radar screen as an important resource.

In our research, we have found that relationships with peers are often identified as important sources of information, guidance, and friendship that help people succeed and feel satisfied in their careers. A newcomer to the trading floor found that her peer who had been at the firm just six months longer than she had knowledge that was invaluable to her as she sought to learn the ropes of being successful in this highly competitive career.

A novice teacher found that that teacher next door had a great deal of wisdom to share regarding teaching approaches in the elementary school grades. He also found that his diverse experiences from his student teaching days were of value to his more experienced colleague. Examples abound from every industry and at every career stage.

In the developmental networks of people who are successful and satisfied in their chosen profession, peers are vital developers who provide guidance and support along the way. The truth is that in times of frequent and rapid change, with flatter, team-based organizations, relationships with peers are more important than ever. Not only are peers potential developers, but they can also help you get your work done.

What Makes Relationships with Peers Unique?

Peer relationships are, by definition, relationships between equals in terms of age and/or status. Two people may occupy similar positions at work, and though they are different in age, they are facing similar challenges because of the role they occupy. Others, because of similarity in age, may not occupy similar work roles, but they share common dilemmas related to balancing work and family responsibilities or to addressing the challenges posed as one becomes more deeply invested in a particular career path. Developmental relationships with peers have the potential to foster learning for both participants. These relationships are often embedded in the workplace, but they can also occur across organizations and industries. The point is that peer relationships present a rich learning opportunity.

Peers Are Available at Every Career Stage

When Kathy first began researching traditional mentoring in the late 1970s, her interviewees did not mention peers as an important source of learning and development. However, Kathy explains, this is because she was seeking to understand the role of relationships with senior colleagues—traditional mentors—who took a personal interest in a junior colleague's learning and well-being. When she went back to the field five years later and asked about relationships with peers (in contrast to relationships with senior developers), she found plenty of evidence for the importance of high-quality connections with peers in fostering and supporting individuals at every career stage.

Peers Are More Accessible

Relationships with peers are far more abundant and accessible than are relationships with senior executives (as the pyramid narrows). In research on peer mentoring and peer coaching with colleagues Tim Hall and Polly Parker, we have found that these are a low-cost alternative to other developmental tools. They are regularly available, and if they have the necessary relational skills, you should include peers in your developmental network.

Peers Provide a Range of Support

As is the case with senior developers, peers can provide both career and psychosocial support (see Chapter 1 for a review). In fact, a continuum of peer mentor relationships (see Figure 8-1) illustrates variations in level of commitment, the intensity of a relationship, and needs satisfied.

As you move from left to right on the continuum shown in the figure, you see that the relationship becomes more comprehensive in terms of the range of support that it provides. So with

Figure 8-1 Continuum of Peer Relationships

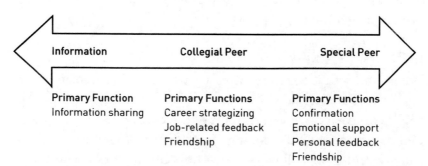

Information	Collegial Peer	Special Peer
Primary Function	**Primary Functions**	**Primary Functions**
Information sharing	Career strategizing	Confirmation
	Job-related feedback	Emotional support
	Friendship	Personal feedback
		Friendship

an information peer your exchange is limited to information that you need in order to get your work done. There is little or no personal relationship, and expectations are quite limited. As you move along the continuum to the right, collegial peer relationships become more valuable, and the range of issues discussed grows to the point where you might receive valuable feedback that can help you move forward in your career. Finally, when you find yourself in a relationship with a peer that feels like a real friendship with depth and intimacy, this is one that provides a level of psychological safety in which you can explore personal and professional dilemmas and get constructive feedback that might be provided by a best friend.

Wendy has two close friends from graduate school, Jamie Ladge and Liz Volpe, who started off as information peers, sharing resources and ideas for how to get through their program. Early on, as Wendy and these peers developed their own research and teaching skills, they shared materials, sources, and practical tips for getting the work done. They got to know each other better and shared personal stories and supported one another through marriages and children. To this day, they continue to check in with one another about their careers, most recently navigating tenure processes at their respective institutions.

Peers Are Easier to Approach

Peers are more accessible than people who relate to you in hierarchical, reporting relationships, which are governed by cultural norms about interacting with those in positions of authority. As a consequence, you may find peers to be more approachable than senior colleagues who may also be potential developers. Depending on your goals and needs, connecting with more approachable peers may be sufficient and easier.

Creating a connection that enables both of you to learn—interactions characterized by mutuality and reciprocity—is easier in the absence of the power differential found across hierarchical levels. We have heard many young professionals and students say that it is empowering to help a peer early in one's career. This may be the first time you have a sense that you have developed expertise that is of value to a colleague, thus confirming your own professional identity.

Be Intentional in Developing Peer Relationships

As with any developmental relationship, you will want to be intentional about creating connections with your peers at work as well as outside of work. The same relational skills that we outline in Chapter 4 are relevant here. Knowing what you need to support your learning and development and clearly expressing your interest in learning from your peers by asking good questions and actively listening to what they bring to the interaction will go a long way to building a connection with meaning and purpose.

Over time, what may have started as a simple request for information (informational peer) may evolve to a point where you are sharing on a deeper level job-related and personal experiences as well as your future goals. With time and deepening trust, your connection may evolve into one that provides unwavering support when you are facing a substantial challenge at work and need the consistent support of someone who knows you well and cares about your success.

Step-Ahead Mentors Are Peers and Role Models

Step-ahead mentors are peers who are more experienced or in the position one level ahead of you in your workplace. These peers can teach you necessary skills, help you access resources, and connect you with key people to help you get your job done. For example, two of Wendy's colleagues, Danna Greenberg and Keith Rollag, both a few years ahead of her, have shared resources for teaching and strategies for productive research time at Babson College. In addition, each provided counsel and helpful advice on preparing for her tenure process. Step-ahead mentors can be critical role models and supporters as you position yourself for promotion.

Where Can You Find Peers Whom You Can Enlist in Your Developmental Network?

Once you see the potential in building developmental relationships with peers, the opportunities to do so will present themselves on a daily basis. Consider the many possibilities at work, peers whom you meet in your life outside of work in your community, and the opportunities that now exist through social media.

In Your Regular Job Interactions

You may be working in a department where there are several individuals about the same age as you. They may or may not be doing the same job that you are doing. Nonetheless, if they are about your age, you may find that you have lots in common. If you differ in age, but occupy similar roles, you may find that discussing how you go about the job may have value. For example, take the case of Raj:

> Raj, a senior market research analyst, explained that he and two of his coworkers "were just always playing off each other in terms of what we think, what career paths we pursue, and what we're looking for in the next position. They have told me that they think I would be very good in sales, and they have been very encouraging." He went on to discuss how these two peers had really turned into close friends as they had worked together for a few years. Raj was comfortable sharing his successes and failures with them. Together the three of them strategized about how to navigate the organization and develop better relationships with their bosses.

In Meetings, on Committees, or on Task Forces

If you find yourself on a task force or committee, consider the other members as potential sources of learning as you get to know them. They may be from other departments and offer perspectives on your work that you hadn't considered before. While at first, assignment to a temporary task force or committee may seem like a distraction from getting your work done, if you approach it as an opportunity to connect with people you might not otherwise have a reason to meet, you can reframe this as an opportunity to expand your developmental network. You may not connect with someone every time, on every committee, but being open to it certainly increases the likelihood that this will happen. As soon as you have a sense that an individual in the group may have a background or skills that you would benefit from learning more about, you can begin to initiate a new connection with the potential for meaning and purpose.

In Training Programs

Educational and training programs offered at work present similar opportunities. In fact, many leadership development professionals are now having peers put in a classroom to work with each other in order to facilitate the relationship building that we are advocating here. So keep in mind that when you sign up for a course at work, not only are you likely to develop new skills and/or attain new knowledge, but you can also seize the opportunity to create new relationships that may become developmental over time. The potential for peer mentoring was recently illustrated at Brigham & Women's Hospital:

> The hospital created the Faculty Mentoring Leadership Program (FMLP) for senior faculty mentors to enhance their skills and grow as leaders. Participants were nominated as "experienced mentors with impact" and required to get a letter of support from their department chair or supervisor. The program ran for nine months, and participants committed to meeting for nine one-and-a-half-hour lunchtime sessions. Three key aspects of the program were (1) its cross-departmental structure, (2) case-based sessions, and (3) the use of facilitators for each peer group. Cases were created based on the participants' experiences as mentors. Two facilitators (one female and one

male) served as coparticipants rather than as instructors since the case material was created by participants. Mentors shared their mentoring skills and furthered their own development through discussion of complex, challenging, and controversial issues.

Audrey Haas, the executive director of the Faculty Development and Diversity division, recently noted, "We are in the midst of our fifth cohort and now have an expanded mentoring network of 80 physician and scientist mentors. They serve as resources within their department for protégés seeking mentors and for other mentors experiencing complex mentoring situations. The interactive online mentoring toolkit, developed for and by participants in the program, is a valuable resource available to mentors at Brigham and Women's and to the broader academic medical community."

Leadership development programs within and across organizations offer similar opportunities for participants to develop strong relationships with peers who share similar career aspirations. Deloitte Chaired Professor Emeritus Deborah Kolb at the Simmons Graduate School of Management has designed and implemented a number of such programs targeted at women leaders. While many have been offered within companies, she now leads a program titled "Leading Women Executives" based in Chicago. High-potential women from major corporations—including Northern Trust, McDonald's, United Airlines, John Deere, Grainger, and Illinois Tool Works—participate in a four-module program spread over three months. A core part of the program is a small peer group (composed of women from different companies at the same level of responsibility) that meets at least once for several hours during each two-day module.

Kolb noted that, "These peer groups are regularly cited in program evaluations as the most valuable part of the entire experience. It is in these established peer groups (with women from different companies) that participants increase awareness of their leadership strengths and potential derailers, and get help from their peers in establishing a meaningful vision for moving forward. It is not unusual for participants to continue to meet with members of their peer group long after the program is completed."

In Communities of Practice

Some organizations are structuring opportunities for peers likely to face similar challenges to interact, either in person or online. These communities of practice offer yet another opportunity to connect with people who can be a source of knowledge and support, and to whom you may have resources to give as well. Internal employee business resource groups and social media groups at companies like Sodexo and PWC make informal peer mentoring easily accessible. These communities are also abundant on public social media sites and through professional associations.

When Traveling for Work

When you are asked to travel to a conference of any kind, consider it an opportunity to meet people who may be potential learning partners down the road. Whether it is a professional society meeting (i.e., IEEE, AMA, etc.), a sales event, or a regional meeting to discuss current and future procedures and practices, you will meet new people. If you are equipped with your relationship-building tactics and skills (see Chapter 4), there is a good chance you may leave the meeting with new connections that have the potential to grow in meaning and purpose.

Outside the Workplace

There are numerous venues outside of work where you may meet people who share your professional interests and values. When you are open to uncovering mutual peer learning opportunities, you will find people in volunteer activities, your house of worship, athletic facilities, recreational activities, and on buses, trains, or airplanes. This "relational mindset" and the appropriate social skills and self-awareness discussed in Chapter 4 are all that you need to identify potential peer developers and to engage them in productive and enjoyable interaction. Here's an example:

> Keisha met Elliot when they were volunteering together at Habitat for Humanity. Painting the interior of a house for the afternoon, they discovered shared interests in music and supporting local businesses. Both were parents, although Keisha's children were still in grade school while Elliot's were in college. Elliot had his own small franchise and was on the local community advisory council. He shared the council's goals with Keisha, who was excited by what she explained as "really thoughtful and meaningful work."

> Elliot wished they had someone with Keisha's strategy background on the council; she was a partner in a Big 4 consulting practice. They kept in touch via LinkedIn, and when there was an opening on the council, Elliot recommended Keisha for the post. With more frequent interaction, Keisha found Elliot to be a great sounding board for some difficult personnel issues she had with her team. In turn, she was able to advise Elliot on upgrading his technology to improve some operational issues.

As illustrated, social media is a potential resource, as many of you reading this book probably already know (see also Chapter 9). Your goal is to identify people with interests and values that align with yours and who have expertise that you would like to acquire. Such people could become peer mentors or peer coaches over time. The key here will be to reach out with good questions as well as good information about yourself in a manner that invites curiosity and a willingness by others to engage with you.

What Are the Most Important Principles for Creating Peer Developmental Relationships?

Some of the principles and skills we outline in Chapters 4 and 6 for developmental relationships with senior colleagues are relevant to building relationships with peers as well. First and foremost, *self-awareness* is essential because it enables you to know what kind of help you are seeking in new connections with others. Are you looking to learn about another area of your company? Do you want to learn more about a hiring manager whom you may talk with about a future position? Are you in sales and wondering if there are ways to improve your sales approach? Are you anticipating having a family and wondering how family-friendly your firm is and how new parents manage the complexities of family and work?

Social skills are important for creating dialogue, building trust, and reaping the benefits of high-quality interactions. Here we go beyond what we have already outlined in the earlier chapters to consider what there is to learn from the coaching field about the mindset and skills that foster helping relationships between peers. We turn to the coaching field because, above all else, good coaches know how to build trusting relationships in which individuals learn and develop in ways that enable them to realize their own personal and professional goals. This is exactly how we see developmental relationships and their meaning and purpose.

Peer Coaching Fundamentals

We've talked about the importance of active listening and asking good questions. More needs to be said about these social skills.

The coaching literature suggests that the fundamentals of effective listening include *curiosity, questioning,* and *deep listening.* We also want to elaborate on the importance of self-awareness to emphasize the importance of *self-management, accountability,* and *intuition.* Together, these six skills are considered fundamental to any helping relationship. (See Table 8-1.)

Fundamentals Create a Shared Story

Keep in mind that as you interact—developing your social skills and self-awareness through peer relationships—you are also creating a "shared story" together. Barnett Pearce in his work on

Table 8-1 Skills in Helping Relationships

Skill	Explanation
Curiosity	The ability to demonstrate sincere interest in another person through positive affect and effective listening and to be open to a variety of outcomes as the relationship unfolds.
Questioning	The ability to ask open-ended, exploratory, nonjudgmental, and nonleading questions for which there are no right answers. The purpose is to prompt reflection, self-disclosure, and deep learning in the other person.
Deep listening	The ability to listen to more than the words by paraphrasing, checking perceptions and assumptions, and assuming that the other person is naturally creative, resourceful, and whole. Here the purpose is to listen for values, passions, motivation, energy, feelings, and perspectives.
Self-management	The ability to monitor your own opinions, beliefs, feelings, and judgments so that they don't get in the way of deep listening and relationship building. This will help you to effectively manage your ego, your impatience, your need to be right, your need to control the agenda, and your willingness to learn.
Accountability	The ability to create and manage routines that will foster mutual commitment to the relationship for particular goals, including agreement on next steps and future expectations. It's important to be willing to reconsider accountability structure over time as needs change.
Intuition	The ability to access and rely upon your intuition (inner knowing) when what to say or ask next is not clear. The purpose is to build trust in your own inner knowing and seeing in order to guide you as you move forward in a relationship. You should assume that your intuition is never wrong. You must also understand that there is no one, right way to proceed.

coordinated meaning making (CMM) describes how each inter-action is shaped by what each of you brings to the table. This includes your different perspectives and influences, the questions you ask of each other, and the social context in which you are interacting.

A relationship that begins at work may look and feel quite different from a relationship that begins at your local athletic center or on a trip to another country. As our colleagues, Ilene Wasserman and Stacy Blake-Beard suggest that whatever the context, paying attention to what each of you brings to the evolving story of your relationship will help you to nurture it along and to deepen your connection with your peer. Paying attention to the questions you ask and the responses you receive, consciously choosing how what you will say next will influence the story you are creating, are all part of creating meaning and purpose. Here's an example of how this works:

> Rosa had been given responsibility to lead the team when her manager was away on medical leave. Although she was an expert in product development, she was struggling with being seen as a leader by her peers and, in fact, seeing herself as a leader. It was difficult for her to be directive in meetings with fellow employees, to turn the conversation into clear instructions about how they should do a task differently or approach their job more effectively. She found a peer coach in colleague Nicole Valliere, manager of leadership development at EMD Serono, a biopharmaceutical subsidiary of Merck KGaA, who was in a different regional office.
>
> Nicole had been trained by Babson College's Coaching Inside the Organization program, and she had the skills to facilitate scenario-based coaching work. She was a new coach seeking to practice and hone her expertise. Most of her interactions with Rosa were virtual, including phone, interactive technology (e.g., Skype, WebEx), or e-mail. Together, they created opportunities for Rosa to exercise her leadership skills, which included rehearsing potential interactions. After working with Nicole for a few months, Rosa attended an EMD Leadership Assessment Center, a three-day leadership assessment involving simulations with peers. Rosa scored the highest in the entire group, indicating she was promotable now, and Nicole was extremely proud. They continue to keep in touch on an as-needed basis.

The REAL Model for Diverse Relationships Supports the Fundamentals

Peer relationships have the potential to transform people when the relationships become high-quality connections. For example, the employee who lacks self-confidence radiates with clarity and confidence after developing relationships with a couple of peers and a senior developer for a few years. This comes about as a result of the psychosocial support and career advice that his or her developmental network provides over time. And in the process, the members of his or her developmental network learn and acquire new insights as well.

In the context of their work on diversity in organizations Ilene Wasserman and Placida Gallegos created the REAL model to guide individuals in creating work relationships and cultures that enable personal and organizational transformation. Consistent with the coaching skills summarized above, the REAL model consists of:

- *Reflecting* on relationships, the assumptions you bring and the context in which they unfold
- *Expanding* awareness of similarities and differences and learning from them
- *Agility* and flexibility in ways of engaging to meaningfully connect, especially with individuals who come from different backgrounds
- *Learning* from the shared stories you create together

These elements are critical to relationships with meaning and purpose.

Both Parties Learn and Grow

In the end, effective helping relationships enable both parties to learn. As Edgar Schein, one of our mentors and senior colleagues, regularly points out in his writing on helping relationships and organizational processes, the key to creating alliances with learning and growing in effectiveness as the primary purpose is coming to such opportunities with humility, good questions, the willingness to take time to reflect on what you are experiencing in your relationships, and the ability to listen deeply.

What Can Organizations Do to Foster Peer Mentoring and Peer Coaching?

In Chapter 7 we discuss how the culture and practices of an organization enhance or undermine opportunities for people to find and establish peer mentoring and peer coaching relationships. When an organization creates opportunities through social events, team meetings, or educational programs, and recognizes people who actively help others learn and develop through their performance management systems, it is much more likely that you will find peers available to help. In a highly competitive environment where only bottom-line results are recognized (and developing others is not officially rewarded), people are much more likely to want to make it on their own rather than taking a collaborative approach to learning as well as task performance.

Offer Both Traditional and Peer Mentoring Simultaneously

We have seen several examples in financial services firms where the business and the culture are highly competitive. One firm that recognized how its culture may be undermining the learning, development, and performance of its new associates took action to create a more supportive environment. Managers realized that associates in the first five years of employment were underperforming and/or leaving the organization because they felt disconnected and unappreciated. A solution to this problem was to make sure that every new associate was assigned a senior mentor as well as a peer mentor. Together, these two relationships have the potential to make a difference in the young associates' onboarding, learning, and retention over the first five years.

Reinforce Peer Programs with Recognition

Creative programs and practices work better in some organizations than others. What seems to make the difference is the extent to which mentors are rewarded for taking the time to meaningfully help to develop their colleagues. When developing others is part of the performance appraisal process and feedback from peers is part of the review process, the quality and value of developmental alliances are greater. In addition, when training is offered on how to create and sustain effective mentoring relationships, people report more satisfaction and effectiveness in these matched relationships.

Integrate Developing Others into Formal Reward Systems

HR practices that formally reward individuals for taking the time to develop others is the highest impact change an organization can make to encourage both hierarchical and peer mentoring. However, far more can be done to encourage peer mentoring and peer coaching. Mentoring and peer coaching circles (see Chapter 6) offer a vehicle for bringing peers together for the primary purpose of supporting each other's learning and development. With an infrastructure that ensures adequate time, training, and recognition, these have proven in recent years to lead to ongoing peer relationships in which individuals support one another through the intermittent challenges that we all face at work.

Foster Peer Relationships through Training

In organizations where leadership development is a significant part of the talent-development agenda, there are many classroom opportunities to foster peer learning. We have seen over and over again that when peer coaching and peer learning (as they are alternatively labeled) are included as part of the learning design, individuals build connections with their peers during the training and are encouraged to stay in touch for three to six months after the experience to make sure that they follow through on the development goals they established.

Frequently these relationships continue far beyond what was suggested at the leadership development program. At CCL (Center for Creative Leadership), a top provider of leadership education, consultants make "learning partners" a regular part of their learning designs. Participants stay connected via e-mail, Skype, and social media as they generally come from different parts of the country and the globe. This can be done equally well within organizations that hold educational events.

Make Developing Others a Criterion for Promotion

Most large organizations have succession-planning processes in place. Committees review candidates and bench strength for management positions throughout the firm. Are candidates for each position assessed, in part, on how well they develop others in their organization? When committee members sponsor particular individuals for a position of greater responsibility and authority, is the individual's willingness and ability to develop others (both peers and juniors) included as an important criterion? These policies and practices do make a difference in who gets promoted and ultimately becomes a steward of the corporate culture. What actually counts in such decision making is usually well-known by people throughout the firm and thus is part of the culture of the organization and substantially influences how people behave.

Create Opportunities for Regular Peer Interaction

Finally, anyone in a supervisory or managerial position can create conditions that foster peer mentoring and peer coaching by creating opportunities for the people they manage to share current challenges in getting their work done at regular staff meetings. We have observed wide variations in how such meetings are structured and facilitated. When regular check-ins regarding current challenges are part of the agenda and time is allocated to hear from each individual and provide feedback and coaching, people begin to help one another and peer coaching becomes a regular part of the work, rather than just something that would be nice to do.

Consider Your Goals and Your Context

Our aim in this chapter is to expand your thinking about the various ways that relationships with peers—inside and outside the workplace—can support learning and development. If you are fortunate enough to work in an organization that has a developmental culture and offers several opportunities to develop mutual helping relationships with peers, by all means, seize them! If on the other hand, the place where you work is highly competitive, characterized by a culture of self-preservation through performing better than anyone else, you will likely need to seek peer support outside of your workplace. There are many potential peer learning opportunities for you to pursue.

Reflection Exercise

Take a few minutes to think about how peer relationships affect your career. Use the following questions to structure your reflection:

1. Go back to the developmental network that you created in Chapter 2.
   a. Do you have peer relationships in your network? What is the quality of these relationships?
   b. Are there missed opportunities to consider, at work or outside of work?
   c. What actions can you take to initiate a new relationship with a peer or to deepen an existing relationship with a peer?
2. If you are in a managerial role, how can you foster peer mentoring among the people who report to you?
3. If you are in a position to introduce peer coaching and peer mentoring into talent development practices, what actions can you take to do so?

PART 3

MENTORING FOR YOU AND YOUR ORGANIZATION

CHALLENGES AND OPPORTUNITIES: DIVERSITY, TECHNOLOGY, AND CHANGE

"For the things we have to learn before we can do them, we learn by doing them." These words were as true when written by Aristotle in *The Nicomachean Ethics* as they are today. Our world continues to present learning challenges and opportunities.

Diversity, globalization, technology, and persistent change are issues that shape our workplaces and our lives. Our hope is that you do not see these as separate from the rest of this book, but rather that you need to be especially attentive as you cultivate your own developmental network or as your organization implements formal mentoring programs,

Over time, working across differences actually increases the potential learning and growth between mentors and protégés. This is an extraordinarily important research finding because it is counterintuitive. We are attracted to people who are more similar to us, a principle called homophily. Thus, early on it may be difficult to build a relationship with someone who is different from you, but these challenges dissipate over time—specifically within nine months.

We also know that context matters—for example, more diversity in an organization generates more supportive peer relationships across people with differences, and a supportive culture fosters better relationships (see Chapter 6). Because of the business benefits of diversity and the inherent challenges of diverse relationships, a network of mentors and sponsors is critical for the career advancement of women and minorities.

In this chapter, we discuss how to foster effective relationships across gender, racial, ethnic, and virtual boundaries so that individuals of all backgrounds can thrive and organizations can develop highly productive and diverse workforces.

Why Do You Need to Know About Implicit Bias?

"Implicit bias" refers to the unconscious attitudes and stereotypes that affect our understanding of and interactions with other people. The key to this concept is that it is unconscious, which means that it is involuntary and unintentional, and it can bias you toward others in a positive or negative way. Implicit bias is part of the reason that we make quick, automatic social judgments that are the basis of stereotypes, first impressions, prejudices, favoritism, sexism, ageism, and so on.

What is remarkable about implicit bias is that your brain makes these associations without your knowledge. Because you are unaware, implicit bias tests often uncover biases even if you are someone who insists you do not discriminate. Since 1998, Mahzarin Banaji and Anthony Greenwald have collaborated with a team of researchers on Project Implicit, exploring implicit biases based on categories such as race, gender, sexual orientation, and political affiliation. You can go to their website and take an implicit bias test for free.

Since we advocate diversity in your developmental network, it is important that you are aware of potential personal biases and how they unintentionally may affect your behavior. For example, informally, mentors tend to select protégés who they see as younger versions of themselves, and protégés tend to select mentors who are role models. These natural tendencies work against diversity. There are also structural challenges based on the composition of people (i.e., the percentage of women or minorities) in organizations and occupations that may affect your ability to connect with diverse others. You, your efforts, and your context will shape your developmental network.

What Is Intersectionality?
A Modern Lens on Relationships

"Intersectionality" is a useful term to describe the complexity of modern identities. It highlights the intersection of multiple identities that may be important for people in the workplace. The roots of intersectionality are in legal and feminist scholarship, which focuses on social inequities based on categories such as gender, race, class, sexual orientation, disability, and so on. These categories are critical for understanding people as individuals and may create challenging dynamics for relationships. For example, if you are a black woman in an organization that has little diversity at the top, access to developmental relationships in the workplace may be limited because two categories—race and gender—are important for your identity and impact your connections with others.

David Thomas pointed out many years ago that mentoring relationships are often plagued by what he calls "racial taboos." He explains that these taboos are conveyed in archetypes that derive from the history of slavery in the United States that may unknowingly fuel our behavior in relationships across racial lines. When this occurs, it is far more difficult to develop a relationship that is mutually beneficial and free of limiting stereotypes.

Intersectionality is becoming even more complex because there are numerous categories that accompany globalization.

The fact of the matter is that all of us have multiple identities, but certain categories may be more or less salient to who you are and how you see yourself. What matters to you in terms of identity categories also depends on your context, particularly the diversity of relationships available in your organization. Multiple strategic relationships have never been more crucial in helping you navigate your career, so having an idea of how complex people are is useful as you think about approaching others who may differ from you in terms of gender, race, ethnicity, social class, or educational background.

We build on the research of Stacey Fitzsimmons to explain the variety of ways people mentally organize their identity (see Table 9-1).

Personal history and current context form the basis for how we think about identity. Given that different people prioritize their identities in different ways, seeking others or matching people based on categories is challenging. The variety alone is daunting—consider, for example, work and nonwork roles, cultural backgrounds, gender, and ethnicity, among others. After all, identity reflects who we are beyond any category and deeply affects how we interact with others.

Table 9-1 Intersectionality at Work: Importance of Identities

Degree of Identity Integration	Hierarchical Identities	Equivalent Identities
Low	One identity is prioritized regardless of context, e.g., woman, manager, Asian	Different identities are important in different contexts, e.g., woman in workplace, Latina in community
High	Different identities are integrated because of context, e.g., woman engineer prioritizes engineer identity but as a clear minority she cannot separate the two.	Integrated identities, e.g., Asian American who feels more similar to other Asian Americans rather than to Asians or Americans.

When you initiate mentoring relationships with people who are different from you in multiple categories (e.g., cross-gender, cross-race, cross-cultural relationships) or have different experiences, you may face challenges in recognizing cultural differences, overcoming stereotypes, developing trust, and managing the perceptions of others. The key is to recognize that these differences pose challenges beyond what you are likely to face when you are in a relationship with someone who is quite similar to you. Making these connections work requires that you make good use of the relational skills we discuss in Chapter 4.

What Are the Benefits of Diverse Relationships?

You are more likely to form a relationship with someone you see as similar, competent, and with whom you feel personally comfortable. Thus you need to be intentional about pursuing diverse relationships. When you interact with people who are different from you, you create new opportunities for learning and support. However, people need time to adapt. Even though diverse relationships are more challenging early on, they expose you to a wider range of information and resources that actually make them more beneficial over time. Take our colleague, Tina Opie, for example:

> Tina Opie was in an MBA class on leadership and ethics taught by Edward Freeman in the Darden School of Business. She recalls how Freeman created an environment of trust and explicitly viewed all students as able and competent. She explained, "He told me that he saw some potential in me. He said, 'You think differently from your classmates; you think about the root cause of things. Would you consider taking a doctoral seminar?'" Opie was surprised that he saw such potential in her and took the time to invite her to another class. She took the seminar and loved it. "He gave me a window into the academic world. It showed me that if this is what getting a PhD is about, then I can do this."

She graduated and worked in banking and consulting for five years. When she decided to get her doctorate, Freeman guided her through the process of applying. This was a cross-gender and cross-race mentoring relationship that had a tremendous impact on the career of the protégé. Now a professor herself at Babson College, Opie says, "It was like opening the black box. He showed me the possibilities and made me feel confident that I could succeed."

Building a relationship despite inherent challenges opens up opportunities for new connections and growth. Our research has shown that different mentors may play different roles in supporting your career. For example, across 41 studies even though men and women were equally likely to have been protégés, researchers found that male mentors provide more career development whereas female mentors provide more psychosocial support. In many organizations, men are more senior in rank and tenure and therefore are more capable of providing career support—particularly sponsorship, exposure, and visibility—critical for career progress and promotion. The importance of mentoring support and insights from those in powerful positions has been linked to the success of women and minorities early in their careers all the way to the corporate board level.

The fundamental principle of developmental networks is to increase the likelihood that you (and your developers) will access the support you need across multiple relationships to succeed in your career. Diversifying your relationships is a key strategy to capturing these benefits.

Benefits of Diverse Relationships
- Awareness of your potential
- Exceeding performance expectations
- Finding a style with which diverse others are comfortable
- Gaining access to informal networks
- Getting tactical advice on navigating the organization
- Advice on challenging assignments

- Awareness of differing perceptions/experiences in the organization
- Increasing opportunities to collaborate and learn

How Do I Make My Developmental Network More Diverse?

Entrepreneurial protégés and mentors should pursue learning relationships purposefully with respect to differences. When you assess your developmental network (see Chapter 3), diversity should be a key component of your analysis. Researchers, especially David Clutterbuck and colleagues, have uncovered several strategies for improving the mentoring process among diverse parties, including:

- Open dialogue
- Suspend judgment
- Identify common interests and values
- Acknowledge your differences
- Make efforts to learn about one another
- Show empathy
- Risk discomfort to make the relationship work

Notably, these are strategies that promote the healthy development of all relationships. It is cultivating a mindset of tolerance and appreciation for differences that can help you overcome any fears or wariness of making such an effort.

Be Transparent in Cross-Gender Relationships

Along with the personal, internal challenges in building relationships, there may be external challenges to pursuing diverse mentoring relationships in the workplace, including managing how your boss and other employees see the relationship. Cross-gender mentoring relationships may be misinterpreted as sexual relationships and open either party to gossip. This can be particularly damaging for the careers of young female protégés. Sylvia Hewlett and the Center for Talent Innovation recommend a few key tips for avoiding misperceptions including:

- Polish your professional presence.
- Meet in public places.
- Choose to meet over lunch rather than dinner.
- Share elements of your private life, including spouses/ significant others or kids.

The key here is to be transparent about the relationship and keep it professional. You do not want to inadvertently damage your own, or anyone else's, reputation or career. It is imperative that senior people take the lead in creating professional dynamics in which it is seen as the norm for mixed gender relationships to develop and thrive.

Be Open in Cross-Race Relationships

Research on cross-race relationships by David Thomas demonstrates that a network of mentors is critical for minority managers competing for access to the top executive jobs. Mentors must be aware of how challenging it is for men and women of color to advance through middle management, and they must be advocates for diversity in their organizations. Minority protégés should build relationships with at least two executives who can sponsor them into the highest ranks. In particular, Thomas found that both parties in cross-race relationships struggle with "protective hesitation" and so refrain from raising sensitive issues. This makes the relationship more fragile and may prevent both parties from reaching their full potential.

Ultimately, Thomas found that black executives consistently benefited from what he calls a "dual support system," where one sponsor is black and the other is white. This has been advocated for women executives as well. In both instances, the kind of support experienced by the protégé when provided by a developer who is similar is different from the support given by a developer who is in a different important identity group. The reality is that a dual support system within many organizations is not possible because of the lack of diversity in senior management. Fortunately deep level similarity—feeling like you are similar to another person in terms of personality, values, and attitudes—has been found to be even more important than actual similarity (same-gender or same-race) in the exchange of support between mentors and protégés. We suggest that you give each other the time to uncover similarities so that you will be able to see yourself in one another, a process called identification, because when you discover meaningful similarities between you and your mentor or protégé, you will feel more supported and more satisfied with the relationship.

Talking about gender, race, and culture is fraught with taboos and societal norms that impede an honest conversation. Derald Wing Sue and his colleagues at Columbia University have studied the challenges of racial dialogues in particular. Here are a few key recommendations for facilitating a constructive conversation:

- Admit your own faults and biases; be vulnerable.
- Validate the perspective of the other person.
- Identify and manage your own emotional reactions and discomfort.
- Understand differences in communication styles.
- Be open to racial blunders and help each other recover.

You need to be open to the other person's perspective and ask a lot of questions. In sharing vulnerabilities, we uncover assumptions about ourselves, other people, and our context.

Manage Expectations in Cross-Cultural Relationships

Much of what we know about cross-cultural mentoring relationships is based on studies of expatriates, those employees who leave for an international assignment and return within the same company. In her study of expatriates in China and Singapore, our colleague Yan Shen found that their developmental networks consistently included three important groups of developers:

(1.) relationships from their home country, (2.) expats in their host country who were similar in background to them, and (3.) host country developers who knew the host country culture and norms better than those in the other groups.

Over the two- to five-year period that the expat worked in the host country, the local developers were extremely important in helping them learn the ropes of the new context and getting to know the local resources. On the other hand, the developmental relationships with those back home became more distant during the period away, but were still very important in helping the individual to repatriate after a time away. Other expats from different countries could be helpful in the cultural transition that had to be made in order for the expat to be successful in the assignment. These findings illustrate the changing needs you may face before, during, and after an international assignment and highlight how different developmental relationships can help you adjust and succeed both personally and professionally. Organizations can facilitate these relationships by providing opportunities for employees to connect at critical junctures in their job changes.

Mentoring relationships embedded in different cultures may have different norms and expectations. Aarti Ramaswami and George Dreher found that supervisors are frequently viewed as mentors in India. In addition, involving protégés in nonwork interactions including family activities was culturally accepted and quite common. Despite a more paternalistic culture, Indian professionals preferred more egalitarian relationships than one might expect.

In Japan, mentoring relationships are viewed as long-term investments characterized by obligation and duty. Protégés feel gratitude and an obligation to repay the favor of their mentors' wisdom. Both parties form strong emotional bonds more similar to those in nonwork relationships than are typically seen in workplace relationships in Western cultures. Such basic differences in assumptions of what constitutes a meaningful relationship need to be surfaced early in cross-cultural relationships in order to avoid frustration, misunderstanding, or disappointment.

Cross-cultural developmental relationships are quite common in today's diverse and global work environment. Challenges in building rapport and getting to know someone who has a different cultural background are equal to those encountered in building relationships with people of the opposite gender or of another race. The possibility of implicit bias exists here, as does the reality of intersectionality. If you are of a particular cultural descent, there are typical stereotypes that may shape what others assume to be your values, goals, and skills. These stereotypes must be transcended if two individuals are to build a flourishing developmental relationship in which mutual learning occurs. In his book *Global Dexterity*, Andy Molinsky points out that learning about another culture is only the first step in figuring out how to build relationships with diverse people. You need to customize your behavior so that you are seen as appropriate yet maintain your own integrity. In cross-cultural relationships, it is especially important to:

- Share your unique experiences and interests.
- Explicitly discuss your cultural similarities and differences.
- Increase interactions to establish trust; consistent contact is most helpful.

Connect with Purpose, and Be Persistent

While it may seem easy to initiate diverse relationships, maintaining and strengthening them may be difficult. Your role is to be clear about the purpose of the relationship and be persistent in connecting over time. Increasing personal disclosure and interpersonal comfort helps facilitate investment in the relationship, and you may simply need to allow more time to build these relationships.

How Can Organizations Support Diverse Developmental Relationships?

Sustaining a developmental culture is the best way to ensure that people are committed to learning relationships. For many organizations, this means investing in both informal and formal initiatives that encourage relationship building with people who are different in terms of gender, race, or ethnicity. In our discussion with Luke Visconti, CEO of DiversityInc, he recommended three key diversity initiatives that are connected to improving organizational performance:

1. Diversity councils with goals
2. Structured mentoring
3. Resource groups

Diversity councils are composed of a strategic group of diverse leaders tasked with developing and overseeing the diversity goals of the organization. These goals are tied to metrics that help the council measure successes and focus on areas for improvement. The strength of your diversity council will be directly related to the visible support it receives from the top (see Chapter 7) and bottom-line benefits.

Structured mentoring is a critical part of effective diversity business practices. All aspects of diversity and inclusion can be harnessed to engage employees, leaders, customers/clients, and stakeholders. Take gender for example, DiversityInc's data indicate that women comprise 25.9 percent of the top five levels of management in their list of the top 50 companies for diversity. In one year, the top 50 outperformed the Standard & Poor's 500 by 29 percent and the Dow Jones Industrial Index by 20 percent. Again and again, we see that diversity improves organizational performance. However, if you are an employee in the minority, it's mathematically impossible to get adequate mentoring, sponsorship, or coaching from people like you.

Visconti shared a story that highlights why structured mentoring is necessary. He was recently in a meeting with the

18-person executive committee of a large, 30,000-employee company. The executive committee included two women and two black men along with 14 white men. Before the meeting, one of the black men pulled Visconti aside and said, "Please, you've got to talk to them about structured mentoring. Because every black person in this company comes to me, and I cannot possibly mentor every black employee."

As the meeting progressed, Visconti facilitated a discussion about diversity and asked a simple question, "Do any of you mentor any black people?" The answer was no, and the committee members were embarrassed. Visconti explains "They weren't racist or anything. They just never thought about it."

Structured mentoring programs with the characteristics we recommend in Chapter 5—particularly active support from senior leaders and training for both mentors and mentees—are one of the best ways to connect people of different races, gender, and ethnicity across different levels of your organization. This will often entail a customized agenda for each meeting or the first few meetings and guidelines on topics to consider. Because all of us have a tendency to be attracted to others like ourselves, it is critical that top-level leaders develop the skills to mentor a range of different employees and role-model these capabilities.

Resource groups are based on shared identities (race, ethnicity, gender, sexual orientation, disability) or experiences (early child development, teleworkers, caregivers to the elderly). Resource groups supported by the organization should make use of a charter that ties the purpose of the group to business to benefit the company. Visconti explains that these have evolved from affinity groups, based on shared interests (food, culture), to become more focused, although the idea is still to link to peoples' passions.

One way for executives to inform themselves of differing perceptions and experiences in their organization is to attend different resource group meetings. By placing yourself in situations where you are interacting with people who are different from you, you increase the possibilities of developing informal mentoring relationships. Leaders should pay particular attention to their role as sponsors, who provide exposure and visibility and advocate for their protégé's promotion.

Why Should I Use Technology to Build Relationships?

The use of technology for relationship development and maintenance poses unique challenges and opportunities. Globalization has necessitated the use of multiple media to facilitate information exchange and collaboration. You are probably already engaged in some e-mentoring, meaning developmental relationship(s) that primarily occur virtually but may also include a face-to-face orientation meeting or technologies such as Skype, FaceTime, Google Hangouts, and so on. Combining mentoring and technology has several advantages including:

- Connecting across geographic and time barriers
- Flexibility to interact asynchronously, on either parties' schedule
- Increasing access to diverse relationships

Face-to-Face Interactions Help to Build Rapport

While virtual communication is convenient and efficient, it is a limited form of expression which may be particularly difficult in the early stages of relationships. Our research has shown that the addition of one phone call or face-to-face interaction improves the support that protégés receive and the satisfaction that mentors feel. When you communicate in-person there is greater richness in the interaction because of the intonations of your voice, your eye contact, your expressions, your posture, and your ability to react in real time to the other party. Some of this richness can be simulated through live streaming technology. However, there is still nothing like actually meeting someone face-to-face to feel connected.

Carol Yamartino, a consultant who coaches leaders and teams for exceptional results, has helped organizations in a variety of industries to create mentoring circles. Her approach is to bring together a group of peers, who share goals, with two senior mentors for the purpose of supporting members' learning and career development. Usually mentoring circles convene once a month, face-to-face for six months, and with a structured agenda to facilitate discussion about how to navigate one's career in the current context. Over time, she has noticed that companies are looking to leverage technology in order to reach a wider range of employees with effective mentoring experiences.

A client recently asked to extend the mentoring circle concept across locations through virtual meetings. As Yamartino told us, "Virtual mentoring—whether one-to-one or in a mentoring circle—doesn't always get the job done. The communication is quite two-dimensional without adequate affective content." Therefore, she recommends a hybrid approach and is helping her client move to a format with one or two initial face-to-face meetings before shifting to an online format such as WebEx or Skype. Over the course of a year, she anticipates that regular face-to-face meetings would be built into the program in order to deepen members' commitment to one another and ensure the success of the mentoring circle.

Make Social Media Part of the Conversation

Technology holds promise for expanding access to mentoring but also introduces new challenges. Social networks, including Facebook, Twitter, and LinkedIn, among others, must be an explicit part of the conversation in any mentoring relationship. These technologies provide an opportunity to connect. However, they often bridge the personal and professional roles for individuals (particularly Facebook) and thus need to be managed thoughtfully.

During program orientations, Wendy always has participants discuss *when* and *if* they will connect to one another via LinkedIn or Facebook. We encourage you to put all these social media options on the table for discussion to foster open dialogue and prevent any awkwardness or problems that may occur with ignored invites or sharing too much information.

How Do Organizations Use Technology for Mentoring?

Many organizations have invested in internal social networks to facilitate knowledge sharing and collaboration, and these systems are also used to establish and build developmental relationships. For example, Intel has a program that matches employees with mentors based on topics or skills they want to learn about regardless of hierarchical position or geographic location. Matching protégés with mentors has been a particularly successful use of technology platforms, often advanced by nonprofits and consulting firms. Technology may connect you to mentors inside an organization, such as KPMG or Sodexo's network strategies (see Chapter 7), or outside of an organization.

How do you personalize the matching process yet keep your mentoring program cost-effective? Technology was the answer when Mentor Resources was looking to help companies grow their mentoring programs. Mentor Resources is a San Francisco–based consulting firm that works with Fortune 1000 companies and government agencies. It helps its partners build formal mentoring programs, match participants, and develop customized activities that enable participants to progress through the program and meet their goals. According to CEO Kim Wise, organizations tend to want mentoring for specific reasons—to support onboarding, enhance diversity initiatives, or improve their talent pipeline, and when they get good results, these programs are often expanded.

Mentor Resources started incorporating technology into its matching process in 2008. After several years of extensively interviewing participants, coding data, and matching by hand, they were looking for a way to scale their capabilities. They found that 18 factors contributed to a successful match, and they replicated these factors through their survey software. Beyond these critical factors, Mentor Resources works with organizations to determine participant compatibilities using unique competencies and functional expertise or specialties. "The key to our matching algorithm is finding synergies that become building blocks for relationships," explains Wise. She calls it a strengths-based model that focuses on similarities in personality, work styles, and learning needs. "In addition, we require participants to meet at least three times before making a decision as to whether or not they want to continue. They need to give each other a chance, and we've found that this is a minimum amount of time for building rapport."

"Mentors keep coming back, and that's a good sign," Wise reports. "These are really smart people and they participate because they are learning something and finding opportunities they never would have thought of otherwise. Many mentors report that they maintain relationships with their mentees long term, and in fact, these relationships turn into a friendship over time." For the organizations that partner with Mentor Resources, establishing or improving their mentoring programs is a learning process. Wise is emphatic that there must be support from the top of the company for participants to dedicate the time necessary for a mentoring program to succeed. One way to assess the success of a mentoring program is to ask for participants' feedback. Through many years of experience and perfecting their software, Mentor Resources now reports a 99 percent satisfaction on matches.

One of Mentor Resources' clients, the U.S. Naval Academy Alumni Mentoring Program (AMP), recently surveyed its participants and confirmed that both mentors and protégés were thriving with their matches. In the past year and a half, 640 alumni both locally and internationally have joined the program, and more get involved every week. AMP started as a way to support U.S. Naval Academy graduates at the end of their service as they were deciding whether to stay in or get out of the navy. Codirector Steve Hudock explains, "We were selected and trained at the U.S. Naval Academy to be leaders. Our mission is to allow individuals to develop to their greatest potential. This means supporting alumni as leaders for our country even out of the navy."

Mentors and protégés are located all over the globe, and AMP enables them to connect so that mentors can support protégés in making informed decisions. Participants commit to an initial meeting and then mutually agree upon further regular contact whether over coffee, on the phone, via Skype, FaceTime, or other technologies. Technology has been critical for providing access and scaling the program. Mentors register through an extensive questionnaire customized in collaboration with Mentor Resources' software. When protégés complete their registration survey, they are matched with three potential mentors and choose one. The program is flexible—if either the protégé or mentor is uncomfortable with the match then either party can opt-out and try another match.

Participants' only criticism of this system is that it is cumbersome. It can be up to a two-hour process to enroll and fill out all the survey information. For some mentors particularly, this approach through technology can be challenging. However once they discuss the process with AMP support staff and get matched, their attitude is overwhelmingly positive. Providing access to mentoring relationships through technology has opened up tremendous opportunities to connect U.S. Naval Academy alumni and provide support at critical junctions in their careers.

When Should You or Your Company Seek External Mentors?

Diversity of relationships, both within your workplace and outside of work, is important for your career development. Organizations and occupations that struggle to attract or promote diverse employees may find that external developmental support for their people is essential. Several companies exist that match women and minority candidates with external mentors (e.g., Menttium Corporation and Mentor Resources), and many professional organizations foster relationships through networking events (e.g., 85 Broads, Minority Professional Network, Young Professionals Association).

Mentors May Be a Scarce Resource

Matching high-potential protégés with external mentors is a strategy that has been effective with senior executives and women managers, particularly when there is a dearth of available mentors. Menttium was founded two decades ago with the primary purpose of helping women professionals benefit from the mentoring of senior executives. At that time, there were few women in senior roles to serve as mentors to young women, and few men in senior roles who were effective at mentoring women. The founders decided to match high-potential women with mentors from companies other than their own. This led to a flourishing mentoring system which regularly matched protégés with mentors from other companies who wanted to help women advance their careers.

Today, Menttium's offerings have expanded considerably. It is now matching minorities with mentors from companies other than their own when the supply within their company is limited or inadequate. They have also added a service to support executives who are approaching the C-suite level and would benefit by being matched with a C-suite executive at another firm who could mentor the aspiring executive on preparing for this movement upward. When we spoke with cofounder and CEO Kim Vappie, she noted that her firm is also helping organizations create mentoring circles composed of eight to ten protégés within one company who are matched with a senior executive mentor from another company. She noted that the renewal rate of external executive mentors is quite high. As Vappie explained, "These mentors take part at first to give back, and after they participate in one of our programs, they discover that they learned as much as their protégés, about a different function, company, or industry."

Mentors May Be in a Different Career Stage

Connecting students to working professionals clearly requires external mentors. Nonprofit MentorNet has connected over 32,000 students to STEM (science, technology, engineering, and mathematics) professionals to facilitate high-quality e-mentoring relationships since 1997. Mary Fernandez, CEO of MentorNet, had a mentor from AT&T Bell Labs when she was in graduate school, so she knows first-hand how important one-to-one mentoring relationships can be in guiding people into STEM careers. She was a mentor herself for 15 years through MentorNet before taking the helm. Fernandez never met most of her protégés in person, but spoke on the phone and then corresponded via e-mail. "In my experience, I would spend about an hour on the phone twice over two weeks at the beginning to bootstrap the relationship. Then we'd start corresponding."

Fernandez sees potential in gathering best practices from master mentors who all have their own methodologies yet rarely share what they know. "We have ample technology behind matching, but there are two other critical components: training and actual engagement. The success of the mentorship depends upon providing developmentally appropriate content that addresses the challenges faced by the student protégé and providing the mentor-protégé pair with guidance on how to recognize and tackle challenges together."

Fernandez and her team have a vision of creating a culture of mentoring in STEM fields in which students develop skill sets and expectations that enable them to succeed. She believes so strongly in the value of technology that her entire executive team works virtually. MentorNet has recently partnered with LinkedIn in the process of reinventing itself as a social network for STEM mentoring.

Persistent Change:
How Relationships Help
with the Pace of Change

With the rise of boundaryless careers, you are likely to experience frequent job changes and movement across organizations. Employee tenure in the United States is about three years for workers between the ages of 25 and 34. Although tenure increases with age, it does not guarantee job security. The boundaries between work and life have also become blurred as we are constantly connected through technology. These trends are compounded by the rapid pace of change and economic uncertainty. Relationships with your developers can provide stability during your own transitions and through workplace upheavals.

Why Are Connections Outside of Work Critical?

In our fast-paced world, relationships outside of work have become a key source of stability and continuity. Developmental networks are a subset of your overall social network. Social networks generally have a core periphery structure with strong relationships that form a close core and weaker ties that come and go in the periphery.

In contrast, a study conducted by Jonathan Cummings and Monica Higgins showed that over time developmental networks take on an inner-core–outer-core structure and are surprisingly unstable. Only 45 percent of relationships in the inner core stayed the same across five years. Stable, inner-core relationships were more likely to be those that provide high amounts of psychosocial support, often those with spouses/partners and friends. These are close relationships that you would be likely to maintain no matter where you work. We also saw this pattern in our own research, in which we found that 56 percent of developers were from outside the workplace. Family members, either a parent or a spouse/partner, were overwhelmingly identified as the most important relationship in people's developmental networks.

As you might expect, nonwork relationships provide more emotional support, whereas work relationships provide more career/instrumental support. However, close relationships all provide some of both types of support and can be essential in helping you through transitions.

When she changed jobs two years ago, Wendy's husband Dan provided emotional support, reminded her of all of the positives that accompanied the risk of a new job, and acted as a sounding board to help her think through how to structure her work-life balance.

Similarly, personal friendships and informal mentors outside of work offer a unique perspective on your current role and can expand your perceptions of what is possible. Both parties in these relationships learn about working in different contexts and are able to think about problems and solutions from a different perspective.

Be Approachable as an Informal Developer

For Dave Templin, senior business manager of the $8 billion earthmoving division at Caterpillar, making himself available as an informal mentor to his employees and the broader Northern Illinois University (NIU) alumni network has been very rewarding. Templin believes it takes someone really caring to mentor others. For him, mentoring is not just about making the business successful, but about the mentees and their careers. Here's a story about one of them:

> Kate, a recent NIU graduate, had kept in touch with Dave after he gave a talk on-campus. She had recently started working as an accountant in an insurance program and reached out again after starting her job to talk about her responsibilities and what she should expect.
>
> After discussions with Dave and other mentors, Kate decided to make a big change, and she joined the Peace Corps. She went

to Africa and worked in business development helping new entrepreneurs start up their businesses. Dave found this incredibly courageous and felt honored to help her think through all her options. "It really impressed me, and I wondered if I would or could ever display that courageousness. She saw something in me, though, that I wouldn't have predicted, and we had some great conversations."

We can say with confidence that it is Templin's authenticity and accessibility that attracts such engaging protégés and continues to deepen his own learning and mentoring skills.

How Do Relationships Help You Cope with Disruption and Steep Learning Curves?

In all sectors, persistent change is a fact of life. Therefore, no matter what your career stage or hierarchical level, you will be a *novice* in one or more arenas at any point in time. This means that learning is more critical than ever before. In order to meet the daily demands of changing circumstances, you must be an active learner and build developmental alliances with peers, seniors, and subordinates both inside and outside the immediate workplace.

Relationships Buffer Stress

If you are thinking about changing jobs or are having a difficult situation at work, it makes sense that you would want to talk to someone outside your organization. Mentors from previous employers, professional organizations, alumni networks, and family or friends provide critical information, support, and resources. These relationships act as a buffer for stress and help decrease work-family conflict thus enabling you to perform better and to feel more satisfied in both your work and nonwork roles.

Relationships Help Redirect Your Career

When Whitney Johnson, an award-winning Wall Street equity analyst, left her job to pursue her own start-up, her husband provided the emotional support and encouragement she needed to "disrupt" her career. She worked through two failed start-ups, all the while growing her network and becoming more involved in her community and church. Then she met Clay Christensen and his son Matt and discovered like-minded colleagues with whom she cofounded Rose Park Advisors. Finding success again as an author of the book *Dare, Dream, Do*, a speaker, and strategic consultant, Johnson attributes her success to both her willingness to dream and her tenacity in pursuing the relationships that would help make her dreams a reality.

Be Proactive in Seeking Support

Seeking connections outside of work with informal mentors and protégés is essential to developing relationships. Leaders at all levels need outside support to help process what goes on within their organization and to provide an external perspective on their leadership growth and development.

Being proactive in initiating relationships is the most effective way to attract and maintain diverse relationships in your network. All of us should seek to enlist a variety of developers outside of work and create a developmental network that fits our career and life goals.

Reflection Questions

Use the following questions to guide your reflections on diversity, technology, and change:

1. How can I diversify the relationships in my current developmental network? Where can I meet interesting people with a different perspective on my business or career?
2. Could I reach out to support diverse employees; how could I help?

3. What initiatives in my organization support diverse relationships, and should I do more to support them or suggest new initiatives?
4. How might I leverage technology in support of mutually enhancing developmental relationships?
5. Do I spend enough time attending to my developmental relationships, inside and outside of work?

10

TOR-MENTORS: WHEN RELATIONSHIPS ARE PROBLEMATIC

Mentoring relationships may become problematic for benign reasons or for more alarming reasons, just like any other relationship. Often, a mentee will outgrow the close guidance of a mentor and want to move in a direction that the mentor does not support. While this may look like dysfunction, it can be reframed as "it's time to move on!"

Problems may occur early if the mentor and mentee have conflicting goals or important value differences that make it very difficult to find common ground and a shared purpose for the relationship. Another possibility is that two people are matched but do not have the relational skills or the time to invest in building the alliance—they become dissatisfied and disillusioned. Problematic relationships are more common than we would like to think. The good news is that in taking action to address the problem(s), you can learn a lot about yourself and position yourself for more satisfying connections with others. Consider Charlie's story:

Jack has been Charlie's formally assigned mentor for about six months. Charlie is a bit disillusioned because they meet very infrequently, and when they do meet, they don't have much to say to each other. They both attended the training required of mentors and mentees, but they are now at a loss as to how to have meaningful and productive dialogue. The relationship feels stilted, and both have the view that the other is responsible for the lack of a good connection.

Negative Experiences Occur in 20 Percent of Formal Relationships

In about one in five formal mentoring relationships a negative experience results. At first glance, you might assume that the negative experience occurred because of a poor match. This is not necessarily the case. All too often, either or both parties don't give a new relationship enough time and attention, or they don't have the necessary relational skills that we outline in Chapter 4. How much has each shared about her goals for the relationship, and what she hopes to bring to the interactions? How consistently has each listened carefully to what the other has said and tried to deepen the connection by identifying and/or posing questions to get at shared experiences and shared values?

In the end, it may very well be that the people like Charlie and Jack don't have enough in common to provide the glue for a developmental relationship. However, we suggest that if you are facing this situation, you investigate further using your self-disclosure and listening skills to the best of your ability. If the dynamic remains stilted and empty in terms of potential for learning, then it is certainly time to move on. If you are in a formal mentoring program, there is usually a coordinator who can help you navigate your way through or away from this particular relationship.

Supervisory Mentor Relationships Are Complex

When a supervisory relationship that has evolved into a mentoring relationship becomes problematic, it may be more difficult to figure out what went wrong. Consider Meg and Pete for example:

> Meg and Pete had a very supportive supervisory and mentoring relationship for several years. Just recently, Pete decided that he wanted to make a significant change in his career path and move from product development to marketing and sales. Meg is feeling betrayed since she brought Pete into the company when he was a novice and actively developed him by providing him with challenging and visible assignments and giving regular feedback along the way.

> Pete is very grateful for the support and guidance that Meg provided but is now becoming resentful because he wants to change his path and Meg is not supporting him in doing so. He feels that she is being selfish about it all and doesn't want to let go of a well-trained member of her team.

While at first glance, it may appear that the relationship has gone awry, it is quite possible that Pete has moved to a new stage of his own development and that he and Meg have entered the separation phase of their relationship (see Table 1-2). If this is true, it means that one or both parties' development needs have changed, and the reciprocity that existed up to now is diminishing and no longer seems helpful to Pete. At the same time, Meg is feeling betrayed (rather than excited) by Pete's change in direction.

Unpacking these negative feelings is a first step toward recognizing the need to move on and to redefine this particular relationship. Each party needs to figure out the best next step, and, when possible, get assistance from trusted others in doing so. Of course, taking such actions to improve or end a developmental relationship is not easy. But it is certainly made easier knowing that you have other developers in your network that you can count on for support.

What Do Problematic Relationships Look Like?

About 15 years ago, scholars identified problematic mentoring relationships as worthy of study simply because such relationships can undermine the career success and personal well-being of both individuals. Terri Scandura introduced us to the idea that problematic relationships can develop even when intentions for the relationship and the other person are good.

As we see above, Meg felt betrayed and Pete felt unsupported, yet both of them had good intentions for the other and for the relationship. Similarly, peer coaching has a predictable set of risk factors that can undermine the quality of this kind of helping relationship. Fortunately, over the past decade we have been able to clarify the nature of problematic relationships to help you to assess the severity of the problem as well as actions that you might take to address the problem. In some instances the relationship will be transformed and become a positive experience once again, and in other instances you will make the decision to leave it behind.

Lillian Eby created a classification of problems in relationships that is useful to consider whenever you find yourself dissatisfied with what you intended to be a thriving developmental relationship. The first thing to note in Figure 10-1 is that most of the issues encountered in developmental relationships are minor and can be addressed through a deeper understanding of the problem and taking actions that will address it. Only infrequently do we encounter relationship problems that are so severe that it is necessary to end the relationship as soon as possible. (See Table 10-1.)

Figure 10-1 Continuum of Relational Problems

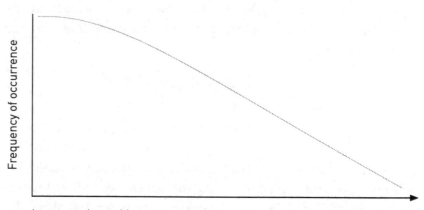

Low-severity problems   High-severity problems

Table 10-1 Degrees of Relational Problems

Minor Relational Problems	Taxing Relational Problems	Serious Relational Problems
Unclear expectations	Failure to engage	Violated expectations
Unmet expectations	Disappointment and regret	Career and personal damage
Superficial interactions	Uncomfortable interactions	Harassment
Lack of self-awareness		Bullying
Lack of relational skills	Submissiveness; overdependence	
	Unwillingness to self-reflect and learn from difficulties	

Minor Relational Problems

Minor problems can usually be addressed with changes in assumptions and behaviors on the part of one or both parties. So, for example, in Jack and Charlie's situation, if one or the other is willing to raise his concern about the lack of fruitful exchanges in the relationship, it is quite likely that they would feel less alone with their dissatisfaction and disillusionment and could find ways to make the relationship more meaningful. Through basic relational skills of genuine curiosity, active listening, and self-disclosure, they would discover that, indeed, they could engage in conversation that would lead to mutual learning. Alternatively, in clarifying their expectations and whether they were or could be met, they might discover with such exploratory conversations that they had little in common and that it might be better to end the relationship so that both would be free to begin other formal alliances. Either outcome would be preferable to a constant state of frustration and disappointment.

It's Easier for the Mentor to Raise Problems, but Sometimes Mentees Have to Do It

Generally, it will be easier for the mentor to raise important questions about expectations and the quality of interactions because of the power differential created by their hierarchical status. However, when we encourage mentees to bring their concerns to their mentors (in spite of the concern or fear they may experience), they usually are pleasantly surprised to find their mentors are receptive and interested in what they have to say. When a mentor is too busy to notice a problem or lacks the relational skills to begin this kind of reflective process, courageous action on the part of a mentee can eliminate the relational problem and move the relationship forward.

Take Risks to Try to Deepen the Connection

If you feel that your relationship remains superficial and that clearly aligned expectations have not been established, the best approach is to use your self-reflective skills to build your self-awareness, and your relational skills to bring your personal learning to the conversation with your developer. While it may feel risky or simply uncomfortable to do, this kind of proactive approach will either deepen your connection or clarify that it may be time to seek meaningful relational learning elsewhere. Often, dialogue with a trusted peer or another developer in your network can be helpful in achieving the self-awareness you need to clarify your next steps.

Understand That Every Developer Is Not a Role Model

Anti–role models may be part of your developmental network. These are people whom you admire for certain skills or who may teach you something, but they also exhibit behavior(s) that you *do not* want to emulate. Anti-role-modeling behavior is most often exhibited by people who devalue relationships (e.g., supervisor who treats employees unfairly or is just not nice) or work-life interface failures (e.g., people who are seen as lacking balance or workaholics).

If you are open-minded, you know that there is something to be learned in every relationship, even if a person demonstrates behavior you don't want to emulate. Sometimes your own identity and career are clarified when you contrast your preferences with someone who has different values. Importantly, sponsors and coaches who offer instrumental support—help with getting promoted or refining your skills—need not be role models. It is worth your effort to uncover what is bothering you about the relationship, and whether the problem needs to be addressed. It may be that you need to accept the relationship for what it is and alter your own expectations.

Use Coaching Skills to Help You Decide If It's Time to End the Relationship

If you have conscientiously brought the coaching skills of *curiosity*, *questioning*, and *deep listening* to this particular relationship and you have practiced *self-management* and *accountability* and you have used your *intuition* to guide your actions, you can conclude that it is time to let go of this connection and direct your energy to building other positive relationships. (See Chapter 8 for a review.)

Taxing Relational Problems

A taxing relational problem may not be solvable, but we are never sure until we take time to reflect on the situation, examine our part in the dynamics, and make a well-considered decision as to whether there are actions that might move the relationship to a more positive footing where both individuals feel as though they are valued and learning from the interactions. In contrast to minor relational problem discussed above, taxing problems are usually characterized by greater negative feelings of disappointment and/or regret, a sense of disengagement from the other person in the relationship, a distinctive lack of mutuality where one party feels overly submissive or overly dominant, and/or a lack of a stance, which might lead to mutual learning from the difficulties encountered in the relationship.

Consider the following relationship which began as a positive one, but over time, became more negative for the mentee.

Susan has had an informal mentor in Beth for about two years. Up until now the relationship has been going very well. Beth has given Susan opportunities to meet other senior managers who might offer her a new position some time in the near future. Susan has just started a family and is concerned about taking on a position of greater responsibility while adapting to her new role as mother. However when Susan tries to raise this concern with Beth, Beth says, "If you want to succeed at this company, you have to seize the opportunities when they are presented to you." Beth seems to have little compassion for the dilemma Susan is currently facing.

This situation is causing Susan considerable stress. She not only feels pressure to take on a position of greater responsibility, but she also feels quite misunderstood by Beth who, up until now, has been her most ardent supporter. Her first attempts to explain her current preferences to her mentor seem to fall on deaf ears. She wonders if she can communicate her needs

206 STRATEGIC RELATIONSHIPS AT WORK

effectively, or whether she will need to find other developers who may be more empathetic to her situation. It is quite likely, too, that Beth is frustrated with Susan since she has invested a lot of time and energy in developing Susan and really wants her to become more visible and more successful. The challenge that Susan currently faces in adapting to new family responsibilities is not something that Beth had a problem with in her own life.

Reflect, Actively Listen, and Self-Disclose to Attempt to Resolve the Problem

For the relational problem between Susan and Beth to be addressed, each individual will have to engage in reflective work in order to consider the multiple factors that may be contributing to the lack of mutual understanding that currently characterizes the relationship. As we note in Chapter 8, different people bring their own story to the relationship—complete with past experiences, enduring assumptions about self and the other, and needs that they hope to fulfill in relating to the other.

The CMM (Coordinated Meaning Making) model reminds us that in order to build a shared story together—which becomes the basis for a strong positive alliance—each party must employ his or her reflective skills, active listening skills, and self-disclosure skills to build mutual understanding and respect.

Ask Questions and Empathize in Order to Move Forward

If Susan and Beth take the time and make the effort to ask questions that invite helpful self-disclosure and use deep listening to convey empathy, acceptance, and understanding, together they will be able to create a shared story in which both of their needs are acknowledged and addressed. Ideally, Susan would become more understanding of the pressure that Beth feels to demonstrate to her superiors her ability to advance the career of another high-potential woman in her organization. And Beth will come to understand and appreciate the challenges that Susan faces at this point in her life journey as a mother and a professional. Together they will consider how to move forward in a manner that supports both of them. Feelings of frustration and regret will diminish, and both parties will begin to learn about the other in a more appreciative way. As a consequence, the quality of the relationship will be enhanced, and both Susan and Beth will feel respected and supported rather than judged negatively.

Use the REAL Model of Communication

Relational work is not easy. Not only are self-awareness and strong social skills a requirement, but often one or both parties will benefit from reflecting on this challenging relationship with another trusted developer or friend. In this manner, for example, Susan and/or Beth get to practice the REAL (reflecting, expanding, agility, and learning) model of communication offered by Ilene Wasserman and Placida Gallegos and discussed in Chapter 8. In doing so, they are better able to bring the same disciplines to their communication in their troubled relationship. If, Susan and/or Beth develop new insights in reflecting with a trusted peer or developer, they may return to the relationship between them with new insight and greater openness to the possibilities. The troubled relationship may be transformed into one with meaning and purpose that supports both individuals as they move forward in their respective career journeys.

If, after applying these communication tools and skills, Susan and/or Beth are still disappointed or frustrated with the lack of mutual understanding and appreciation, it may be time to move away from the relationship. This is never easy, yet such a decision frees up space and opportunity for new relationships to form and to flourish. It is at moments like these that a robust developmental network is critical as it ensures that the loss of one important connection can be compensated for by the support of other strong developmental relationships.

Serious Relational Problems

Severe relational problems are usually born of bad intentions or lack of self-awareness that leads to destructive behavior toward one or both people in the relationship. Fortunately, these do not occur often. More often than not, however, when they do occur, it is best to let go of the relationship so that you minimize harm to yourself and create the space to enlist others in your developmental network. The question for all of us when we face such difficulties is, "How do we know whether this is a minor, taxing, or serious problem?" The short answer is that we cannot know without implementing the communications tools we outline in Chapters 4 and 8, and review them along with the examples presented in this chapter.

Let's consider one more case.

Tom was asked by his boss, the executive vice president of operations, to actively sponsor one of the company's high-potential female engineers. For the first two years, Abby was most appreciative of Tom's support and attention. She noticed over time, however, that his attitudes and behaviors started to bother her. She began to question whether his intentions were good and uniformly supportive of her career advancement. He rarely asked her to take on an assignment that required traveling abroad, and when he traveled with her to other cities in the United States, his behavior toward her became uncomfortably flirtatious. All of the discomfort that she experienced went unexpressed until one day, after the prodding of a female colleague, she decided to bring it to Tom's attention. He was embarrassed and angry, and felt unjustifiably accused.

If we put ourselves in Abby's shoes, we really don't know whether Tom's intentions are bad—that he is not seriously supporting and promoting her career but simply enjoying the opportunity to be around a bright and attractive woman—or whether he simply has had too little experience working closely with young, competent women, that he hasn't developed the social skills to keep the relationship on an appropriate professional level. What we do know is that Abby is very uncomfortable and is beginning to doubt whether this relationship is really serving her career development goals.

The REAL model of communication prompts Abby to reflect on her own experiences and to acknowledge her discomforts with the interactions to date. It also encourages her to explore the dynamics she and Tom are experiencing by herself, with a trusted other, and with Tom to see if she and he can learn from the difficulties she has experienced in this particular mentor relationship. So far, Tom has reacted defensively when she raised the issue of her discomfort, and he does not seem receptive to exploring what may be contributing to the relational problem. We might ask Abby whether she is genuinely curious, whether she is asking good questions, and whether she has applied deep listening in bringing the issue to Tom's attention. Did she begin by blaming Tom or did she begin by sharing her experience and the discomfort she was carrying around?

While we don't know the answers to these questions, we do know that when strong feelings are evoked in conversation, there is more going on than meets the eye. And it is only by knowing the full range of factors that may be affecting Tom and Abby's communication that Abby can effectively uncover Tom's intentions and assess whether the relationship can be repaired to a point that both can continue to benefit from the alliance.

In their book *Difficult Conversations*, Douglas Stone, Bruce Patton, and Sheila Heen identify several elements of a conversation that we should consider when we feel vulnerable (e.g., possible harassment, possible career derailment), and when the outcomes of such a conversation are uncertain. Whenever a mentoring relationship starts to feel very uncomfortable, as is the case with Tom and Abby, thinking through the elements of a difficult conversation can help you attempt to address the situation effectively.

Uncover differing perceptions about *"what happened?"* First, in any difficult conversation there are actually three conversations going on that we must attend to. First, is the *"what happened?"* conversation—what's the story here? This usually consists of struggling with who's right (the truth), who meant what (intentions), and who's to blame. In difficult conversations one or both parties can get stuck in a position of assuming they are right, the other person is wrong, or the other's intentions were bad. This stance will not enable healthy curiosity or deep listening and is very likely to result in no forward movement.

Understand Your Feelings and Manage Identity Issues

The second conversation is the *"feelings"* conversation—what we should do with our emotions? You need to be clear about your feelings and clear about whether to share them with your developer. And the third is the *"identity"* conversation—what does this interaction and my reactions to it say about me? Here the work is to see how the relationship is affecting your self-esteem and your sense of who you are in the world.

The point is that when a mentoring relationship gets difficult and leads to discomfort and other negative feelings, examining these three conversations will prepare you to approach your mentor or mentee with compassion and a genuine interest in learning in order to benefit from a reflective conversation in which the primary purpose is to learn, not to blame.

Determine Whether the Risk of a Difficult Conversation Is Worth It

It is a tall order to expect Abby to have a difficult conversation with Tom. She may decide after examining the three conversations above that it doesn't make sense to suggest further conversations with Tom. Or she may decide that she really doesn't know what his motives and intentions are, that he has been consistently supportive of her career advancement up until recently, and that perhaps her behavior has in some way and unknowingly contributed to the current dynamics. Perhaps a conversation would help to develop better ways of their interacting with each other. The choice that you have to make is between blaming the other person and taking a judgmental stance (e.g., assuming that Tom's intentions were bad) and engaging in a learning conversation where you decide to shift your internal orientation from certainty to curiosity, debate to exploration, and simplicity to complexity.

As we consider this serious relational problem from Abby's point of view, we should also consider the possibility that Tom has choices to make as well. If his intentions are actually good and he wants to actively support Abby's career development and success and if he has developed self-reflective and communication skills, he will be in a position to approach interactions with Abby with curiosity, compassion, and a desire to learn. He will also recognize that she is very uncomfortable and is experiencing much frustration, dissatisfaction, and a sense of betrayal in their relationship. Armed with the principles regarding how to have a difficult conversation, Tom and Abby, together, may find a way to move to a more positive situation in their relationship. We cannot know the outcome, but we can prepare for the work.

You Must Decide to Engage or Disengage

Ultimately, it is your decision whether to further engage or disengage from the relationship. In reviewing the three conversations above, you will learn a lot about yourself and whether the challenge of engaging in yet another difficult conversation is a wise and worthwhile thing to do. It makes sense to discuss your options with a trusted peer or another developer who can actively listen and help you to reflect on these options. We have seen over and over again that when people take the time to reflect on these relational problems with curiosity, compassion, and self-awareness, they learn important things about themselves and others as well as how to nurture effective developmental relationships.

What Are the Consequences of Staying in Problematic Relationships?

There are significant negative consequences of staying in problematic relationships too long. These range from consequences for one or both people in the relationship to consequences for the organization as a whole. We urge you to attend to problems as soon as they arise so that the following consequences can be minimized.

In each of the scenarios we discuss in this chapter so far, one or both parties are likely to experience the frustration that they are not able to build or sustain a positive relationship with their mentor or mentee. Whether it be Jack and Charlie who were matched in a formal mentoring program, or Pete and Meg whose mentoring relationship evolved from a supervisory relationship, or Susan and Beth who are in an informal mentoring relationship, or Abby and Tom's relationship where Tom was asked to actively sponsor Abby, we see the potential for negative consequences for these individuals and their organizations if no actions are taken to improve the relationship dynamics. These actions are summarized in Table 10-2.

What Can Organizations and Leaders Do to Minimize Relational Problems?

The negative consequences discussed in Table 10-2 are quite substantial and, if left unrecognized and unattended, will have corrosive effects on the individuals involved as well as on the organization as a whole. There are a number of actions that managers, leaders, and those who oversee Human Resources development or talent development can take to minimize these negative consequences.

Establish a Supportive Culture for Relationship Building

It is most important that your organizational culture and practices support attention to relationship-building efforts. Individuals need to be given opportunities to develop the self-awareness, self-regulation, and social skills to effectively initiate, build, and sustain high-quality developmental relationships characterized by mutual learning, trust, and a deepening commitment to one another. When this kind of "developmental culture" exists (see Chapter 7), these problematic relationships will be minimized.

Table 10-2 Consequences of Problematic Relationships

Relationship	Relational Problem	Individual Consequences	Organizational Consequences
Jack and Charlie (formal match)	Minor	Frustration Lowered job satisfaction Anxiety/stress	Absenteeism Turnover Lowered performance
Pete and Meg (supervisory)	Minor to taxing	Frustration Lowered self-esteem Lowered job satisfaction Lowered performance Lack of trust	Absenteeism Turnover Lowered performance Lowered level of trust and loyalty
Susan and Beth (informal)	Taxing	Lowered self-esteem Lowered job satisfaction Lowered commitment Lowered performance Anxiety/stress Feeling of betrayal	Absenteeism Turnover Lowered performance Lowered level of trust and loyalty Less propensity to help others
Abby and Tom (informal by request)	Serious	Lowered self-esteem Lowered performance Heightened anxiety/stress Lowered level of loyalty and commitment Feeling of betrayal Damaged reputation	Absenteeism Turnover Lowered performance Lowered level of trust and loyalty Less propensity to help others Legal issues

We suggest the following strategies for creating and sustaining a developmental culture that supports high quality relationships:

- Encourage and reward personal learning.
- Encourage and reward relationship-building efforts.
- Be a role model for reflective learning, effective communication, and active engagement of developmental relationships, and be attentive to both problems and opportunities.
- Offer education as part of formal mentoring programs.
- Offer education and training on emotional competence, CMM, the REAL model, mentoring, coaching, and developmental networks as part of ongoing employee development.
- Offer third-party support when individuals need help in dealing with relational problems.

Offer Third-Party Consultation and Support

In informal relationships, you should seek the support of other developers in order to get a third-party perspective. In a formal mentoring program, the coordinator can act as a third-party consultant. Lisa Bonner shared how important a third party can be in mitigating and resolving problems from her experience as the coordinator of the reverse mentoring program at The Hartford.

An executive mentee told Bonner that his reverse mentor had shared details of a confidential project with others in the company, and he was extremely angry. She stepped in and talked to the mentor, who was alarmed and denied a role in the information leak. Bonner investigated and as it turned out, it was a member of the executive's own team who had told other employees about the project. This misunderstanding could have undermined both the relationship and the reverse mentor's career. Having a third party step in who is trusted and viewed as a resource to the mentoring program can be invaluable.

What Can You Do to Address Problems in Your Relationship with a Developer?

Most of us will encounter relational problems throughout our working lives. This is a reality of human interaction. It would be helpful if you anticipate that expectations will not always be aligned, trust will have to be built and sustained, and misunderstandings can and do occur occasionally. In this chapter we discuss four relationships that had much developmental potential at the outset and for various reasons became difficult and frustrating to varying degrees. The next time you encounter misunderstanding, conflict, or a lack of satisfying communication, consider making use of the tools and strategies we have outlined here. Such preparation will ensure that you take effective action to address the problematic situation, and you can choose to leave or continue the relationship knowing that you have carefully considered the options available to you. Don't forget to:

1. Reflect on your experiences to enhance your self-awareness.
2. Look at your own contributions to the relationship.
3. Consider your partner's situation with compassion and empathy.
4. Approach what may be a difficult conversation with a willingness to learn.
5. Prepare for the conversation and enlist a trusted third party, as needed.
6. Weigh the positive and negative aspects of the relationship.

Relationships can go awry and as the one in charge of your own development, it is critical that you regularly address your concerns directly with your developer. What we know for sure is that a problematic relationship generally does not improve without concerted efforts to make it better. Depending on the nature of the difficulty, simply spending more face time together can make a positive difference. You can use your healthy connections with others to spot-check whether there are problems that need to be addressed. If you are concerned about how things are going in a particular relationship, you can explore ways to examine the problem systematically with a trusted peer, an HR professional, or an external developer.

Reflection Questions

When you reach out to a new developer, contemplate deepening a relationship, or consider participating in a new mentoring initiative, mitigate the chances of a "tor-mentoring" relationship by thinking through the following:

1. As you initiate or try to strengthen relationships, can you anticipate problems and take steps to minimize the occurrence of challenges?
2. Who can serve as a sounding board and help you through difficult conversations?
3. When you encounter challenges, do you enlist the help of a peer?
4. Assessing your current developmental network, to what extent are you using the REAL model—reflecting, expanding, agility, and learning—to maximize your learning?

EVERYONE SHOULD BUILD DEVELOPMENTAL NETWORKS

Everyone has something to learn and teach. Relationships enable us to learn new skills, exchange ideas, collaborate, give and receive feedback, and envision new possibilities for our work and lives. Because we now live and work in a world characterized by volatility, uncertainty, complexity, and ambiguity (VUCA), it is impossible to effectively address the problems and challenges we regularly face without enlisting the wisdom and knowledge of others.

The macro trends of globalization, workforce diversity, new technology, and an increasing pace of change not only influence relationships, but they also elevate the need for relationships characterized by personal and task-related learning. Your ability to foster dynamic and high-quality connections with others through multiple platforms presents new opportunities for continuous learning. A network approach to development is now critical for the success of both individuals and organizations.

So far we have emphasized the importance of building and sustaining high-quality relationships and developmental networks so that individuals can thrive (in terms of performance and satisfaction) at work. In doing so, we have outlined what actions you can take to proactively enlist others in your developmental network, as well as what organizations can do to facilitate this process through education, appropriate performance management systems, a variety of formal programs, and a developmental culture. In this chapter we highlight the following core principles that will ensure that the potential of relationships will be realized:

Seven Core Principles for Leveraging Relationships
1. Assume that connecting comes naturally.
2. Seize mentoring moments.
3. Seek mutuality in relationships.
4. Encourage reciprocity through developmental networks.
5. Create opportunities for in-person relationship building.
6. Expect managers to develop others.
7. Foster mentoring across organizations and industries.

Assume That Connecting Comes Naturally

We spend a lot of time thinking about our social world, more than 10,000 hours—that magic number needed for expertise—before the age of 10. In his book, *Social*, neuroscientist Matthew Lieberman explains that our brains are literally wired to be social. Our neural networks for social thinking enable us to make sense of other people and ourselves.

Lieberman's research using fMRI scans demonstrates that in our downtime, those moments between active tasks, our brains take on a default neural configuration—a default network—and this default network is almost identical to our social thinking network.

Relational learning, the key to successful mentoring relationships, turns out to be a natural fit. You should find comfort in the fact that a combination of platforms now exists to facilitate our social connections. And technology unlocks efficiency in accessing relationships when you need help with your work and your career.

Keep Reaching Out Despite Your Discomfort

Even with conditions that are supportive, there are many people who don't find reaching out to potential developers or potential protégés very natural or easy. There are many life experiences as well as personality traits and preferences that may contribute to minimizing the social contact that could otherwise lead to a strong developmental network.

If you've experienced a very destructive relationship, you may be wary of relying on others for career or psychosocial support; self-reliance may be the more comfortable choice for you. The good news is that as you come to know yourself (see Chapters 2 and 4), you will get to know your preferences and your skills. In order to benefit from high-quality connections, you may need to try new behaviors that may feel uncomfortable at first.

You Will Build Your Inner, Other, and Outer Focus

In his most recent book, *Focus*, Daniel Goleman demonstrates how we need to attend to inner, other, and outer focus. The first two types of attention directly embody the critical competencies of self-awareness and social skills. The third, outer focus, is about the organizational or social context that surrounds you at work.

As we take the time to practice the right skills and effective self-inquiry, we develop new neural pathways that enable us to build high-quality connections more easily. We come to understand our development needs and to identify who might be good learning partners given their roles in the organization and what it takes to be successful in this particular context. Goleman's earlier work on emotional intelligence also suggests that as we practice such behaviors, people with whom we interact will be affected by our experiences. Thus in honing your approach to relationship building, you are likely to enhance the relational experiences of others.

The good news here is that the earlier research on emotional intelligence and the latest neuroscience reinforce the principle that, if given the opportunity, you can build connections with others that will support your personal learning and career development. And this applies whether you are just beginning your career journey or beginning to build your career legacy.

Seize Mentoring Moments

When you approach every relationship as an opportunity to learn and an opportunity to help, you create the potential for "mentoring moments." These are short, uplifting interactions when you feel connected with someone who expresses genuine concern for you and helps you in the moment. Our colleague Belle Rose Ragins describes these as "mentoring episodes" in which both parties experience positive benefits, including heightened self-esteem, new knowledge or skills, mutual positive regard, zest, and a desire for more connection.

The key to seizing such moments is to be open to learning opportunities in every relationship, regardless of age, hierarchical status, or location. Just as careers have become boundaryless, relational learning and development need to be viewed as boundaryless. Mentoring moments happen when you are intentional about learning from relationships. As Ragins explains, mentoring episodes can accumulate to a point where a developmental relationship has been established, and both parties have become invested in the learning partnership.

When You Are Intentional, You Learn

Every conversation has the potential to be a mentoring moment. Our colleague, Richard Boyatzis, has developed a model of "intentional change." He shows that trusting relationships are central when you are trying to develop new competencies and skills. When you make it a habit to seize mentoring moments, you begin to build more enduring relationships that will support you in your learning and development. These relationships—including those with coaches, mentors, bosses, peers, and subordinates—can become steady sources of support and encouragement at each step of the learning process. Take Marcus, for example:

Marcus is an executive in a large insurance company. He consistently walks the floor where most of his employees work in open cubicles. He makes it a point to stop and talk with people. Tony, one of his employees, was quite frustrated with what seemed like unnecessary red tape holding up completion of the processing of large claims. In listening to Tony, Marcus was made aware of unnecessary aspects of the approval procedures and asked one of his direct reports to come up with a better way. Tony felt appreciated and listened to, and as a result, became more willing to talk with Marcus and other managers about other aspects of the workflow that seemed less than optimal. Both Tony and Marcus benefited from the interaction and mutual trust deepened in the relationship.

Building Relationships Improves Performance

Mentoring moments can turn into relationships. For example,

Janice supervised a group of nurses in a hospital and realized that she could enhance her leadership effectiveness by building stronger ties with her direct reports. Up to that point, she held bimonthly meetings with her staff where current challenges would be discussed and goals for the future reviewed and updated. She observed that these meetings were very effective in building her team and her staff members' relationships with each other. She decided that it would be beneficial to focus on her relationship with each of the five people in her unit.

Janice began to find (or create) opportunities for informal conversations—over lunch, at the end of the day, or at mid-afternoon when the work tended to hit a lull. As she looks back at this minor change in her behavior, Janice notes that she is now informally coaching three of her five direct reports on career-related matters. At the same time she notes that her unit's overall performance is improving on critical elements.

These short-term, as needed, helping relationships certainly do not fit the definition of traditional mentoring relationships.

However in a fast-paced world, temporary connections give us access to new information and resources to complete tasks and enable us to move forward in our work and lives. When you experience learning and mutual regard, and you have a mindset that there are opportunities to learn in every interaction, such a moment can encourage you to reach out more often and to take the time to learn and teach several times a day. Of course any connection has long-term mentoring potential if there is value in the relationship for both parties.

Seek Mutuality in Relationships

The knowledge that in a developmental relationship both mentor (or sponsor, coach, developer, etc.) and protégé learn and grow is an essential building block for engaging in multiple mentoring relationships. Engaging in a developmental network is a mutually beneficial endeavor. However relationships change over time, so it is likely that the time investment and exchange among your developers will vary.

Mutuality Means That Both People Learn and Grow

When you build mutuality in a relationship, you are committed to both of you learning. Whether you are learning about career opportunities, being coached on a particular assignment, or developing self-awareness as a result of getting candid feedback from your learning partner, you are also aware of how you can support the other's learning as well. This comes about as a result of what our colleagues, Joyce Fletcher and Belle Ragins, call "fluid expertise." When each of you is taking care to actively listen to the other and share your own experience in order to deepen the help that you can give and take, you may at moments be the teacher and at other moments be the student.

Each Person Contributes Expertise

In a formal mentoring program that Kathy helped to develop at a large oil company, senior male executives were matched with high-potential female engineers in order to actively develop these women (by creating better access to mentoring). A secondary goal for the program was to help senior male executives better understand the challenges that women engineers face in a male-dominated environment. In most instances, both parties reported that they had learned quite a bit in their matched relationships. Not only did female engineers get promoted more rapidly as a result of the exposure, coaching, and sponsorship they received from their senior male mentors, but mentors reported having a much better understanding of the challenges that women face as well as how their own behavior could be modified to better support them.

Mutuality Is Not Necessarily Equal in Each Relationship

You may experience different levels of mutuality across the developmental relationships in your network. This is expected because each person in your developmental network will have a unique set of needs and capabilities. Whether the relationship occurs naturally or comes about as a result of a formal program, it is possible to strive for mutuality. Seeking mutuality means making the effort to build a relationship in which both parties benefit. What is critical is that both of you feel valued and empowered by the interactions that you have. Commitment to learning and to the relationship deepens as a result.

Entrepreneurial protégés reach out to new relationships whenever their development needs and opportunities change, which we predict will happen with increasing frequency. Each of us will need to seek the right balance of close relationships for those intimate career conversations and more distant developers for occasional help and insights. Your contributions to your developers' learning will support their contributions to their own developmental network, creating a virtuous network of learning and growth.

Encourage Reciprocity Through Developmental Networks

Organizations are beginning to use a network approach to mentoring, encouraging people at all levels to seek the support they need from each other. This is truly a developmental network approach to mentoring. Fostering an environment in which people can connect and learn, both face-to-face and virtually, capitalizes on the skills and experiences of your current workforce.

Technology can connect people to others whom they would otherwise not interact with, facilitate a platform for knowledge sharing and skill development, and provide access to a diverse perspective on the company and their career. When employees participate, every individual has multiple opportunities to learn and to teach—the essence of reciprocity.

Social Media Can Foster Developmental Networks

Cognizant, a multinational IT consulting firm, has created its own internal social media platform that integrates knowledge management, work management, and client engagements. Social media serve to help employees accomplish work tasks, build internal relationships to share knowledge, and build client relationships.

Our colleagues Bala Iyer, Sal Parise, and Tom Davenport have worked closely with executives at Cognizant to understand and assess how the company benefits from a social approach to learning. Employees build their personal brands in the company by sharing their research with others and participating in discussions with industry experts and practitioners. The give and take of dialogue and shared learning strengthens existing relationships and builds new connections. Why does this approach work?

1. Technology fits and reinforces the organizational culture.
2. Senior management participates.
3. People consume as well as contribute information and resources.

This give and take of contributing new content (e.g., blogs, answers on discussion boards, tweets) and learning by consuming others' content reflects how reciprocity is the foundation of relational learning. Mutual benefits accrue through the thoughtful exchange of ideas and a supportive developmental culture.

How Triple Creek Creates Dynamic Learning Networks with River

Triple Creek, a social learning software company focused on modern mentoring through their web-based River platform, helps a variety of organizations establish electronic mentoring relationships and foster learning through social networks. President and CEO Randy Emelo describes the approach as "releasing the dynamics of chaos theory to create learning networks." By breaking down barriers to communication, River encourages people to connect based on their interests and experience. In a large corporation, this approach enables employees to figure out, "Who are the right people to talk to right now."

The objective is to capitalize on natural learning needs and give permission for people to access the network on an ongoing basis. Participants build their profiles and can connect to one another in learning engagements, which are goal-centered relationships created around topics of interest that last for as long as participants want or need them to. They can be open or restricted to permit access to the engagement based upon the participants' preferences. Many learning engagements tend to focus on what's new and fresh, which stimulates generative connections through field-based learning where users post questions and collaborate with people to get their work done. It's a productivity tool as well as a relational learning tool.

How do learning engagements work? Imagine that you are a new data analyst who has been working for a global company for six months. You have a question about the best way to present your data to a client. You start a learning engagement titled, "Data Analytics and Visualization," you search for advisors in the River database who can help you based on matching factors such as competencies, you look for other people in the system who may also want to learn about this topic, and you invite them to join your learning engagement. You post a technical question about the best options for visualizing the dataset you are analyzing to get the conversation and collaboration started. Within days, 140 people across every business unit of your company, including managers and individual contributors around the world, have joined your learning engagement. Several people have offered you ideas and provided links to other resources for your reference. In addition, new questions have been added for discussion, and there is a lively dialogue generating new content about this important topic.

These learning conversations happen asynchronously and provide opportunities for people to share their tacit knowledge and to improve one another's capabilities. Typically, there is a flurry of activity in any learning engagement, but as participation winds down, it may be time to end it. Learning engagements run from six to nine months on average. Some may be as short as three weeks while other topics are permanently relevant. If an engagement ends, because of a lack of activity or because a topic has simply run its course, it is archived so that you can search it in the future.

The network that you create as a participant can help you learn new skills and take on new job roles faster. It places a premium on experiential learning and reinforces an appreciative developmental culture through a kudos system. The system encourages you to tag people with up to three behavioral strength indicators, such as creative, methodical, or analytical, and you can be recognized for sharing knowledge through badges. By contributing to others' learning, you build a reputation organically beyond the organizational hierarchy.

Emelo explains, "In this system, everyone is both an advisor and a learner. It is a broad-based learning practice of relational knowledge sharing." This is a truly modern mentoring approach characterized by:

- Open and egalitarian relationships
- Diverse connections—cross-functional, cross-geographical, cross-generational
- Flexibility—people move in and out of mentoring communities as needed

These characteristics facilitate short-term connections to help people with immediate task needs and through the exchange of tacit knowledge shared in learning engagements. Long-term networks of relationships are also created through permanent personal profiles. As a result, employees are more engaged and productive. Organizations also benefit from increased retention as well as employee and customer satisfaction. Triple Creek is at the forefront of establishing mentoring relationships through dynamic learning networks in Fortune 1000 companies around the globe.

Create Opportunities for In-Person Relationship Building

Building relationships through technology is one avenue for extending your developmental network, but there are other avenues as well. Professional conferences, networking events, alumni events, and affinity groups exist to support your development and connect you with others who share your interests. We know that mentoring relationships are stronger when people have the opportunity to meet face-to-face even just once.

Despite the widespread adoption of technology, people still seek opportunities for in-person human connections. Edward Hallowell explains that human moments have two prerequisites: your physical presence and your cognitive and emotional attention. Your focus and capacity to engage with others in the moment enable connections that thrive.

Human Moments Connect Us

One creative new approach to creating human moments is a *mentoring mashup* event. The idea of a "mashup" comes from web design where content from multiple sources can be displayed together. Applied to people, "mashup" can be translated to "meet-up," which inspired Heatherjean MacNeil, associate director of programs for the Center for Women's Entrepreneurial Leadership (CWEL) at Babson College, to apply it to mentoring.

The CWEL now sponsors "mentor mashup" events for its MBA women with local professional groups (e.g., Wonder Women of Boston) and companies (e.g., Liberty Mutual).

Susan Duffy, executive director of the CWEL, explains that the format of a mentor mashup session is education-networking-action. Participants learn something new, attend a presentation by an expert guest speaker, have an opportunity to meet people, and leave with something to do. This often includes connecting again with people they met or making a change based on what they learned. These events are open to current MBA women, friends of the CWEL, the cosponsoring company or group, and Babson alumni—literally a meet-up of people with mutual interests from different organizations.

The idea of a mentoring mashup capitalizes on in-person relationship building within a geographic region, an important component of feeling connected and getting connected to your community.

Find Times to Meet In Person and Follow Up Virtually

In recent years we have seen organizations try different venues to create opportunities for individuals to meet face-to-face with potential mentors or protégés. In some instances, events sponsored by employee resource groups can serve this purpose, where individuals who have much in common have the opportunity to begin getting to know each other around a guest lecture or some other event. We have seen organizations implementing hybrid mentoring circles which begin with one or two face-to-face meetings, and then the participants meet virtually on a regular basis.

Consultant Carol Yamartino shared that one of her clients is pulling individuals from several geographic areas together for a mentoring circle experience. "This is an experiment, and we will solicit ongoing feedback from the group to determine how often face-to-face meetings are needed to make sure the quality of interactions continues to deepen."

Experiment to Learn

We are all experimenting and continuing to learn about human connection and the possibilities and limitations of virtual technology communities. Of course, exclusively virtual relationships can flourish, but occasional face-to-face interactions can help establish a deeper sense of connection.

Expect Managers to Develop Others

Creating a developmental culture involves leaders at every level (see Chapter 7). Effective managers develop talent by building learning relationships with employees and other managers that enable them to get their work done and grow in each role. Recent research within Google showed that the number one behavior that characterized the most effective managers was being a good coach. In our own research and consulting work, we have seen how managers can make a big difference in a subordinate's performance and potential. Amy's story is a good example:

> Amy is a fast-rising engineering manager in a large consumer products company. Her name has come up a few times as a good candidate for promotion to director level. However, over the years she has alienated a few senior people because of how strongly she pushes her ideas. Her firm values a consensus-based approached to decision making. She is expected to build networks with others, even those who might not agree with her, explain her situation, hear how her ideas impact their situation, and work out an agreement, all before going to the CEO.
>
> Amy finds this process enormously frustrating and one that takes her out of her comfort zone. She sees all this as "playing politics" and knows that she's not particularly good at it. She has trouble asking useful questions and waiting for a response, so she often never finds out about the concerns of those whom she is trying to influence.
>
> As Amy's boss, Hetty has given Amy feedback regarding her style from past managers and more recent observations. Hetty

understands Amy's ambition to move up in the company and could see that there is a lack of fit between Amy's approach and the culture of the organization. She began meeting regularly with Amy to "coach" her for several months.

Hetty gave Amy a few readings on influence tactics and theory, and these seemed to make sense to Amy. The notion of finding out what others want seemed only fair, although she still needed to build some skills. She was working on a project that would challenge her influence skills and this provided fertile grounds for a number of coaching discussions. She and Hetty would simply rehearse how the conversations might go. Since Hetty was her boss and familiar with some of the people with whom Amy would be conversing, Hetty was able to provide an effective role-play partner for Amy.

Amy learned to ask questions and relax more in the process, trying to focus on what she was really hearing from potential partners rather than preparing her rebuttal. Over time, she began to see the power in this approach and was able to successfully add the idea of "asking useful questions and listening" to her repertoire. She was still as hard driving as ever, but her style was subsequently seen by others as being more well-rounded and consistent with "the way we do business here."

Implement Strategies That Support a Developmental Culture

Many leaders and talent development practitioners struggle with how to support a developmental culture in their organizations. In observing the efforts of companies in several different industries to encourage their managers to coach, we have identified critical elements of a strategy to support a developmental culture in which every manager sees it as part of his or her role to actively develop others:

1. Include "developing others" as a competence that is regularly assessed as part of the annual performance review.

2. Make sure that every manager receives periodic feedback from subordinates and/or peers about how they are doing developing others as part of their work.
3. Provide multiple educational opportunities on the fundamental relational skills that managers need to effectively develop others.
4. Publicly recognize managers who are outstanding developers of others in order to reinforce the importance of this competence for overall performance and the well-being of employees and the organization as a whole.

Good Questions Invite Reflection, Feedback, and Self-Disclosure

At a recent meeting of the Boston University Executive Development Roundtable (EDRT), our Center for Creative Leadership colleague Michael Campbell discussed the power of good questions in helping managers be effective coaches to those who work for them. Whether it is a matter of questions that invite reflection, specific feedback on observable behavior, or disclosure of a personal story that shows people that you identify to deepen your connection, these actions strengthen managers' repertoires as coaches. During this conversation, talent development practitioners from several industries reflected on how their efforts to foster mentoring and developmental networks through interest groups as well as formal matching programs consistently offered opportunities for employees to practice these critical relational skills. This kind of practical education will have great impact if it is supported and reinforced as we note above.

Entrepreneurial Protégés Make Better Managers

Learning to develop yourself through relationships will help you become a better manager. Google's talent analytics team found that its best managers express interest and concern for people's well-being and help with career development. So being an entrepreneurial protégé, which requires self-awareness and social skills, has the added benefit of preparing you to manage others more effectively.

Foster Mentoring across Organizations and Industries

Organizations can and do mentor each other, particularly small entrepreneurially ventures poised for growth. This happens in Silicon Valley and Greater Boston where start-up incubators foster connections between high-potential start-ups and expert venture capitalists. Often, these incubators host several organizations in the same building where they may interact and share information or resources, such as how to access capital, manage talent, or develop sales and marketing skills.

Create Ecosystems That Support Mentoring

Silicon Valley exemplifies an ecosystem with a culture of mentoring, where the norm is for experienced professionals to help newcomers who have interesting ideas without the expectation of direct reciprocity; the community reciprocates. As newcomers gain experience, they offer mentoring to new entrepreneurs themselves. These new forms of mentoring are fostering the growth of organizational leaders who actively learn from one another and discover the skills and resources that will enable their firms to thrive.

Our colleague Peter Cohan has interviewed hundreds of entrepreneurs about the mentoring that helped them succeed. Elad Gil, a serial entrepreneur talks about cohorts of peers or "graduating classes of alumni from Google each year" that comprise his network. These connections are kept alive through social media and face-to-face gatherings. He and Aydin Senkut, in Gil's cohort, co-organize events for Google alumni to share practical insights on starting and building ventures. Google alumni trade insights on issues such as, "How to grow revenues faster, how to sell a company, and whom to contact if you want to raise capital."

Community Mentoring Through Hiive

Just recently, we learned about Hiive, an online platform in beta testing designed to serve people in the creative industries (e.g., advertising, film, music, etc.) in the United Kingdom by providing various mentoring opportunities. The trade name "Hiive" suggests the idea of a hive community and the idea of "Hi, I've . . ." as a way of introducing yourself to people with your skills. Susie Goldring and Tom Turcan, working on behalf of the U.K. Sector Skills Council, explained that, "On a high level, Hiive is a community mentoring environment, containing resources, tools, and most importantly, like-minded members." They are developing protocols and tools to guide members in choosing how they want to participate. Passive mentoring, active mentoring, group mentoring, and extended mentoring are the four basic alternatives that have been defined:

- Passive mentoring occurs when one member picks up advice from another without any interaction, through reading a useful post or listening to a member's response to another member's question.
- Active mentoring occurs when one member poses a question to another and is helped by the interaction.
- Extended mentoring exists for a predetermined number of months and/or meetings, after which you decide whether to continue or not.
- Group mentoring brings up to six individuals together to learn from each other, much like we might find in mentoring circles (see Chapter 6).

Different communication media will be available through the Hiive website. Some communications will be made public (with the consent of the participants) to benefit others in the community. Perhaps most unique is the additional alternative which Hiive designers call "business mentoring." It is a form of extended mentoring where the mentee is a small business owner or CEO, and the mentor is a business owner or CEO who wants to help less experienced entrepreneurs be successful with their start-ups. Thus both individuals and companies in the creative industry will benefit from participating in this mentoring community.

We are particularly impressed with the deep design work that has been done to ensure that relationships are characterized by mutuality and reciprocity. When members register to become a mentor, they provide a statement about what they can offer, as well as what they would like to gain from mentoring on Hiive. In addition, they provide up to five key words indicating the areas for which they believe they have experience to act as a mentor. This information (along with comparable information from mentees) will be used in a matching algorithm to bring people together who have shared interests and can learn from each other. Finally, resource materials are in development, including mentoring guidelines; mentoring principles; self-assessment tools to clarify values, career interests, preferences, and talents; and ongoing supplements from relevant experts.

Your Strategic Relationships at Work and Beyond

Your understanding of the following seven core principles for leveraging relationships will enhance your own developmental network as well as that of those around you. To build your strategic relationships at work and beyond, we encourage you to:

1. Assume that connecting comes naturally.
2. Seize mentoring moments.
3. See mutuality in relationships.
4. Encourage reciprocity through developmental networks.
5. Create opportunities for in-person relationship building.
6. Expect managers to develop others.
7. Foster mentoring across organizations and industries.

Each principle will help you establish yourself as an entrepreneurial protégé and mentor. The key to fostering strategic relationships is a mindset that this is a continuous process in which you reflect, experiment, learn, and teach.

Reflection Questions

Are you prepared to build your developmental network and encourage others to do the same? Consider the following questions to prepare yourself for the work ahead:

1. How well do you align with the first three core principles of (a) assume that connecting comes naturally, (b) seize mentoring moments, and (c) see mutuality in relationships? Are there areas where you might improve?

2. If you have responsibility for a unit, department, or division of your organization, what are you doing to align with the remaining four core principles of (d) encourage reciprocity through developmental networks, (e) create opportunities for in-person relationship building, (f) expect managers to develop others, and (g) foster mentoring across organizations and industries? Are there areas where you might improve or opportunities for your organization to improve its practice?

3. If you are an internal or external talent development specialist, how well are you educating your employees or clients so that they can leverage the seven core principles outlined here?

CONCLUSION: STRATEGIC RELATIONSHIPS AT WORK AND BEYOND

What should you take away from this book on developmental relationships? In today's fast-paced, global economy, every one of us needs to be an entrepreneurial protégé. Continuous learning through strategic relationships at work and beyond is now essential for your success and the success of your organization.

Since everyone is a learner and everyone can be a teacher, each and every one of us has the opportunity to be an entrepreneurial protégé and mentor. Here is how you can become more entrepreneurial yourself:

- **Increase your self-awareness.** The better you understand your goals, values, preferences, strengths and weaknesses, and interests, the better equipped you will be to seek out developers who will be able to support and guide you. Make use of the assessment tools offered in Chapters 1–4, and those that are often available at work or on the web.

- **Be intentional.** Build your network to support your development. "True mentors" who provide all the support you need to succeed are rare today. And we recommend you diversify your efforts anyway. Each developer may provide one or many types of support, but combined your network of relationships will offer you the help you need.
- **Reach out proactively.** Initiate new relationships that have potential. Ask good questions, ask for feedback, actively listen to responses, and share your personal goals and aspirations. Cultivate each relationship and see where it goes, but spend your time wisely.
- **Practice your relational skills.** Seize the opportunity in every interaction to hone your relational skills. This means listening deeply, asking good questions, and sharing your own experience with others in order to deepen trust and invite their engagement with you. Strive to understand others' points of view and experiences. These skills will become more of a habit as you practice them.
- **Seek mutuality.** People in high-quality relationships foster mutual learning, inspire growth, and care about the whole person. Form more high-quality relationships by preparing before reaching out, carefully considering who is approachable, using your relationship-building skills, and giving relationships time to develop.
- **Strive for diversity in your developmental network.** Diversify your network by reaching out to developers with different backgrounds and experience from yours, across hierarchical levels, both within and outside of your workplace. They will enrich your career and life.
- **Periodically reassess your developmental network.** At least once a year, review your developmental network and consider how well it is supporting your current goals. Consider whether it is time to enlist one or more new developers in your network, and whether you may want to serve as a developer to one or more others who would benefit from your experience. Ask yourself whether your

developmental relationships are of high quality and whether there are actions you can take to deepen some of the ties.

Since persistent learning is critical to success in the knowledge economy, it is imperative that leaders and organizations foster *developmental networks*. To improve the potential for high-quality connections within your organization, you should:

- **Provide opportunities for relationship building.** Formal programs can connect people who would otherwise not connect with one another through informal interactions. There are a variety of mentoring roles—mentors, sponsors, coaches, mentoring circles—that may be a good fit for your organization. The goals of any initiative must align with the organizations' strategy and have the active support of senior leaders. Education and training may be necessary to ensure that everyone shares the same set of expectations and that everyone has the self-awareness and social skills to participate effectively.
- **Create a developmental culture.** Initiatives to create relationship-building opportunities will only be effective if the culture and practices of your organization encourage, recognize, and reward efforts to build high-quality relationships with others. So any effort to facilitate developmental relationships and developmental networks must include a systematic assessment of HR systems and practices as well as employees' perceptions of what is expected and valued by the organization. This assessment may point to specific needs for changes in policy and practice to better align the culture with efforts to enhance learning through relationships at work. It is equally important for leaders at all levels to model the behavior they want to see throughout the organization.
- **Support peer relationships.** Relationships among people of a similar age or in parallel roles at work can present rich learning opportunities. Peer mentoring relationships are

more accessible than others and support employee development by providing another perspective on work issues, offering fresh ideas, and/or access to different organizational relationships and resources. They often offer friendship and can act as nonjudgmental sounding boards for a myriad of issues. Enlisting peers into developmental networks helps each of us access the full range of support we need from relationships at work.

- **Encourage everyone to learn from new challenges and opportunities.** Diversity, globalization, technology, and persistent change present challenges and opportunities for all of us. Over time, working across differences actually *increases* the potential learning and growth between people. A supportive culture fosters more and better relationships, but it is worth extending yourself and encouraging others to reach out to diverse others both inside and outside your workplace. Extending efforts beyond the usual also means leveraging technology in new ways, particularly when it enables people in different geographic areas to connect and learn from one another. It also means reaching out to people with whom you don't necessarily have an easy rapport, but where you see potential to learn from someone with a different perspective or set of skills or to help someone who might benefit from your talents and experience. It is important to remember that sometimes relationships are difficult, but armed with the necessary relational skills (that can be learned), such difficulties can be transcended, and in the process much task-related and personal learning can occur.

- **Minimize difficulties in or disengage from problematic relationships.** It is not possible to avoid problematic relationships entirely. However, with an understanding of the underlying causes—including misaligned expectations, lack of relational skills, unrealistic needs, or poor motives for engaging in the first place—problems can be minimized. The same relational skills necessary to initiate and build your developmental network will enable you to address minor and more taxing problems. The key is to assess the sources of the problem and address them immediately. If efforts to improve communication and the quality of the relationship fail, it is time to disengage and move on to relationships with potential. Organizations benefit from acknowledging that such problems will occur and may offer education and support regarding how best to address them.

- **Remember the core principles for leveraging relationships.** Just as individuals need to be mindful of how best to leverage relationships to support their career development, leaders and organizations should keep these same principles in mind when creating policy, making critical decisions, and implementing new programs. We encourage you to seize opportunities for mentoring moments and mutual learning, encourage relationship building, expect managers to develop others, and use the strategic approach to identify those opportunities that align with your organization's context. While these core principles may seem simple, taking the actions that align with them is not always easy.

Finally, whether you are at the beginning of your career journey or a seasoned professional, part of an organization or a solo practitioner, an organizational leader, or a talent development specialist, remember to take a strategic approach:

- **Reflect, experiment, learn, teach.** A strategic approach means that you begin by reflecting on your current relationships and context. You will systematically assess what is, and identify a vision for yourself or your organization that fosters learning partnerships. When such a vision is shared with your colleagues and friends and throughout your organization, everyone can share ways to help each other create and sustain robust developmental networks that contribute to both individual and organizational performance. For you, it will be a continuous cycle of reflection, relationship initiation and change, learning and growth, and reassessment. For your organization it will also be a continuous process in which pilots are designed, implemented, and then evaluated so that learning is maximized. Over time, experiments become regular practice when it is clear through evidence generated in learning and performance outcomes that relational initiatives support career development and business strategy, which are, of course, one and the same.

Our hope is that you have found some new ideas, tools and inspiration that will empower you to build relationships with meaning and purpose that support your personal success in work and in life. After researching, observing, and working with people in many different industries on the challenge of building sustainable developmental networks, we are convinced that there are many fruitful avenues to pursue. We invite you to begin now with what makes sense to you, given your goals, current challenges, and work role. All it takes is practice, reflection, and more practice. You will undoubtedly learn, and teach, and create opportunities for others to do the same.

RECOMMENDED READING

Introduction: What Are Strategic Relationships?

Kopelman, S., Feldman, E. R., McDaniel, D. M., and Hall, D. T. (2012). "Mindfully negotiating a career with a heart." *Organizational Dynamics* 41: 163–171.

Kram, K. E. and Higgins, M. A. (2009). "A new mindset on mentoring: Creating developmental networks at work." *Sloan Management Review,* online.

Petrie, N. (2011). "Future trends in leadership development." *Center for Creative Leadership,* white paper, November.

Chapter 1: Why Relationships Matter

Benson, G. (2007). "Making relationships work: A conversation with psychologist John. M. Gottman." *Harvard Business Review,* December: 45–50.

Dutton, J. (2005). *Energize Your Workplace: How to Build and Sustain High-Quality Connections at Work.* San Francisco: Jossey-Bass.

Goleman, D. (2006). *Social Intelligence: The new science of human relationships.* New York: Bantam Books.

Kram, K. E. (1988). *Mentoring at Work: Developmental Relationships in Organizational Life.* Lanham, MD: University Press of America.

Chapter 2: How-to: Map Your Developmental Network

Hill, L., and Lineback, K. (2011). "The three networks you need." HBR Blog Network: March 3. Online.

Sigetich, A., and Leavitt, C. (2008). *Play to Your Strengths: Stacking the Deck to Achieve Spectacular Results for Yourself and Others.* Pequannock, NJ: ReadHow YouWant.com, Ltd.

Chapter 3: Analyze Your Developmental Network

Gallo, A. (2011). "Demystifying mentoring." HBR Blog Network: February 1. Online.

Rollag, K., Parise, S., and Cross, R. (2005). "Getting new hires up to speed quickly." *Sloan Management Review* 46(2):35–41.

Chapter 4: Taking an Entrepreneurial Approach to Relationships

Chandler, D. E., Hall, D. T., Kram, K. E. (2009). "A developmental network and relational savvy approach to talent development: A low-cost alternative." *Organizational Dynamics* 39(1): 48–56.

Drucker, P. (2005). "Managing oneself." *Harvard Business Review*, January: 100–109.

Goleman, D. (2000). *Working with Exceptional Intelligence*. New York: Bantam.

Schein, E. (2009). *Helping: How to Offer, Give, and Receive Help*. San Francisco: Berrett-Koehler.

For more reading on reflection:

Daudelin, M. W., and Hall, D. T. (1997). "Using reflection to leverage learning." *Training and Development*, December: 13–14.

Seibert, K., and Daudelin, M. (1999). *The Role of Reflection in Managerial Learning*. Westport, CT: Quorum Books.

Chapter 5: Formal Programs for Professional Development

Allen, T. D., Finkelstein, L. M., and Poteet, M. L. (2009). *Designing Workplace Mentoring Programs: An Evidence-Based Approach*. Malden, MA: Wiley-Blackwell.

Ragins, B. R., and Kram, K. E. (2007). *The Handbook of Mentoring at Work: Theory, Research, and Practice*. Thousand Oaks, CA: Sage Publications.

Chapter 6: Mentoring Alternatives: Sponsors, Coaches, Reverse Mentors, and Mentoring Circles

Coutu, D., and Kauffman, C. (2009). "What can coaches do for you?" *Harvard Business Review*, January: 91–97.

Hewlett, S. A. (2013). *(Forget a Mentor) Find a Sponsor: The New Way to Fast-Track Your Career*. Cambridge, MA: Harvard Business Review Press.

Hunt, J. M., and Weintraub, J. R. (2011). *The Coaching Manager: Developing Top Talent in Business*, 2nd edition. Los Angeles: Sage.

Ibarra, H. (2010). "Women are over-mentored (but under-sponsored)." HRB Blog Network, August 26. http://iblogs.hbr.org/2010/08/women-are-over-mentored-but-un/

Murphy, W. M. (2012). "Reverse mentoring at work: Fostering cross-generational learning and developing millennial leaders." *Human Resource Management* 51(4): 549–574.

Chapter 7: Creating and Sustaining a Developmental Culture

McCauley, C. D., DeRue, D. S., Yost, P. R., and Taylor, S. (2014). *Experience-Driven Leader Development: Models, Tools, Best Practices, and Advice for On-the-Job Development*. San Francisco: Wiley.

Schein, E. (2013). *Humble Inquiry: The Gentle Art of Asking Instead of Telling*. San Francisco: Barrett-Koehler.

Schneider, B., and Barbara, K., *The Handbook of Organizational Climate and Culture: Antecedents, Consequences, and Practice*. New York: Oxford University Press.

Zachary, L. J. (2005). *Creating a Mentoring Culture: The Organization's Guide*. San Francisco: Jossey-Bass.

Chapter 8: Making the Most of Relationships with Peers

Kimsey-House, H., Kimsey-House, K., Sandahl, P., and Whitworth, L. (2011). *Co-Active Coaching: Changing Business, Transforming Lives*. Boston: Nicholas Brealey Publishing.

Parker, P., Hall, D. T., and Kram, K. E. (2008). "Peer coaching: A relational process for accelerated career learning." *Academy of Management Learning and Education* 7(4): 487–503.

Parker, P. Kram, K. E., and Hall, D. T. (2012). "Risk factors in peer coaching: A multilevel approach." *Journal of Applied Behavioral Science*, 1–27.

Chapter 9: Challenges and Opportunities: Diversity, Technology, and Change

Banaji, M. R., and Greenwald, A. G. (2013). *Blind Spot: Hidden Biases of Good People*. New York: Delacorte Press. See https://implicit.harvard.edu/implicit/.

Clutterbuck, D., Poulsen, K. M., Kochan, F. (2012). *Developing Diversity Mentoring Programmes: An International Casebook*. New York: Open University Press.

Molinsky, A. (2013). *Global Dexterity*. Cambridge, MA: Harvard Business Review Press.

Chapter 10: Tor-Mentors: When Relationships Are Problematic

Pearce, W. B. (2007). *Making Social Worlds: A Communication Perspective*. Malden, MA: Blackwell.

Stone, D., Patton, B., and Heen, S. (1999). *Difficult Conversations: How to Discuss What Matters Most*. London: Penguin Books.

Chapter 11: Everyone Should Build Developmental Networks

Emelo, R. (2013). "Mentoring without Barriers." *Chief Learning Officer*, October: 27–29.

Harrington, B. and Hall, D. T. (2007). *Career Management and Work-Life Integration: Using Self-Assessment to Navigate Contemporary Careers*. Thousand Oaks, CA: Sage Publications.

NOTES

All people we discuss are research participants or colleagues. First names are occasionally used to maintain anonymity, particularly in early chapters.

Introduction

2 **One of the most important findings from the extensive academic literature:** For reviews of research on mentoring and developmental networks, see T. D. Allen and L. T. Eby (2007), *The Blackwell Handbook of Mentoring: A Multiple Perspectives Approach,* Malden, MA: Blackwell Publishing; S. Dobrow, D. E. Chandler, W. M. Murphy, and K. E. Kram (2012), "Developmental networks: A review and prospects for future research," *Journal of Management* 38(1): 210–242; M. C. Higgins and K. E. Kram (2001), "Reconceptualizing mentoring at work: A developmental network perspective," *Academy of Management Review* 26(2), 264–288; K. E. Kram (1985), *Mentoring at Work: Developmental Relationships in Organizational Life,* New York: Scott, Foresman and Company; B. R. Ragins and K. E. Kram (2007), *The Handbook of Mentoring at Work: Theory, Research, and Practice,* Thousand Oaks, CA: Sage.

4 **In Homer's *Odyssey*:** Mentor is one of the forms that Athena, the goddess of war and wisdom, takes in her interaction with Telemachus. This character's role was expanded in the 1699 book *Les Adventures de Telemaque* by Francois Fenelon, to encompass the qualities of wisdom, support, and guidance associated with mentoring today. See A. Roberts (1999), "Homer's mentor: Duties fulfilled or misconstrued?" *History of Education Journal,* 81–90.

Mentors and mentoring were identified as critical components of career development in the writings of Daniel Levinson. See D. J. Levinson, C. N. Darrow, E. B. Klein, M. H. Levinson, and B. McKee (1978), *The Seasons of a Man's Life,* New York: Knopf. And furthered by his student K. E. Kram's research—particularly her book: K. E. Kram (1985), *Mentoring at Work: Developmental Relationships in Organizational Life,* Lanham, MD: University Press of America.

5 **"the boundaryless career":** M. B. Arthur and D. M. Rousseau (1996), *The Boundaryless Career: A New Employment Principle for a New Organizational Era,* New York: Oxford University Press.

6   **the protean career:** D. T. Hall (2002), *Careers in and out of Organizations.* Thousand Oaks, CA: Sage.

8   **protégés need relational savvy:** D. E. Chandler, D. T. Hall, and K. E. Kram (2010), "A relational approach to talent development: An under-utilized and low-cost alternative, *Organizational Dynamics* 39(2), 48–56.

12 **But you can call them:** P. Claman (2010), "Forget mentors: Employ a personal board of directors," *HBR Blog Network,* accessed August 15, 2012, http://blogs.hbr.org/cs/2010/10/forget_mentors_employ_a_person .html

Chapter 1

19 **Decades of research on workplace relationships:** S. Dobrow, D. E. Chandler, W. M. Murphy, and K. E. Kram (2012), "Developmental networks: A review and prospects for future research," *Journal of Management* 38(1): 210–242; R. M. Ryan, and E. L. Deci (2001), "On happiness and human potentials: A review of research on hedonic and eudaimonic well-being," *Annual Review of Psychology* 52, 141–166; S. E. Seibert, M. L. Kraimer, and R. C. Liden (2001), "A social capital theory of career success," *Academy of Management Journal* 44(2): 219–237.

20 **A commonly cited statistic is that we all have seven separate careers:** e.g., The Numbers Guy (2010). "Seven careers in a lifetime? Think twice, researchers say. *Wall Street Journal*, Sept. 4, http://online.wsj.com/news/articles/SB10001424052748704206804575468162805877990. See also *U.S. Bureau of Labor Statistics*, http://www.bls.gov/ for recent statistics.

21 **How do developers provide support?:** For a thorough review of the fundamentals of mentoring, including developmental functions, phases of relationships, and outcomes of developmental relationships, see K. E. Kram (1985), *Mentoring at Work.* Researchers added to Kram's functions in the context of developmental networks in the following articles: W. M. Murphy and K. E. Kram (2010), "Understanding non-work relationships in developmental networks," *Career Development International* 15(7): 637–663; R. D. Cotton, Y. Shen, and R. Livne-Tarandach (2011), "On becoming extraordinary: The content and structure of the developmental networks of major league baseball Hall of Famers," *Academy of Management Journal* 54(1): 15–46; Y. Shen and K. E. Kram (2011), "Expatriates' developmental networks: Network diversity, base, and support functions," *Career Development International* 16(6): 528–552.

23 **30 years of systematic, empirical research shows:** D. E. Chandler, K. E. Kram, and J. Yip (2011), "An ecological systems perspective on mentoring at work: A review and future prospects," *Academy of Management Annals* 5(1): 519–570; S. Dobrow, D. E. Chandler, W. M. Murphy, and K. E. Kram (2012), "Developmental networks: A review and prospects for future research," *Journal of Management* 38(1): 210–242.

25   **all developmental relationships go through four phases:** K. E. Kram
      (1983), "Phases of the mentor relationship," *Academy of Management Jour-*
      nal 26(4): 608–625.

26   **being proactive:** D. E. Chandler and K. E. Kram (2010), "Enlisting Others
      in Your Development as a Leader," in M. G. Rothstein and R. J. Burke
      (eds.), *Self-Management and Leadership Development*, New York:
      Edward Elgar, pp. 336–360. For additional citations, see reference in
      Chapter 5.

27   **High-quality relationships:** J. E. Dutton and E. D. Heaphy (2003), "The
      Power of High Quality Connections," in K. Cameron, J. E. Dutton, and
      R. E. Quinn (eds.), *Positive Organizational Scholarship*, San Francisco:
      Berrett-Koehler Publishers, pp. 263–278. For an introduction to positive
      relationships, see J. E. Dutton and B. R. Ragins (2007), *Exploring Positive*
      Relationships at Work: Building a Theoretical and Research Foundation, New
      York: Lawrence Erlbaum Associates. For an overview of the POS domain,
      see K. S. Cameron and G. M. Spreitzer (2011), *The Oxford Handbook of*
      Positive Organizational Scholarship, New York: Oxford University Press.

28   **formal continuum of quality in mentor-mentee relationships:**
      B. R. Ragins and A. K. Verbos (2007), "Positive Relationships in Action:
      Relational Mentoring," in J. E. Dutton and B. R. Ragins (eds.), *Exploring*
      Positive Relationships at Work: Building a Theoretical and Research Foundation,
      Mahwah, NJ: Erlbaum, pp. 91–116.

29   **Quality of Developmental Relationships:** We created this figure based
      on a graph and table in B. R. Ragins and A. K. Verbos (2007), "Positive
      relationships in action," p. 98.

30   **This is in sharp contrast to typical work relationships:** Social exchange
      theory suggests that people will develop relationships if the benefits
      outweigh the costs. For a comprehensive review, see R. Cropanzano
      and M. S. Mitchell (2005), "Social exchange theory: An interdisciplinary
      review," *Journal of Management* 31: 874–900.

30   **mental models (or schemas) that individuals bring to relationships:**
      B. R. Ragins (2011), "Relational Mentoring: A Positive Approach to
      Mentoring at Work," in K. S. Cameron and G. M. Spreitzer (eds.), *The*
      Oxford Handbook of Positive Organizational Scholarship, New York: Oxford
      University Press, pp. 519–536.

32   **Shared values and perspectives are the glue:** Deep-level similarities
      include values and attitudes whereas surface-level similarities refer to
      demographics such as age, race, or gender. For more on deep similarities,
      see D. A. Harrison, K. H. Price, and M. Bell (1998), "Beyond relational
      demography: Time and the effects of surface and deep level diversity or
      work group cohesion," *Academy of Management Journal* 41: 96–107. And
      for a review of the similarity-attraction hypothesis, see T. D. Allen (2007),
      "Mentoring Relationships from the Perspective of the Mentor," in B. R.

Ragins and K. E. Kram (eds.), *The Handbook of Mentoring at Work: Theory, Research, and Practice*, Thousand Oaks, CA: Sage, pp. 123–147.

32   **Avoid Dysfunctional Relationships:** L. T. Eby (2007), "Understanding Relational Problems in Mentoring: A Review and Proposed Investment Model," in B. R. Ragins and K. E. Kram (eds.), *The Handbook of Mentoring at Work: Theory, Research, and Practice*, Thousand Oaks, CA: Sage, pp. 323–344.

34   **Social Roles of Developers:** Our table was created based on M. C. Higgins (2001), "Changing careers: the effects of social context," *Journal of Organizational Behavior* 22: 595–618, as well as W. M. Murphy and K. E. Kram (2010); Cotton et al. (2011). In addition, in an unpublished paper by R. D. Cotton, Y. Shen, and K. E. Kram, it was found that more than 75 percent of developers came from one's current organization, family, and or support in one's community.

Chapter 2

39   **Career communities:** P. Parker, M. B. Arthur, and K. Irkson (2004). "Career communities: a preliminary exploration of member-defined career support structures," *Journal of Organizational Behavior* 25(4): 489–514.

40   **The dictionary gives:** *Free Dictionary* (http://www.thefreedictioary.com. Acessed September 15, 2013.

40   **Taking initiative involves some risks:** M. C. Higgins, D. E. Chandler, and K. E. Kram (2007), "Developmental Initiation and Developmental Networks," in B. R. Ragins and K. E. Kram (eds.), *The Handbook of Mentoring at Work: Theory, Research, and Practice*, Thousand Oaks, CA: Sage, pp. 349–372.

40   **The best protégés have relational savvy:** D. E. Chandler (2009), "Relational savvy: why some individuals are more adept with developmental relationships," Unpublished dissertation, Boston University.

41   **The "knowing" career competencies** were first articulated in R. J. DeFillippi and M. B. Arthur (2004), "The boundaryless career: a competency-based perspective," *Journal of Organizational Behavior* 15(4): 304–334.

Chapter 3

44   **formal mentoring can contribute a lot to your career development:** T. D. Allen, L.T. Eby, M. L. Poteet, E. Lentz, and L. Lima (2004), "Career benefits associated with mentoring for protégés: A meta-analysis, *Journal of Applied Psychology* 89: 127–136.

44   **informal mentors are more effective:** B. R. Ragins and J. L. Cotton (1999), "Mentor functions and outcomes: A comparison of men and women in formal and informal mentoring relationships," *Journal of Applied Psychology* 84(4): 529–550.

45 **Your career will transition:** Current career trends were assessed from
several sources—Bureau of Labor Statistics (2012), "Number of Jobs, Labor
Market Experience, and Earnings Growth: Results from a National Longitudinal Survey News Release." Accessed May 23, 2013. http://www.
bls.gov/news.release/nlsoy.htm; European Labour Force Survey. 2012.
Accessed May 23, 2013. http://epp.eurostat.ec.europa.eu/portal/page/
portal/microdata/lfs.; Rhein, T. (2010). "Is Europe on the way to becoming
a 'high-speed labour market?'" Institute for Employment Research: IAB
Brief Report; International Labour Organization (2013), *Global Employment
Trends 2013*. Geneva: International Labour Office.

46 **Relationships outside of work can be sturdy during change:** M. Hig-
gins (2001), "Changing careers: the effects of social context," *Journal of
Organizational Behavior* 22: 595–618; W. M. Murphy and K. E. Kram (2010),
"Understanding non-work relationships in developmental networks,"
Career Development International 15(7): 637–663.

46 **Decades of work-family research:** For a comprehensive review of social
support and stress, see C. Viswesvaran, J. I. Sanchez, and J. Fisher
(1999), "The role of social support in the process of work stress: A meta-
analysis," *Journal of Vocational Behavior* 54(2): 314–334.

46 **when people cannot talk shop to a parent, spouse, or partner:** W. M.
Murphy, (2007), "Individual and relational dynamics of ambition in
careers," Boston College: Unpublished dissertation.

48 **Developmental Network Characteristics:** M. C. Higgins and D. A.
Thomas (2001), "Constellations and careers: Toward understanding the
effects of multiple developmental relationships," *Journal of Organizational
Behavior* 22: 223–247; C. Kirchmeyer (2005), "The effects of mentoring on
academic careers over time: Testing performance and political perspectives, *Human Relations* 58: 637–660; J. V. Peluchette and S. Jeanquart (2000),
"Professionals' use of different mentor sources at various career stages:
Implications for career success," *Journal of Social Psychology* 140: 549–564;
I. J. H. van Emmerik (2004), "The more you can get the better: Mentoring
constellations and intrinsic career success," *Career Development International* 9: 578–594.; for a comprehensive review of developmental networks, see S. R. Dobrow, D. E. Chandler, W. M. Murphy, and K. E. Kram
(2012), "A review of developmental networks: Incorporating a mutuality
perspective," *Journal of Management* 38(1): 210–242.

48 **The more the merrier?:** M. Higgins (2000), "The more, the merrier? Multiple developmental relationships and work satisfaction, *Journal of Management Development* 19(4): 277–296.

48 **extraordinarily successful people have an average of 16 developers:**
R. D. Cotton, Y. Shen, and R. Livne-Tarandach (2011), "On becoming
extraordinary: The content and structure of the developmental networks
of major league baseball Hall of Famers," *Academy of Management Journal*
54(1): 15–46.

48   **plugging into support at the right moments across an evolving career:**
M. C. Higgins (2007), "A Contingency Perspective on Developmental
Networks," in J. Dutton and B. R. Ragins (eds.), *Exploring Positive Relation-
ships at Work: Building a Theoretical and Research Foundation*, Hillsdale, NJ:
Lawrence Erlbaum, pp. 207–224.

50   **Broaden your range:** S. R. Dobrow et al. (2012), "A review of developmental networks," for a review of the benefits of having a range of
developers. In addition, see T. D. Allen and L. Finkelstein (2003), "Beyond
mentoring: Alternative sources and functions of developmental support,"
Career Development Quarterly 51: 346–355.

52   **career communities:** P. Parker, M. B. Arthur, and K. Irkson (2004), "Career
communities: a preliminary exploration of member-defined career
support structures," *Journal of Organizational Behavior* 25(4): 489–514. For
a summary of research on network density, see pp. 64-65 in E. H. Volpe
and W. M. Murphy (2011), "Married professional women's career exit:
Integrating identity and social networks, *Gender in Management* 26(1):
57–83.

52   **Brokers connect you to people:** This is because brokers occupy "structural holes," which means that without a connection to them you would
not be connected to a particular person or network, R. S. Burt (1992),
Structural Holes: The Social Structure of Competition, Cambridge, MA:
Harvard University Press.

53   **Strong relationships form over time:** Strong ties make up the core of a
developmental network, whereas weak ties tend to make up the periphery. See J. Cummings and M.C. Higgins (2005), "Relational instability at
the core: Support dynamics in developmental networks," *Social Networks*
28: 38–55.

53   **Weak ties connect you to new opportunities:** The classic piece on weak
ties in sociology is M. S. Granovetter (1973), "The strength of weak ties,"
American Journal of Sociology 78(6): 1360–1380.

Chapter 4

58   **more confident about relationship-building:** M. C. Higgins, D. E.
Chandler, and K. E. Kram (2007), "Developmental Initiation and Developmental Networks," in B. R. Ragins and K. E. Kram (eds.), *The Handbook
of Mentoring at Work: Theory, Research and Practice*, Thousand Oaks, CA:
Sage, pp. 349–372.

58   **Over a decade of research on developmental networks:** S. Dobrow, D. E.
Chandler, W. M. Murphy, and K. E. Kram (2012), "Developmental networks: A review and prospects for future research," *Journal of Management*
38(1): 210–242.

58   **mentors and coaches like helping:** J. E. Dutton and B. R. Ragins (eds.)
(2007), *Exploring Positive Relationships at Work: Building a Theoretical and
Research Foundation*, Mahwah, NJ: Erlbaum, especially pp. 91–116.

60   **core competencies contribute to career success:** R. J. DeFillippi and M. B. Arthur (2004), "The boundaryless career: a competency-based perspective," *Journal of Organizational Behavior* 15(4): 304–334.

61   **self-awareness is the first building block:** D. T. Hall (2002), *Careers in and out of Organizations,* Thousand Oaks, CA: Sage.

63   **self-awareness also generates the confidence:** D. Goleman (1998), *Working with Emotional Intelligence,* New York: Bantam.

63   **Guidelines for Structured Reflection:** M. W. Daudelin and D. T. Hall (1997), "Using reflection to leverage learning," *Training & Development,* December, pp. 13–14. See also M. W. Daudelin (1996), "Learning from experience through reflection," *Organizational Dynamics* 24(3): 36–48.

64   **DiSC:** The DiSC behavioral style assessment can be accessed through Wiley: http://www.everythingdisc.com/Disc-Personality-Assessment-Become-a-Partner.aspx?gclid=CPzNsrTNl7wCFRPxOgodbzAAdQ. For a free, short version, accessed July 16, 2013: http://discpersonalitytesting.com/free-disc-test/

64   **MBTI:** The MBTI can be accessed through Myers & Briggs Foundation (2003). My MBTI Personality Type. Accessed July 16, 2013. http://www.myersbriggs.org/my-mbti-personality-type/

64   **LPI:** The LPI can be accessed through Pfeiffer Assessments (2007). LPI = Leadership Practices Inventory. Accessed July 16, 2013. http://www.pfeiffer.com/WileyCDA/Section/id-811878.html. See also J. M. Kouzes and B. Z. Posner (2007). *The Leadership Challenge,* 4th ed. San Francisco: John Wiley & Sons.

65   **discover your "personal genius":** H. Shepard (1984), "On the Realization of Human Potential: A Path with a Heart," in M. Arthur, L. Bailyn, D. J. Levinson, and H. Shepard (eds.), *Working with Careers,* Center for Research in Career Development, Graduate School of Business, Columbia University.

66   **When there's a good fit:** B. Harrington and D. T. Hall (2007), *Career Management and Work-Life Integration: Using Self-Assessment to Navigate Contemporary Careers.* Thousand Oaks, CA: Sage.

68   **10,000 hours of deliberate practice:** M. Gladwell (2008), *Outliers,* New York: Back Bay Books. The study citation is K. A. Ericsson, R. T. Krampe, and C. Tesch-Romer (1993), "The role of deliberate practice in the acquisition of expert performance," *Psychological Review* 100: 393–394

68   **build on their strengths:** L. M. Roberts, G. Spreitzer, J. Dutton, R. Quinn, E. Heaphy, B. Barker (2005), "How to play to your strengths," *Harvard Business Review,* January, 75–80; T. Rath (2007), *Strengths Finder 2.0,* New York: Gallup Press.

68   **caveat that others are willing to help:** D. E. Chandler and K. E. Kram (2010), "Enlisting Others in Your Development as a Leader," in M. G. Rothstein and R. J. Burke (eds.), *Self-Management and Leadership Development,* New York: Edward Elgar, pp. 336–360.

69 **Neuroscience shows:** M. Bowman, K. M. Ayers, J. C. King, and L. J. Page (2013), "The Neuroscience of Coaching," in J. Passmore, D. B. Peterson, and T. Freire (eds.). *The Wiley-Blackwell Handbook of the Psychology of Coaching and Mentoring*, Malden, MA: Wiley-Blackwell.

69 **serendipitous interactions that change how you think or act:** S. J. Wells (2009), "Tending talent," *HR Magazine*, May: 53–60. See also J. Fletcher, J. and B. R. Ragins, "Stone Center Relational Cultural Theory: A Window on Relational Mentoring," in B. R. Ragins and K. E. Kram, *The Handbook of Mentoring at Work: Theory, Research, and Practice*, Thousand Oaks, CA: Sage, pp. 373–399.

70 **if you proactively initiate relationships:** D. B. Turban and T. W. Dougherty (1994), "Role of protégé personality in receipt of mentoring and career success," *Academy of Management Journal* 37(3): 688–702.

70 **never eating lunch alone:** *Never Eat Alone* is the title of Keith Ferrazzi's popular book about networking (New York: Crown, 2005).

71 **Initiating Relationships Self-Assessment:** Based on a scale developed for research on developmental relationship initiation in W. M. Murphy (2011), "From e-mentoring to blended mentoring: Increasing students' developmental initiation and mentors' satisfaction," *Academy of Management Learning and Education* 10(4): 606–622.

72 **When you create a good connection:** T. D. Allen, R. Day, and E. Lentz (2005), "The role of interpersonal comfort in mentoring relationships," *Journal of Career Development*, 31(15): 155–169.

72 **manage these interactions most effectively:** D. Goleman (2007), *Social Intelligence: The New Science of Human Relationships*, New York: Bantam Books. See also D. Goleman (2000), "Leadership that gets results," *Harvard Business Review*, March–April; R. Boyatzis and D. Goleman (2008), "Social intelligence and the biology of leadership, *Harvard Business Review*, September, and Chandler, D. (2009), Relational savvy: why some individuals are more adept with developmental relationships, unpublished dissertation, Boston University.

74 **growth-enhancing relationships:** J. Baker-Miller (2004), "Preface," in J. Jordan, I. Hartling, and M. Walker (eds.), *The Complexity of Connection.* New York, N.Y.: Guilford Press. See also J. B. Miller and I. Stiver (1997), *The Healing Connection*, Boston: Beacon Press.

74 **They actually release positive energy:** R. W. Quinn (2007), "Energizing Others in Work Connections," in J. E. Dutton and B. R. Ragins (eds.), *Exploring Positive Relationships at Work: Building a Theoretical and Research Foundation*, New York: Lawrence Erlbaum, pp. 73–90.

74 **energy sets in motion a virtuous cycle:** J. Dutton (2003), *Energize Your Workplace: How to Build and Sustain High Quality Connections at Work,* San Francisco: Jossey-Bass. See also J. Dutton and E. Heaphy, "The Power of High Quality Connections," in K. Cameron, J. Dutton, and R. Quinn

(eds.), *Positive Organizational Scholarship: Foundations of a New Discipline,* San Francisco: Berrett-Koehler, pp. 263–278.

74 **"Will you be my mentor?":** S. Sandberg (2013), *Lean In: Women, Work, and the Will to Lead*, New York: Alfred A. Knopf.

74 **determination based on your performance:** R. Singh, B. R. Ragins, and P. Tharenou (2009), "Who gets a mentor? A longitudinal assessment of the rising star hypothesis," *Journal of Vocational Behavior* 74(1): 11–17; T. Allen, M. L. Poteet, J. E. A. Russell (2000), "Protégé selection by mentors: What makes the difference?" *Journal of Organizational Behavior* 21(3): 271–282.

78 **Extensive research on goal-setting:** E. A. Locke and G. P. Latham (1990), *A Theory of Goal Setting and Task Performance*, Englewood Cliffs, NJ: Prentice-Hall; E. A. Locke and G. P. Latham (2002), "Building a practically useful theory of goal setting and task motivation: A 35-year odyssey," *American Psychologist* 57: 705–717.

Chapter 5

83 **Over 70 percent of Fortune 500:** T. Gutner (2009), "Finding anchors in the storm: Mentors," *Wall Street Journal*, January 27. Retrieved from http://online.wsj.com/article/SB123301451869117603.html.

83 **informal relationships generally more effective:** C. M. Underhill (2005), "The effectiveness of mentoring programs in corporate settings: A meta-analytical review of the literature," *Journal of Vocational Behavior* 68: 292–307.

85 **idea of mentoring is a much broader:** In her original study on the topic of mentoring, K. E. Kram did not use the term "mentor"; instead she asked people to describe a person who had contributed to their individual growth and career advancement. She described how "true mentoring" relationships were rare because organizations were highly competitive and people were busy, so it was more likely that less intensive relationships, like sponsorship, would be more easily available. See K. E. Kram (1985), *Mentoring at Work*, Glenview, IL: Scott Foresman.

85 **program roles and define general responsibilities:** For a scholarly perspective on the definition of mentor, see D. L. Haggard, T. W. Dougherty, D. B. Turban, and J. E. Wilbanks (2011), "Who is a mentor? A review of evolving definitions and implications for research," *Journal of Management* 37(1): 280–304.

88 **benefits of mentoring relationships:** There are several reviews of the literature on mentoring and its benefits. For an overview, see D. E. Chandler, K. E. Kram, and J. Yip (2011), "An ecological perspective on mentoring at work: A review and future prospects," *Academy of Management Annals* 5: 519–570. See also C. M. Underhill (2005), "The effectiveness of mentoring programs in corporate settings: A meta-analytical review of the literature," *Journal of Vocational Behavior* 68: 292–307.

89   **Here are some specifics:** M. J. Lankau, and T. A. Scandura, (2002). "An investigation of personal learning in mentoring relationships: content, antecedents, and consequences," *Academy of Management Journal* 45(4):779–790.

89   **did not think of Sandberg as a mentor:** See the story of the mentee who missed the career support offered in S. Sandberg (2013), *Lean In: Women, Work, and the Will to Lead*. New York: Knopf, pp. 70–71.

91   **increases job embeddedness:** There is a growing stream of literature on job embeddedness as a key reason people stay. For an overview, see K. Jiang, D. Liu, P. F. McKay, T. W. Lee, and T. R. Mitchell (2012), "When and how is job embeddedness predictive of turnover? A meta-analytic investigation," *Journal of Applied Psychology* 97, 1077–1096. See also W. M. Murphy, J. P. Burton, S. C. Henagan, and J. P. Briscoe (2013), "Employee reactions to job insecurity in a declining economy: A longitudinal study of the mediating role of job embeddedness," *Group and Organization Management* 38: 512–537.

91   **administered internally or cross-functionally:** K. Giscombe (2007), "Advancing Women through the Glass Ceiling with Formal Mentoring," in B. R. Ragins and K. E. Kram (eds.), *The Handbook of Mentoring at Work*, Thousand Oaks, CA: Sage, pp. 549–571.

91   **Voluntary participation:** For extensive discussion and exercises for formal programs, see T. D. Allen, L. M. Finkelstein, and M. L. Poteet (2009), *Designing Workplace Mentoring Programs: An Evidence-Based Approach*, Malden, MA: Wiley-Blackwell.

96   **Not surprisingly:** On the mentors' perspective, see studies by W. M. Murphy (2011). From e-mentoring to blended mentoring: Increasing students' developmental initiation and mentors' satisfaction," *Academy of Management Learning and Education* 10(4): 606–622; and F. J. Weinberg and M. J. Lankau (2011), "Formal mentoring programs: A mentor-centric and longitudinal analysis," *Journal of Management* 37(6): 1527–1557.

97   **Get participants' input on matching:** T. D. Allen, L. T. Eby, and E. Lentz (2006), "Mentorship behaviors and mentorship quality associated with formal mentoring programs: Closing the gap between research and practice," *Journal of Applied Psychology* 91(3): 567–578.

97   **Matching Methods:** For a thorough discussion of matching, especially how orientation to a program is different from the initiation phase of informal mentoring relationships, see S. D. Blake-Beard, R. M. O'Neill, and E. M. McGowan (2007), "Blind Dates? The Importance of Matching in Successful Formal Relationships," in B. R. Ragins and K. E. Kram (eds.), *The Handbook of Mentoring at Work: Theory, Research, and Practice*, Thousand Oaks, CA: Sage, pp. 617–632.

98   **similarity of interests to make pairings:** See K. Giscombe (2007), "Advancing Women through the Glass Ceiling with Formal Mentoring," in B. R. Ragins and K. E. Kram (eds.), *The Handbook of Mentoring at Work*, Thousand Oaks, CA: Sage, pp. 549–571.

98 **While bosses can be great informal mentors:** W. A. Gentry, T. J. Weber, and G. Sadri (2008), "Examining career-related mentoring and managerial performance across cultures: A multilevel analysis," *Journal of Vocational Behavior* 72: 241–253.

99 **quality of training:** On perceptions of formal programs, see analysis in T. D. Allen, L. T. Eby, and E. Lentz (2006), "Mentorship behaviors," pp. 573. Findings show that training quality is related to protégés' perceived quality of the program, career support, and role modeling received, whereas hours of training is related to psychosocial support.

101 **Ask for feedback regularly:** See Allen, Finkelstein, and Poteet (2009), *Designing Workplace Mentoring Programs*, Hoboken, NJ: Wiley.

105 **culture that will support implementation:** For more exercises from an organizational perspective, see L. J. Zachary (2005), *Creating a Mentoring Culture: The Organization's Guide*, San Francisco: Jossey-Bass.

107 **shared reflection and peer coaching:** See P. Parker, D. T. Hall, and K. E. Kram (2008), "Peer coaching: A relational process for accelerating peer learning," *Academy of Management Learning and Education* 7(4), 487–503. Also see P. Parker, K. E. Kram, and D. T. Hall (2012), "Exploring risk factors in peer coaching: A multilevel approach," *Journal of Applied Behavioral Science* 7 (4), 487–503.

Chapter 6

111 **critical to women's and minorities' success:** H. Ibarra (2010), "Women are over-mentored (but under-sponsored)," *HBR Blog Network*, August 26, http://blogs.hbr.org/2010/08/women-are-over mentored-but-un/

111 **Sylvia Hewlett's recent book:** S. A. Hewlett (2013), *Find a Sponsor: The New Way to Fast-Track Your Career*, Cambridge, MA: Harvard Business Review Press.

112 **Comparison of Developmental Roles:** The definitions of sponsors, coaches, reverse mentors, and mentoring circles here are the most widely shared. However, each company has its own definitions, shaped by its particular culture and practices. Therefore, you should inquire about what is offered by your employer so that your expectations are aligned with the company's offerings.

113 **delivering 110 percent on objectives:** S. A. Hewlett, M. Marshall, and L. Sherbin (2011), "The relationship you need to get right: How to be an effective sponsor—and a good protégé—throughout your career," *Harvard Business Review*, October: 131–134.

113 **a sponsor provides high instrumental support:** M. C. Higgins (2007), "A Contingency Perspective on Developmental Networks," in J. E. Dutton and B. R. Ragins (eds.), *Exploring Positive Relationships at Work: Building a Theoretical and Research Foundation*, New York: Lawrence Erlbaum.

114 **Luke Visconti of DiversityInc consults with many organizations:** DiversityInc also ranks in the Top 50 companies who implement success-ful diversity-management programs, see http://www.diversityinc.com/.

115 **Ted Childs:** Ted Childs, LLC, consults for many organizations on the role of mentorship and sponsorship in promoting minority, female, and disabled talent. While he uses the term "mentor," he is including sponsor-ship as a key role in getting talented people of diverse backgrounds into senior positions. He emphasizes that sponsors do not have to be of the same background. Shared values are key.

115 **executive with power:** S. A. Hewlett (2013), "The right way to find a career sponsor," *HBR Blog Network*. Accessed October 16, 2013, at http://blogs.hbr.org/2013/09/the-right-way-to-find-a-career-sponsor/.

116 **the coaching industry:** D. Coutu and C. Kauffman (2009), "What can coaches do for you?" *Harvard Business Review*, January: 91–97. See also in the Harvard Business Essentials series, Harvard Business School (2004), *Coaching and Mentoring: How to Develop Top Talent and Achieve Stronger Performance*, Boston, MA: Harvard Business School Press.

119 **a prestigious New York financial services firm:** This team was put together by the Simmons Graduate School of Management's Center for Gender in Organizations, Boston, MA. Dr. Deborah Kolb was the project leader. See http://www.simmons.edu/som/research/centers/cgo/.

120 **At the Center for Creative Leadership:** For more information, see www.ccl.org.

121 **Establish a coaching dialogue:** J. M. Hunt and J. R. Weintraub (2011), *The Coaching Manager: Developing Top Talent in Business*, 2nd edition. Thousand Oaks, CA: Sage.

121 **Coaching Inside the Organization:** For more information, see http://www.babson.edu/executive-education/open-enrollment-programs/Pages/coaching-inside-the-organization.aspx.

122 **The practice of reverse mentoring:** W. M. Murphy (2012), "Reverse mentoring at work: Fostering cross-generational learning and developing millennial leaders," *Human Resource Management* 51(4): 549–574.

124 **The Hartford's Reverse Mentoring Program:** see also K. L. DeAngelis (2013), *Reverse Mentoring at the Hartford: Cross-Generational Transfer of Knowledge about Social Media*, Chestnut Hill, MA: Sloan Center on Aging and Work, Boston College.

127 **began working in 2006 with WFD Consulting:** WFD Consulting works with organizations concerned with career development practices for women, as well as the work-family challenges that individuals and orga-nizations face. For more information, see www.wfdconsulting.com.

129 **Dr. Dennis Ceru teaches at Babson College and has served as mentor to circles of CEO/entrepreneurs:** Strategic Management Associates provides tools and services for executive development. For more information, see http://strategicma.com/.

Chapter 7

131 **embraced by leaders at every level:** R. Emelo (2013), "Creating a modern mentoring culture," *Infoline*, 1309, September. Alexandria, VA: ASTD Press.

131 **What is a developmental culture?:** D. T. Hall and P. H. Mirvis (1996), "The New Protean Career: Psychological Success and the Path with a Heart," in D. T. Hall and Associates (ed.), *The Career Is Dead—Long Live the Career*. San Francisco: Jossey-Bass.

133 **These programs span the firm:** Data provided by Barbara Wankoff, director of workplace solutions in KPMG, October 11, 2013.

133 **KPMG carefully defined sponsors:** Based on the research of H. Ibarra, N. M. Carter, and C. Silva (2010), "Why men still get more promotions than women," *Harvard Business Review*, September: 80–85; Catalyst (2011), *Fostering Sponsorship Success among High Performers and Leaders*, New York: Catalyst.

136 **Climate is about how people perceive the systems:** B. Schneider, M. G. Ehrhart, and W. H. Macey (2013), "Organizational climate and culture," *Annual Review of Psychology* 64: 361–388.

136 **an organizational climate is stronger when:** These factors are all considered moderators of organizational climate. See B. Schneider, M. G. Ehrhart, and W. H. Macey (2013), "Organizational climate and culture," *Annual Review of Psychology* 64: 368.

136 **Developmental Climate Assessment:** Some items from this assessment are adapted from P. H. Mirvis and D. T. Hall (1996), "New Organizational Forms and the New Vareer," in D. T. Hall and Associates (ed.), *The Career Is Dead—Long Live the Career*. San Francisco: Jossey-Bass, pp. 95–99.

138 **to create a developmental culture is found at Wilhelmsen Lines:** D. O'Connell, J. McCarthy, and D. T. Hall (1997), *Ingar Skaug and Wilhelmsen Lines: Leadership in Organizational Transformation (A),(B), and (C)*. Boston, MA: Boston University School of Management. For more detail on Skaug's leadership style, see J. McCarthy, D. O'Connell, and D. T. Hall, (2004), "Leading beyond tragedy: the balance of personal identity and adaptability," *Leadership and Organization Development Journal* 26(6): 458–475.

139 **Action Learning develops people:** J. O'Neal and V. J. Marsick (2007), *Understanding Action Learning*, New York, NY: AMACOM.

140 **AL is often used as a tool in formal leadership:** J. Raelin (2010), *The Leaderful Fieldbook: Strategies and Activities for Developing Leadership in Everyone*, Boston: Davies-Black, imprint of Nicholas Brealey Publishing.

140 **The appreciative inquiry process mobilizes:** D. L. Cooperrider and D. Whitney (2007), "Appreciative Inquiry: A Positive Revolution in Change," in P. Holman and T. Devane (eds.), *The Change Handbook*, San Francisco: Berrett-Koehler Publishers, pp. 245–263.

141 **An AI approach begins with structuring an organizational analysis:** I. Wasserman, (2012), "The wholeness principle and stories of diversity

and inclusion: A reflexive approach, *Appreciative Inquiry Practitioner*, November.

142 **Many studies of culture focus on the leader's role:** E. H. Schein (2010), *Organizational Culture and Leadership*, 4th edition, San Francisco: Jossey-Bass.

143 **leaders who display their weaknesses:** R. Goffee and G. Jones (2000), "Why should anyone be led by you?" *Harvard Business Review*, September–October: 62–70.

144 **the "Spirit of Mentoring" at Sodexo:** Sodexo has won several awards for these mentoring initiatives. Recent honors include the prestigious 2012 Catalyst Award in North America for Diversity and Inclusion, achieving the #1 ranking on the 2013 Top 50 Companies for Diversity list by DiversityInc, and being named the "Best Company for Hourly Workers" in 2013 by *Working Mother* magazine.

146 **on-the-job experience plays a key role in learning:** D. A. Kolb (1984), *Experiential Learning Experience as a Source of Learning and Development*. Englewood Cliffs, NJ: Prentice Hall.

146 **three characteristics of a challenging assignment:** C. D. McCauley, D. S. DeRue, P. R. Yost, and S. Taylor (2014), *Experience-Driven Leader Development: Models, Tools, Best Practices, and Advice for On-the-Job Development*, San Francisco: Wiley.

149 **championed the construction of Deloitte University:** B. Groysberg, M. Gibbons, and J. Bronstein (2010), "Building a developmental culture: the birth of Deloitte University," *Harvard Business School*: Case Study #411059.

Chapter 8

152 **mentoring has been a hot topic:** G. R. Roche (1979), "Much ado about mentors," *Harvard Business Review*, January; K. E. Kram (1985), *Mentoring at Work*, New York: Scott-Foresman; D. E. Chandler et al. (2011), "An ecological perspective"; S. Dobrow et al. (2012), "Developmental networks."

152 **In our research:** K. E. Kram and L. Isabella (1985), "Mentoring alternatives: The role of peer relationships in career development, *Academy of Management Journal* 28(1): 110–132; W. M. Murphy, and K. E. Kram (2010), "Understanding non-work relationships in developmental networks," *Career Development International* 15(7): 637–663.

153 **developmental networks of people who are successful:** R. D. Cotton, Y. Shen, and R. Livne-Tarandach (2011), "On becoming extraordinary: The content and structure of the developmental networks of major league baseball Hall of Famers, *Academy of Management Journal* 54(1): 15–46.

154 **peer coaching and peer mentoring are a low-cost alternative:** P. Parker, D. T. Hall, and K. E. Kram (2008), "Peer coaching: A relational process for accelerated career learning, *Academy of Management Learning and Education* 7(4): 487–503.

154 **continuum of peer relationships:** K. E. Kram and L. Isabella (1985), "Mentoring alternatives: The role of peer relationships in career development, *Academy of Management Journal* 28(1): 110–132; see also K. E. Kram (1985), "Mentoring at work."

157 **just always playing off each other in terms of what we think:** W. M. Murphy, (2007), "Individual and relational dynamics of ambition in careers," Boston College, unpublished dissertation, p. 58.

158 **having peers put in a classroom:** C. D. McCauley and V. A. Guthrie (2007), "Designing Relationships for Learning into Leader Development Programs," in B. R. Ragins and K. E. Kram (eds.), *Handbook of Mentoring at Work: Theory, Research, and Practice,* Thousand Oaks, CA: Sage, pp. 573–592.

158 **peer mentoring was recently illustrated at Brigham & Women's Hospital:** L. C. Tsen, J. F. Borus, C. C. Nadelson, E. W. Seely, A. Haas, A. L. Fuhlbrigge (2012), "The development, implementation, and assessment of an innovative faculty mentoring leadership program," *Academic Medicine* 87(12): 1–5.

159 **programs targeted at women leaders:** For more information on Women's Leadership Programs, see R. Ely, H. Ibarra, and D. Kolb (2011), "Taking gender into account: Theory and design for women's leadership programs, *Academy of Management Learning and Education* 10(3): 474–493.

160 **communities of practice offer yet another opportunity:** For more information, see http://wenger-trayner.com/resources/publications/cops-and-learning-systems/; see also E. Wenger (1998), *Communities of Practice: Learning, Meaning, and Identity,* Cambridge, UK: Cambridge University Press.

162 **coaching field about the mindset and skills that foster helping relationships between peers:** For more in-depth information about coaching skills, see J. Whitimore (2009), *Coaching for Performance: Growing Human Potential and Purpose,* Boston: Nicholas Brealey Publishing; see also K. Kimsey-House, H. Kimsey-House, P. Sandahl, and L. Whitworth (2011), *Co-active Coaching: Changing Business, Transforming Lives,* Boston: Nicholas Brealey Publishing.

162 **six skills are considered fundamental to any helping relationship:** A. Sigetich and C. Leavitt (2008), *Play to Your Strengths*. Franklin Lakes, NJ: Career Press.

162 **Barnett Pearce in his work on coordinated meaning making (CMM):** W. B. Pearce (2007), *Making Social Worlds: A Communication Perspective,* Malden, MA: Blackwell Publishing.

164 **the evolving story of your relationship:** I. Wasserman and S. Blake-Beard (2010), "Leading Inclusively: Mindsets, Skills, and Actions for a Diverse, Complex World," in K. Bunker, D. T. Hall, and K. E. Kram (eds.), *Extraordinary Leadership: Addressing the Gaps in Senior Executive Development,* San Francisco: John Wiley, pp. 197–212.

165 **The REAL model:** I. Wasserman and P. Gallegos (2009), "Engaging Diversity: Disorienting Dilemmas That Transform Relationships," in B. Fisher-Yoshida, K. D. Geller, and S. A. Schapiro (eds.), *Innovations in Transformative Learning: Space, Culture, and the Arts*, New York: Peter Lang, pp. 156–176.

166 **coming to such opportunities with humility, good questions, the willingness to take time:** E. Schein (2010), *Helping: How to Offer, Give, and Receive Help*, San Francisco: Berrett-Koehler; E. Schein (2013), *Humble Inquiry: The Gentle Art of Asking Instead of Telling*, San Francisco: Berrett-Koehler.

168 **learning partners:** See www.ccl.org for more information about the Center for Creative Leadership.

Chapter 9

173 **working across differences actually increases the potential learning:** D. B. Turban, T. W. Dougherty, and F. K. Lee (2002), "Gender, race, and perceived similarity effects in developmental relationships: The moderating role of relationship duration," *Journal of Vocational Behavior* 61: 240–262.

174 **a principle called homophily:** J. M. McPherson, L. Smith-Lovin, and J. M. Cook (2001), "Birds of a feather: Homophily in social networks," *Annual Review of Sociology* 27: 415–444.

174 **challenges dissipate over time—specifically within nine months:** Based on the findings of F. J. Weinberg and M. J. Lankau (2011), "Formal mentoring programs: A mentor-centric and longitudinal analysis," *Journal of Management* 37(6): 1527–1557.

174 **We also know that context matters:** For example, see S. B. Bacharach, P. A. Bamberger, and D. Vashdi, (2005), "Diversity and homophily at work: Supportive relations among white and African-American peers," *Academy of Management Journal* 48(4): 619–644.

174 **a network of mentors and sponsors is critical for the career advancement of women and minorities:** See D. A. Thomas (2001), "The truth about mentoring minorities: Race matters," *Harvard Business Review* 79(4): 98–112.

174 **on Project Implicit:** M. R. Banaji and A. G. Greenwald (2013), *Blind Spot: Hidden Biases of Good People*, New York: Delacorte Press. For more information, see https://implicit.harvard.edu/implicit/

175 **informally, mentors tend to select protégés who they see as younger versions of themselves:** B. R. Ragins and J. L. Cotton (1999), "Mentor functions and outcomes: A comparison of men and women in formal and informal mentoring relationships," *Journal of Applied Psychology* 84: 529–550.

175 **Intersectionality:** First introduced through a legal lens in K. Crenshaw (1991), "Mapping the margins: Intersectionality, identity politics, and violence against women of color," *Stanford Law Review* 43(6): 1241–1299. The work of feminist scholar Patricia Collins also forwarded these ideas in several articles and books, particularly in P. Collins (2004). *Black Sexual Politics: African Americans, Gender, and the New Racism.* New York: Routledge.

175 **what he calls racial taboos:** D. Thomas (1989), "Mentoring and irrationality: The role of racial taboos," *Human Resource Management* 28: 279–290. See also D. Thomas (1993), "Racial dynamics in cross-race developmental relationships," *Administrative Sciences Quarterly* 38: 169–194.

176 **variety of ways people mentally organize their identity:** S. R. Fitzsimmons (2013), "Multicultural employees: A framework for understanding how they contribute to organizations," *Academy of Management Review* 38(4): 525–549.

177 **diverse relationships are more challenging early on, more beneficial over time:** D. B. Turban, T. W. Dougherty, F. K. Lee (2002), "Gender, race, and perceived similarity effects in developmental relationships: The moderating role of relationship duration," *Journal of Vocational Behavior* 61: 240–262. See also F. J. Weinberg and M. J. Lankau (2011), "Formal mentoring programs."

178 **Our research has shown that different mentors may play different roles in supporting your career:** S. Dobrow, D. E. Chandler, W. M. Murphy, and K. E. Kram (2012), "A review of developmental networks: Incorporating a mutuality perspective," *Journal of Management* 38(1): 210–242.

178 **across 41 studies:** K. E. O'Brien, A. Biga, S. R. Kessler, and T. D. Allen (2010), "A meta-analytic investigation of gender differences in mentoring," *Journal of Management* 36(2): 537–554.

178 **The importance of mentoring support and insights from those in powerful positions:** M. L. McDonald and J. D. Westphal (2013), "Access denied: Low mentoring of women and minority first-time directors and its negative effects on appointments to additional boards," *Academy of Management Journal* 56(4):1169–2298.

179 **strategies improving mentoring process among diverse parties:** D. Clutterbuck, K. M. Poulsen, and F. Kochan (2012), *Developing Diversity Mentoring Programmes: An International Casebook.* New York: Open University Press.

179 **Cross-gender mentoring relationships may be misinterpreted as sexual relationships:** S. D. Blake-Beard (2001), "Taking a hard look at formal mentoring programs: A consideration of potential challenges facing women," *Human Resource Management* 20(4): 331–345.

180 **few key tips for avoiding misperceptions:** S. A. Hewlett (2013), "Make yourself safe for sponsorship," *HBR Blog Network*, October 7. http://blogs.hbr.org/2013/10/make-yourself-safe-for-sponsorship/.

180 **Research on cross-race relationships:** D. A. Thomas (2001), "The truth about mentoring minorities: Race matters," *Harvard Business Review*, April: 98–107.

181 **Fortunately, deep-level similarity:** E. A. Ensher, and S. E. Murphy (1997), "Effects of race, gender, perceived similarity, and contact on mentor relationships," *Journal of Vocational Behavior* 50: 460–481. See also D. A. Harrison, K. H. Price, and M. Bell (1998), "Beyond relational demography: Time and the effects of surface and deep level diversity or work group cohesion," *Academy of Management Journal* 41: 96–107.

181 **challenges of racial dialogues:** D. W. Sue (2013), "Race talk: The psychology of racial dialogues," *American Psychologist* 68(8): 663–672.

181 **In her study of expatriates:** Y. Shen and K. E. Kram (2011), "Expatriates' developmental networks: network diversity, base, and support functions," *Career Development International* 16(6): 528–552. See also J. M. Mezias, and T. A. Scandura (2005), "A needs-driven approach to expatriate adjustment and career development: A multiple mentoring perspective," *Journal of International Business Studies* 36: 519–538.

182 **mentors in India:** A. Ramaswami and G. F. Dreher (2010), "Dynamics of mentoring relationships in India: A qualitative exploratory study," *Human Resource Management* 49(3): 501–530.

182 **In Japan, mentoring relationships:** M. I. Bright (2004), "Can Japanese mentoring enhance understanding of Western mentoring?" *Employee Relations* 27(4): 325–339.

183 **In his book *Global Dexterity*, Andy Molinsky points out:** A. Molinsky (2013). *Global Dexterity*. Cambridge, MA: Harvard Business Review Press.

184 **DiversityInc's data:** M. M. Smith (2013), Web Seminar: DiversityInc Top 50 Best Practices from Merck, EY. Accessed October 20, 2013: http://www.diversityinc.com/diversityinc-top-50/web-seminar-diversity-best-practices-from-merck-ernst-young/

186 **one phone call or face-to-face interaction:** W. M. Murphy (2011), "From e-mentoring to blended mentoring: Increasing students' developmental initiation and mentors' satisfaction," *Academy of Management Learning & Education* 10(4): 606–622.

186 **When you communicate in-person there is greater richness:** R. L. Daft and R. H. Lengel (1984), "Information richness: A new approach to managerial behavior and organizational design, *Research in Organizational Behavior* 6:191–233.

187 **Carol Yamartino:** See www.yamartino.com for more information on The Yamartino Group.

188 **Intel has a program:** Warner, F. (2002). Inside Intel's mentoring movement. *FastCompany*, 57: 116-121.

188 **Mentor Resources:** See http://www.mentorresources.com/.

189 **U.S. Naval AMP:** Dr. Steve Hudock and his colleagues coordinate the U.S. Naval Academy Alumni Mentoring Program. It is notable that the AMP is funded through generous donations of alumni, particularly the Class of 1969 in anticipation of their 50th anniversary in 2019.

191 **Menttium:** See: http://www.menttium.com/.

192 **MentorNet:** See http://www.mentornet.org/organization/mission.

193 **Employee tenure is about three years:** Bureau of Labor Statistics (2012), "Employee tenure in 2012," *U.S. Department of Labor News Release*, September 18, 2012, http://www.bls.gov/news.release/tenure .nr0.htm

193 **developmental networks take on an inner core–outer core structure:** J. N. Cummings and W. C. Higgins (2006), "Relational instability at the network core: Support dynamics in developmental networks," *Social Networks* 28: 38–55.

193 **Family members, either a parent or a spouse/partner, were overwhelmingly identified:** W. M. Murphy and K. E. Kram (2010), "Understanding non-work relationships in developmental networks," *Career Development International* 15(7): 637–663. See also W. M. Murphy (2007), "Individual and relational dynamics of ambition in careers," Boston College: unpublished dissertation.

196 **Being proactive in initiating relationships:** C. Ya, K. M. Thomas, C. E. Lance (2008), "Intentions to initiate mentoring relationships: Understanding the impact of race, proactivity, feelings of deprivation, and relationship roles," *Journal of Social Psychology*, 148(6): 727–744.

Chapter 10

201 **Mentoring relationships may become problematic:** For conceptual clarity on dysfunctional mentoring, see T. Scandura (1998), "Dysfunctional mentoring relationships and outcomes," *Journal of Management* 24(3): 449–467.

201 **predictable set of risk factors:** P. Parker, K. E. Kram, and D. T. Hall (2012), "Exploring risk factors in peer coaching: A multilevel approach," *Journal of Applied Behavioral Science* 49(3): 361–387.

202 **Continuum of Relational Problems:** adapted from L. T. Eby (2007), "Understanding Relational Problems in Mentoring," in B. R. Ragins and K. E. Kram (eds.) (2007), *The Handbook of Mentoring at Work*, Thousand Oaks, CA: Sage, p. 325.

204 **Anti–role models:** See W. M. Murphy and K. E. Kram (2010), "Understanding non-work relationships in development networks." Career *Development International* 15(7): 637–663 and Y. Shen and K. E. Kram (2011), "Expatriates' developmental networks: network diversity, base, and support functions." *Career Development International* 16(6) 528–552.

204 **conscientiously brought the coaching skills:** For discussion of skills essential to helping relationships, see A. Sigetich and C. Leavitt (2008), *Play to Your Strengths*, Franklin Lakes, NJ: Career Press.

206 **CMM (Coordinated Meaning Making) model:** W. B. Pearce (2007), *Making Social Worlds: A Communication Perspective*, Malden, MA: Blackwell Publishing.

207 **REAL model:** I. Wasserman and P. Gallegos (2009), "Engaging diversity: Disorienting Dilemmas that Transform Relationships," in B. Fisher-Yoshida, K. D. Geller, and S. A. Schapiro (eds.), *Innovations in Transformative Learning: Space, Culture, and the Arts,* New York: Peter Lang, pp. 156–176.

209 **identify several elements of a conversation:** D. Stone, B. Patton, and S. Heen (1999), *Difficult Conversations: How to Discuss What Matters Most,* London, U.K.: Penguin Books.

Chapter 11

217 **VUCA:** An acronym for "volatility, uncertainty, complexity, and ambiguity," created by the U.S. Army to characterize the current environment in which we live and work.

218 **In his book, *Social*:** Lieberman, M.D. (2013), *Social: Why Our Brains Are Wired to Connect*, New York: Crown.

219 **In his most recent book, *Focus*:** D. Goleman (2013). *Focus: The Hidden Driver of Excellence*, New York: Harper Collins.

219 **Goleman's earlier work on emotional intelligence:** D. Goleman (2006), *Social Intelligence*, New York: Bantam Books. See also D. Goleman (2002). *Working with Emotional Intelligence*. New York: Bantam Books.

220 **mentoring episodes in which both parties experience positive benefits:** B. Ragins, and A. Verbos (2007), "Positive Relationships in Action: Relational Mentoring and Relational Schemas in the Workplace," in J. Dutton and B. R. Ragins (eds.), *Exploring Positive Relationships at Work*, Mahwah, NJ: Lawrence Erlbaum, pp. 91–116.

220 **mentoring episodes can accumulate:** J. Fletcher and B. R. Ragins (2007), "Stone Center Relational Cultural Theory: A Window on Relational Mentoring," in B. R. Ragins and K.E. Kram (eds.), *The Handbook of Mentoring at Work: Theory, Research, and Practice,* Thousand Oaks, CA: Sage, pp. 373–400.

220 **model of "intentional change":** The intentional change model suggests that trusting relationships are an essential part of the process by which individuals change their behavior and learn new competencies. R. Boyatzis (2007), "Mentoring for Intentional Behavioral Change," in B. R. Ragins and K. E. Kram (eds.), *The Handbook of Mentoring at Work: Theory, Research, and Practice*, Thousand Oaks, CA: Sage, pp. 447-469. See also

R. F. Boyatzis, M. Smith, and N. Blaize (2006), "Sustaining leadership effectiveness through coaching and compassion: It's not what you think," *Academy of Management Learning and Education* 5(1): 8–24.

222 **fluid expertise:** J. Fletcher and B. R. Ragins (2007), "Stone Center Relational Cultural Theory: A Window on Relational Mentoring," in B. R. Ragins and K. E. Kram (eds.). *The Handbook of Mentoring at Work: Theory, Research, and Practice.* Thousand Oaks, CA: Sage, pp. 373-400.

224 **Cognizant to understand and assess:** B. Iyer, S. Parise, S. Rajagopal, and T. H. Davenport (2011), "Putting social media to work at Cognizant," *Ivey Business Journal*, July–August.

225 **How Triple Creek creates:** For more information, see http://www .triplecreekriver.com/.

226 **modern mentoring approach:** R. Emelo (2013), "Mentoring without barriers," *Chief Learning Officer*, October: 27–29.

227 **human moments have two prerequisites:** E. Hallowell (1999), "The human moment at work," *Harvard Business Review*, January–February: 58–66.

227 **Center for Women's Entrepreneurial Leadership (CWEL) at Babson College:** For more information, see http://www.babson.edu/academics/ centers/cwel/pages/home.aspx.

228 **Carol Yamartino:** See www.yamartino.com.

229 **Recent research within Google:** D. A. Garvin (2013), "How Google sold its engineers on management," *Harvard Business Review*, December: 74–82.

229 **Amy's story is a good example:** This coaching example was provided by Prof. James Hunt, coauthor of *The Coaching Manager*, Thousand Oaks, CA: Sage, 2007.

231 **Boston University Executive Development Roundtable (EDRT):** EDRT brings 40 member companies to campus twice a year to discuss leading edge issues in leadership development. The Center for Creative Leadership is now a partner with Boston University in this roundtable. Michael Campbell (from CCL) was a guest speaker during the fall meeting on "The Power of Relationships and Developmental Networks." See http:// www.bu.edu/edrt/meetings

232 **Elad Gil, a serial entrepreneur:** P. Cohan (2013), "Why Elad Gil gives back to Silicon Valley," Blog accessed October 23, 2013, http://www .forbes.com/sites/petercohan/2012/07/23/why-elad-gil-gives-back-to- silicon-valley/

INDEX

ABOUT THE AUTHORS

Wendy Marcinkus Murphy is Associate Professor of Management at Babson College. Her research interests are in the area of careers, particularly developmental networks, learning, and the work-life interface. Her work has appeared in such journals as the *Academy of Management Learning and Education, Career Development International, Gender in Management, Group and Organization Management, Human Resource Management, Journal of Management,* and the *Journal of Vocational Behavior* among others. She has served as a representative-at-large for the Careers Division of the Academy of Management. She is also a member of the American Psychological Association, the Society for Industrial and Organizational Psychology, and the Organizational Behavior Teaching Society. Murphy teaches organizational behavior, leadership, managing talent, and negotiation for undergraduate, MBA, and Executive Education programs. She also serves as the faculty advisor for the Mentoring Programs through the Center for Women's Entrepreneurial Leadership (CWEL). In 2014 she was recognized by Poets and Quants as one of the "40 Most Outstanding B-School Profs Under 40 in the World." Prior to joining the faculty at Babson College, she taught at Boston College and Northern Illinois University. She and her husband Dan delight in their three young children and enjoy family time swimming and exploring nature.

Kathy E. Kram is the Richard C. Shipley Professor in Management at Boston University. Her primary interests are in the areas of adult development, relational learning, mentoring and developmental networks, leadership development, and change processes in organizations. In addition to her book, *Mentoring at Work*, she has published in a wide range of journals including *Organizational Dynamics*, *Academy of Management Journal*, *Academy of Management Review*, *Harvard Business Review*, *Business Horizons*, *Qualitative Sociology*, *Mentoring International*, *Journal of Management Development*, *Journal of Management Education*, *Journal of Management Inquiry*, *Organizational Behavior and Human Performance*, *Career Development International*, and *Psychology of Women Quarterly*. She is coeditor of *The Handbook of Mentoring at Work: Theory, Research and Practice* with Dr. Belle Rose Ragins. In 2011 she was awarded the premier Everitt Cherrington Hughes Award from the careers division of the Academy of Management for building bridges between research and practice. In 2013 she received the Boston University Executive Development Roundtable Marion F. Gislason Award for Leadership in Executive Development. She is a founding member of the Center for Research on Emotional Intelligence in Organizations (CREIO). During 2000–2001, she served as a visiting scholar at the Center for Creative Leadership (CCL), during which time she worked on a study of executive coaching and its role in developing emotional competence in leaders. She served as a member of the Center's Board of Governors from 2002 to 2009. She and her husband, Peter Yeager, enjoy hiking, traveling, and listening to their musician son, Jason, perform in a variety of venues.

CPSIA information can be obtained at www.ICGtesting.com
Printed in the USA
LVOW07*0025291115

464063LV00008B/270/P